HUSBAND-LOVING LESSONS

A SERIES OF LESSONS FOR WIVES OF ANY AGE FROM THE PERFECT "MARRIAGE MANUAL"—THE WORDS OF GOD

By
Yvonne S. Waite

Edited By
Pastor D. A. Waite, Th.D., Ph.D.
Director, THE BIBLE FOR TODAY, INCORPORATED

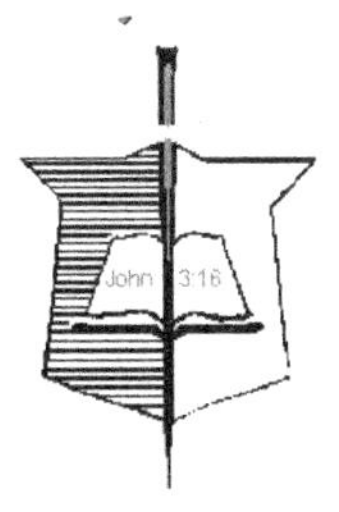

900 Park Ave.
Collingswood, N.J., 08108
U.S.A.

ISBN 978-1-56848-128-9

Published By
THE BIBLE FOR TODAY PRESS
900 Park Avenue
Collingswood, New Jersey 08108,
USA

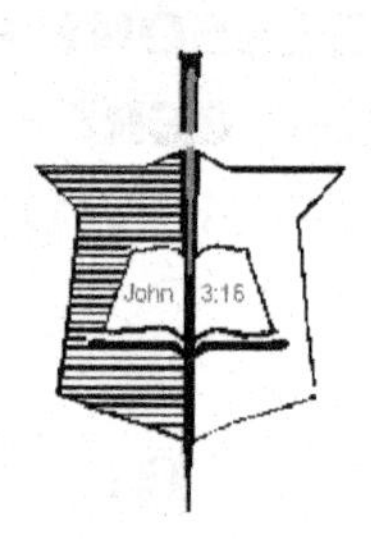

Church Phone: 856-854-4747
BFT Phone: 856-854-4452
Orders: 1-800-John 10:9
e-mail: BFT@BibleForToday.org
Website: www.BibleForToday.org.
Fax: 856-854-2464

BFT #3488

Formatted by **TOP**:
The **O**ld **P**aths Publications, Inc.
Directors: H. D. & Patricia Williams
142 Gold Flume Way
Cleveland, GA 30528
Web: www.theoldpathspublications.com
Email: TOP@theoldpathspublications.com
Jeremiah 6:16

DEDICATION

I dedicate this book to the memory of my mother, Gertrude Barker Sanborn, and my mother-in-law, Helen Peirce Waite, who taught me by example how to be a good wife. No woman could have had better human patterns for wifemanship.

My mother's first allegiance to the Words of God was followed by her love and wifely obedience to her husband, my father, R. O. Sanborn. A daughter could not have a better example than I had in Mother. She taught me how to hold my head up high in life's conflicts, how to walk, and how to trust and obey God. Often she would say, "If you do not obey me, you will not obey God!" Her admonition taught me to be a law-abiding person, and to obey God's Words found in the Bible. It was she who led me to Jesus Christ as my personal Saviour. It is an introduction I'll never forget and it has shaped my whole life!

My mother-in-law taught me by example how to be a "Mrs. Waite." I saw her submit to her husband, Virgil Henry Waite, and be his champion, even when it was not easy. She was a woman of strong fortitude and courage, a leader among women—but always a country-town girl at heart. She taught her son how to be a man and care for his family, encouraging his future leadership as a husband and a father. I will always be grateful for my mother-in-law, who at first frightened me with her authoritative manner and uncomplaining spirit. She was a woman I can try to emulate, but never would be able to, even if I live to be one hundred. She was good and merciful, an example for me all of our sixty-five years of marriage (since August 27, 1948).

TABLE OF CONTENTS

INTRODUCTION

THE AUTHORITY TO TEACH

MY AUTHORITY TO BE BOLD ENOUGH TO TEACH SUCH LESSONS IS FOUND IN TITUS 2:3-5:

> *The aged women...teach the young women to be sober, to love their husbands, to love their children, to be discreet, chaste, KEEPERS AT HOME, good, OBEDIENT TO THEIR OWN HUSBANDS, that the word of God be not blasphemed!*

THESE LESSONS HAVE HELPED COUPLES

A few years ago, my husband and I were eating in a nearby restaurant. As we sat there, a woman kept looking at me. She was with her husband. Soon she asked if I were Mrs. Waite. She said she knew me from the past. While pointing at me, she turned to her husband and said, ***"HONEY, THIS IS THE WOMAN WHO SAVED OUR MARRIAGE!"***

It turned out that she had been in one of the HUSBAND LOVING CLASSES which had been held in one of the homes in South Jersey many years ago. I can tell you it was a humbling experience! I was amazed!

THE PERFECT TEXT

After I wrote these *HUSBAND-LOVING LESSONS*, I sent my teaching manual to my mother, expecting her to comment on the lessons. There was no comment–only silence. I wondered about her silence. She lived far from me, so I did not see her often, but we corresponded almost weekly. So the next time I visited her, I asked: "*Mother, what do you think about the HUSBAND-LOVING LESSONS?*" Usually she commented on my writing with approval. This time was different. Mother said something like this: ***"YOU HAVE NOT LIVED LONG ENOUGH."***

As the years have flown by since last she so spoke, I realized she was right. I had not lived long enough! At the writing of these lessons, I had been married twenty-eight years. Compared to her many years of marriage, mine was in its infant stage. My parents had sixty-five years of marriage and my husband's parents had decades. Now that I have been married sixty-five years at this printing, I have realized how wise my mother's statement was. Yet, I still maintain, as I did back in 1977, when these lessons first came into being, that I then had, and now have, the *perfect* textbook for marriage. That text was and is THE BIBLE, God's Holy Words! From Its pages, the youngest bride, to the oldest great-grandmother-wife, can sit at Jesus' feet and learn how to be a godly wife.

THE LIFE MATE DECISION

Most of us come into marriage completely ignorant of its pitfalls and difficulties. We have seen our parents pattern the subject, and often that was good; but when you and I walked down that wedding aisle, we had not the faintest idea of the life ahead of us. Most often our choice of a husband was made when we were young, innocent, and completely unaware of what our needs really were or would be. We made our "LIFE-MATE DECISION" when we had barely made *any* life-choices of any importance at all. Sometimes the very attribute that drew us to our choice of a husband so many years ago is the very characteristic that disturbs us most after marrying him.

AN OPEN DOOR TO TEACH MARRIAGE PRINCIPLES

I remember well the day I met DOLLY BERRY, and when she asked me to teach her how to be a good Christian wife. She had recently been born-again out of the Catholic Church and desired to do God's will in all areas of her life, beginning with her marriage. Only a few weeks prior to meeting Dolly, I had prayed that God would open a door of service for me to teach women. So she and her friends gathered around my dining room table as we searched the Scriptures together to see what they had to say to help us be the Christian wives God wanted us to be.

Every week, women with marriage needs would sit at that table to learn. Most were women I had never met. Soon the classes extended to other homes and other neighborhoods. It was a season in my life of great surprise and blessing to be used of God in such a way. It was a time of personal challenge for me to live the lessons that I was teaching. Marriage is hard. It is difficult. We are ever-learning how to be godly wives. The lessons will not cease until our marriages end–not in divorce, but in our deaths or that of our mates. If a marriage ends in divorce, it is an incomplete marriage and an incomplete life, snuffed out before it had a chance to be "perfected" by God's Words.

At the time, I was not *"aged."* For some reason at that time of my life, I considered myself as one of the *"older women"* of Titus 2:3-5. I had been married twenty-eight years to the same husband. We had five children—four were adults. Though I had much living and sorrow in my life; MY MOTHER WAS RIGHT! I had not lived long enough!

Yet, I felt, at the time, that the LORD would have me teach women what He had taught me and continues to teach me from His Scriptures on HUSBAND-LOVING. I do believe those classes and those lessons were from God because they were taken from the Bible. Then my students could teach others the same truths as to HOW other wives could learn to love their husbands. It was a challenge for pupils and teacher.

THANKFUL HUSBANDS

What an amazing time in my life! Husbands came up to me in the supermarkets to thank me for the lessons. Women would introduce me to their little babies or children and relate, *"Mrs. Waite, this is my HUSBAND-LOVING CHILD."* Just a few weeks ago, a woman wrote me thrilled that she had discovered my *HUSBAND-LOVING LESSONS.* She had found my *JUST*

FOR WOMEN radio programs on our **BibleForToday.org** internet site.

I remember a young man in California who came to me, thanking me for writing *HUSBAND-LOVING LESSONS.* I mentioned to him that I was having doubts about an article I was contemplating on I Corinthians 7. I thought I might be overdoing it. He implored me, *"Mrs. Waite, you MUST write it! YOU MUST BE BOLD!"*

When the *HUSBAND LOVING LESSONS* first began, I was over forty years old *"in the Lord,"* as a born-again believer. I had been married twenty-eight years. The Lord had blessed Dr. Waite and me with four sons and a daughter. Our second-born son went HOME to be with the Lord in April of 2008. I miss him. We have eight grandchildren, and thirteen great grands at this writing. They are a joy to me!

My husband and I graduated together in 1945, from Berea High School in Berea, Ohio. We were married on August 27, 1948, and traveled on our honeymoon to Dallas, Texas. My husband was a student at DALLAS THEOLOGICAL SEMINARY–the old Dallas–earning his Th.M. and Th.D. degrees.

It was as a new bride, living in our twenty-six foot trailer behind the seminary, that God began to unfold His teaching on WIFELY SUBMISSION. It was there that I began my long journey down the road in *HUSBAND-LOVING LESSONS.*

SOME THANK-YOU'S

I want to thank my husband of sixty-five years (1948-2013), Pastor D. A. Waite, Th.D., Ph.D., for encouraging me in publishing this book. Years ago, he would come home from teaching school and type the *HUSBAND-LOVING LESSONS* on his electric typewriter, putting it into a better form, helping me with spelling, and checking out any doctrinal errors.

For this second printing of the book, Dr. Waite has worked with me and my proof readers, MARILYN STOUT and ANNE MARIE NOYLE, who corrected many

errors and Scripture passages. Thank you, Marilyn, for all your work which was far above the call of duty for any proofreader. Thank you, Anne Marie for the hours of reading and re-reading you did, and for the corrections you made for a better understanding of the book. I want to thank my husband, too, for the hours and hours he has taken to copy these corrections into the body of the book.

Thank you, Editor H. D. Williams, for your diligence and editorial wisdom crafting an old copy-machine manuscript into a book of marriage wisdom to be used for God's glory in the lives of Christian women wherever they may be. Also, I appreciate all that Patricia Williams has done to make the book attractive with her inventive cover artistry.

This humble book has turned itself into a marriage answer for success and blessing for all to learn and practice to glorify God in their homes.

Lastly, **my acknowledgments would not be complete, if I did not thank DOLLY BERRY for asking me to teach her how to be a good Christian wife.** She encouraged me and invited many of her friends to sit around our teaching table those many years ago. *To God be the glory!*

I THANK THEE, MY HEAVENLY FATHER, FOR SUCH A PRIVILEGE TO TEACH THY MARRIAGE RULES TO OTHERS. IT HUMBLES ME TO THINK THAT THOU CANST USE THIS BOOK TO BLESS MANY MARRIAGES AND HOMES.

Yvonne S. Waite (Mrs. D. A. Waite)
BIBLE FOR TODAY MINISTRIES
Collingswood, NEW JERSEY
November, 2013

HUSBAND-LOVING LESSON #1

THE CHALLENGE OF SUBMISSION

I think the grandest portion of SCRIPTURE for a wife to anchor her HUSBAND-LOVING to is found in 1 Peter 2:20-3:6. A wife should read these verses until she knows what they say by heart and can bounce back upon them in her everyday living with her spouse.

A POINT TO REMEMBER

Always remember that GOD'S instructions to a woman, a wife, are for her and her only. She should not be concerned with the instructions given to the man, her husband. It is her duty to follow the wife's rules and it is her husband's duty to follow the husband's rules. If her mate does not respond to God's commands, this is not her fault, nor should she throw the fact up to the husband. Her concern is to keep her part of the bargain. Her commands are from the LORD and she should follow them and continue to walk in that path no matter what her husband does or does not do. THIS IS THE HARD PART, for we are prone to want to quit when the rest of the players are not following the rules. Not so in HUSBAND-LOVING. We must continue on, following our "marriage manual"—God's Words—even if we are the only ones reading or heeding it.

THE BEHAVIOR METHOD OF HUSBAND-LOVING (1 Peter 2:20-3:6)

Let us first have before us the definition of "behavior." It is as follows:

1. *mode of conducting oneself; deportment;*

2. *The way in which an organism, organ, or substance acts, esp. in response to a stimulus; as, the behavior of glands; activity or change in relation to environment; as, the behavior of steel under stress.*

syn. Bearing, demeanor, comportment—behavior, conduct. BEHAVIOR applies to our mode of acting in the presence of others or toward them, and often refers to purely eternal relations or to particular instances; it is especially used with reference to children. CONDUCT applies rather to the general tenor of our actions (particularly in their ethical relations) in the more serious concerns of life; when used of specific actions, it implies their moral aspects more definitely than behavior. (Webster's New International, Dictionary)

THE PIVOTAL VERSE (1 Peter 3:1)

Verse one of chapter three of First Peter (1 Peter 3:1) is the PIVOTAL VERSE of this portion of the SCRIPTURES. All that precedes explains how to be in subjection to one's husband, how to behave by our conduct; all that follows embellishes this behavior or subjection.

BUFFETED FOR FAULTS

In 1 Peter 2:20, it is pointed out that if we are "*BUFFETED*" FOR A FAULT—a real fault—and "*take it patiently.*" So what? But if we "*suffer*" for doing right AND "*TAKE IT PATIENTLY*"—this is "*ACCEPTABLE WITH GOD.*"

Doesn't this verse remind us of marriage? How often a wife is blamed when innocent. The proof of our good CHRIST-LIKE BEHAVIOR is how we take this buffeting. Is our response "*ACCEPTABLE WITH GOD*"? This is a good question and often our answer is embarrassing to ourselves.

JESUS CHRIST—OUR SUBMISSION EXAMPLE

How did Jesus Christ respond to revilers? Look at 1 Peter 2:23. He "*reviled not again.*" "*When He suffered, HE threatened not.*" But what did He do? He "*committed Himself to HIM that judgeth righteously.*" Doesn't this refer us back in our thinking to verse 20?—"*but if, when ye do well and suffer for it, ye take it patiently, "THIS IS ACCEPTABLE WITH GOD"* (1 Peter 2:20).

Was Christ a sinner? No. Was guile found in His mouth? No.

GUILE: 1. Deceitful cunning, craft and treachery.
2. Obs. A stratagem; a trick.

GUILELESS: (adj.) Lacking guile; hence, innocent.

This innocent SON OF GOD bore my sins in His own body on the Tree. He bore your sins so you could have a righteousness before GOD. Because Jesus Christ took our sins in His own body, we, therefore, can be dead to sins. We should live unto righteousness, for His sufferings on the cross made this kind of life possible if we have been "*born-again*" (John 3:3).

FAILING TO FOLLOW HIS EXAMPLE IN THIS MATTER

How often Christian (born-again) women fail the LORD in this area of living before our husbands as righteous ones. Even if our husbands know the LORD, we should have a manner of living which radiates CHRIST.

We were not given the example of JESUS CHRIST as the TEMPLE-CLEANSER, nor were we told to "*follow His steps*" (1 Peter 2:21) in His rebuking of Jerusalem. We—as CHRISTIAN HUSBAND-LOVERS—were exhorted, however, to pattern our wifeship after CHRIST on the cross with a closed mouth. How this rebukes my soul.

ARE YOU BORN-AGAIN?

Before I was born-again, I was like a lost sheep (1 Peter 2:25), but since accepting Jesus Christ as my Saviour—my sin-bearer, the One who took my place at the cross, the One who bore in His body all my badness—as a young child of eight or nine years of age, I have returned back to my GOOD SHEPHERD and my soul OVERSEER (Bishop). How about you? Has there ever been a time in your life when you came to Jesus Christ and said, "Come into my life, Lord Jesus"? Has there ever been a day that you left all your good works behind and said, "Nothing in my hand I bring, simply to Thy cross I cling"?

Did you think your prayers could get you to heaven? Are you under the unbiblical belief that your good works and kind deeds can gain entrance to God's eternal life? If you are depending on your goodness, you will burn in eternal Hell.

When I was a little girl, my mother taught me a verse in the book of Titus, Chapter 3, verse 5, and I shall never forget it:

> *Not by works of righteousness which we have done, but according to his mercy he saved us . . .* (Titus 3:5a).

Ephesians Chapter 2, verses 8 and 9, reads like this:

> *For by grace are ye saved through faith; and that not of yourselves: it is the gift of God: Not of works, lest any man should boast* (Ephesians 2:8-9).

WORKS CANNOT SAVE YOUR TROUBLED SOUL

I am so glad that my works are not what God is looking upon for my eternal life. WHY? Because I'm not a very good "works" person. I get all worn out baking cakes for people or running around cleaning other people's houses. I just couldn't rake enough leaves for crippled old ladies to make it to heaven, nor could I go to church every day of the year and pray to make it. How thankful I am that my merit is nothing—just filthy rags.

For ALL (that means you, too) have sinned, and come short of the glory of God (Romans 3:23).

ETERNAL LIFE A GIFT

God tells us in His Words that ETERNAL LIFE is a GIFT. What can you and I do for a gift? We cannot work for it. We cannot pay for it. We must take it in our hands, possess it, unwrap it, enjoy it, and rejoice in it.

I have had to learn to accept earthly gifts from earthly fathers. Contrary to what you may think, it is not always easy. There is a submission, a lowering, a humbling connected with taking a gift. Has anyone ever given you a new car? Well, I recall when my father-in-law gave us a new car. At first we did not want it. In fact, we rejected the offer for one whole year. Then, we accepted it. All of a sudden, sitting in our driveway, was a new station wagon. We had not paid for it, for we couldn't have done it at the time. We didn't work for it at all. We just took it, enjoyed it, and said, "Thank you, Dad." He paid for it. He worked hours to let his money work for him to buy that station wagon. Nothing we did brought it into our family (except, we accepted the gift). THIS IS WHAT SALVATION IS ALL ABOUT. Accepting and not rejecting what has already been paid for by Jesus Christ shedding His blood on the cross for your sins.

For the wages of sin is death, but the GIFT OF GOD is eternal life through Jesus Christ, our LORD (Romans 6:23).

YOU MUST SEE YOURSELF AS A SINNER

So, you know you are a sinner. Who hasn't done something contrary to the law of God, the Ten Commandments? Did you know that in this state of sin that you found yourself when the Spirit of God convicted you that really you were a sinner—are a sinner—did you know that God loved you? Yes He did and He does.

> *But God commendeth His love toward us in that, while we were yet sinners, Christ died for us* (Romans 5:8).

"Yet sinners." This reminds me of the condemnation which is every human being's if they do not accept Christ as Saviour. God knew of this condemnation. And because He knew that everyone without Jesus Christ was CONDEMNED ALREADY (John 3:18), HE showed His love towards us while we were yet sinners.

> *For God so loved the world, that He gave His only begotten son, that whosoever believeth in Him should not perish, but have everlasting life* (John 3:16).

ONLY BELIEVE AND LIVE

Dear wife, trying to be the HUSBAND-LOVER that God wants for you to be, have you ever placed your name in that space that says "WHOSOEVER"? WHOSOEVER means you. Read again John 3:16 and say your name, and see how much God loved you, how much He doesn't want you to perish, how much He yearns that you accept the free gift of ETERNAL LIFE which comes wrapped up in Jesus Christ.

> *For God sent not His Son into the world to condemn the world, but that the world through Him might be saved. He that believeth on Him is not condemned; but he that believeth not is condemned already, because he hath not believed in the name of the only begotten Son of God* (John 3:17-18).

"ONLY BELIEVE AND LIVE"

Lift up your eyes to Calvary,
Only believe and live;
On yonder cross your Saviour see—
Only believe and live.

It was for you He bled and died,
On that dread cross was crucified,
He suffered sore, Your sins He bore—
Only believe and live.

Great is God's love in Him revealed,
Only believe and live;
Fully your pardon has been sealed,
Only believe and live.

Seek now forgiveness full and free,
Pardon and peace and liberty,
Come to Him now, Before Him bow,
Only believe and live.

Naught can you do His love to win,
Only believe and live;
Open your heart and let Him in,
Only believe and live.

Works cannot save your troubled soul,
Only His blood can make you whole,
Simply accept, No more reject,
Only believe and live.

Robert Harkness

WHAT DOES SUBJECTION MEAN?

Once again we find ourselves as wives "smack dab" up against the first verse of Chapter 3 in 1 Peter. So, before we go any further, I think we'd better settle in many minds what this difficult word, SUBJECTION, means. We had better understand it, chew on it, meditate upon its meaning, and then be prepared to act upon what the SCRIPTURES say about subjection without throwing up.

"SUBJECTION" IN WEBSTER'S LARGE DICTIONARY

If we look into the *Webster's New International Dictionary*, we find:

> *SUBJECTION: N. (see subject) 1. Act of subjecting or subduing; subjugation; also Obs. domination; government.*
> *2. State of being subject, or under the power, control, and government of another; a state of obedience or submissiveness; as, subjection to the laws.*
> *3. Obligation, as by a contract, pledge, etc.; liability; condition of being under some obligation or necessity. Obs.*
> *4. Logic. Attachment of a subject to a predicate; correlative to predication.*

"SUBJECTION" IN THE THESAURUS

Let us look further into the *Roget's International Thesaurus* for help. This book suggests we look into three areas for words similar in meaning: (1) Inferiority, p. 37.2; (2) Subjugation, p. 762; and (3) Submission, p. 763.1 [The numbers following the words are the page numbers where to find the helps].

I don't think I will give a long list, but just a few words which I have chosen under SUBMISSION (nouns):

1. *Submittal, yielding, compliance, acquiescence, obedience, subjection; resignation, resignedness, deference, subservience; passivity, passiveness, non-resistance.*
2. *Surrender, cessation; capitulation; renunciation, abandonment, relinquishment, backdown (coll.), recession, recedence.*
3. *Submissiveness, docility, tractability, yieldingness, compliableness, pliancy, pliability, flexibility, plasticity, facility.*
4. *Manageability, governability, controllability, corrigibility, towardness, towardliness, un-*

troubledsomeness.

5. *Meekness, gentleness; tameness, mildness; quietness, lamblikeness, humility.*

SUBJECTION EVIDENCED IN THE "ACT OF MARRIAGE"

One of the most interesting thoughts on SUBJECTION and SUBMISSION was given me when I was reading *THE ACT OF MARRIAGE*[1] by LaHaye, that during the "act of marriage" true SUBJECTION can be discovered by a wife in the fulfillment of her sexual being in orgasm.

"IN THE SAME MANNER" (1 Peter 3:1)

What does this mean, "in the same manner"? This means, I believe, that a wife should be in SUBJECTION to her man as Christ was to the CROSS.

We love the Lord Jesus because of His vicarious suffering, because He became SIN for us, because He was SUBMISSIVE to the FATHER, because He was SUBJECT to the death of the cross. "*He committed Himself to Him that judgeth righteously*" (1 Peter 2:23b). Right?

So it is with this abandonment that we should be SUBJECT to our own husbands.

SUBJECTION TO ONE'S OWN MAN

Here is an important truth: SUBJECTION TO ONE'S OWN MAN. How easy it is to be caught in the snare of thinking another man, another woman's husband, is "it." Sometimes another man will give a woman more attention than her own husband does. Why is this? And the woman who is so glad for some attention begins to think, "This man is really something."

---

[1] Tim and Beverly LaHaye, *The Act of Marriage* (Zondervan, 1998). This book is referred to often throughout *Husband-Loving Lessons* by reference to chapters and specific pages. It may also be purchased on Amazon if still in print.

This is wrong. This is sin—even when it is just friendliness. I don't mean a Christian wife should not be friendly, but she should always be aware that her inner self should be for the one she married.

True, one's husband may neglect and pay no attention to her, but still a wife's subjection is to be to her OWN HUSBAND, and as time continues in her life and as she applies the SCRIPTURAL teaching to her own personal life and marriage, God will bring fruit into that marriage of a loving husband who will want to be with her more than any other thing in his life.

ACTIONS SPEAK LOUDER THAN WORDS

Peter wrote that:

> *If any* [husband] *obey not the word, they also may without the word be won by the conversation of the wives;* (I Peter 3:1b)

What does this mean? In other words, if your husband is unsaved, he can become born-again just by seeing how you as a believing wife behave. He may, like the jailer of Philippi, (Acts 16:25-34), ask, "*What must I do to be saved*?"

If this power is in the hands of a believing wife—her behavior, her SUBJECTION to her own husband—how much would be the blessing towards a believing wife with her relationship with her believing husband!

WHAT DOES A HUSBAND-LOVER LOOK LIKE?

The husband who is properly "husband-loved," will see the "*CHASTE*" *(virtuous, pure in thoughts and action, modest, simple in design and expression, not ornate)* CONDUCT of his wife and her fear or reverence or awe of him, and he can't help but love her and wonder at her FAITH (1 Peter 3:2).

The adornment which interests a husband most of all is his wife's inner clothing; all that inner robing which shows her husband she is "*chaste*" (see above

paragraph).

It is that hidden woman of the heart, "the inside you;" that part of a human being that loves, hurts, cries, misses, loves, grieves, and leaves the body when the body dies and decays.

We have all met beautiful women who are nothing but shells, covering a starving, empty inner person. What a shame and waste of a life.

WHAT DOES GOD THINK ABOUT THE INNER WOMAN?

Have you thought of what God sees in us and what He thinks about these virtues or lack of virtues in our inner woman? When He sees the meek and quiet spirit of the wife in subjection, God sees an expensive (great price) garment. Why is it (the meek and quiet spirit) of great price in the sight of God? At this reading, I feel it must be the price that a woman, like Sarah—our example—or women like we are have paid in our SUBJECTION to our own husbands.

WHAT SUBJECTION BRINGS

What does subjection bring to a woman? A meek and quiet spirit. (Lest you think we will have no starch left when we reach the "SUBJECT-TO-HER-LORD-HUSBAND-STATE," do not fear. Moses was said to have been the "meekest" man whoever lived; yet he had much gumption and get-up-and-go. Often God had to harness Moses though, so let us take care.)

A QUESTION FOR YOU

Or does a meek and quiet spirit bring about subjection? Just asking. Perhaps it does. Dressing, adorning, have much to do with behaving. Let us get out that MEEKNESS, that quiet spiritness, and put it on this week and see if subjection will be the fruit of such primping.

> *For after this manner (the inner adorning) in the old time (the Old Testament DAYS) the holy (sanctified) women also, who trusted (hoped) in God, adorned themselves (something a woman can do—she can't work for her salvation, but she can dress her inner self) being in subjection unto their own husbands: Even as Sara (who forsook her native land to be with Abraham, who lived in a tent to traipse after him, who watched him worship a God who was foreign to her for years, who fell in love with that same God (and believed) obeyed Abraham, calling him lord: (A wife can't work for her salvation, but she can work for her SUBJECTION. She can place her husband in the proper place in her life first by saying it with her mouth and talking up her man as her "head" and letting her "heart" follow her reason.) whose daughters ye are (follow this Mother Subjection—if there ever was a Mother Superior, Sarah was it.) as long as ye do well, and are not afraid with any amazement* (1 Peter 3:5-6).

SOME THINGS TO REMEMBER AND DO IN HUSBAND-LOVING

1. **You married a man. Don't expect his reactions to be that of a woman.**

2. Praise The Lord for his manliness. Take the advantages that such a being can bring to you as a wife.

3. **Be sexually aggressive with your husband**. Remember, "all is fair in love and war."

> ***"Marriage is honorable in all, and the bed undefiled:"* (The act of marriage is undefiled.) (Hebrews 13:4a)**

4. **Do not admonish him—unless he asks,** but remember he really doesn't want to hear anything contrary to what he believes. RE-ENFORCE his thinking (unless he is going to rob a bank).

ADMONISH:

- *To warn of a fault; to reprove gently or kindly, but seriously; to exhort; also, to put (one) in mind of something forgotten, by way of a warning or exhortation; as he was admonished not to go.*
- *To enjoin by a warning; as to admonish silence. Syn. & Ant. see REPROVE—admonisher; noun—admonishment, noun.*

Remember, a man does not want an ADMONISHER; he wants a MEEK AND QUIET SPIRIT. ADMONISH could be put in less kindly words by the definition of NAG . . . at least it would seem that way to a husband.

5. Read *THE ACT OF MARRIAGE* by Beverly and Tim LaHaye.

6. **READ in GENESIS the beginning of God's ways with Man and Woman,** and meditate on the verses to bring thoughts with you when we meet again.

HUSBAND-LOVING LESSON #2

BACK TO THE BEGINNINGS

ASSIGNMENT

Read, study, and ponder 1 Peter 3:1-6 with the following questions in mind:

(1) Is a wife in SUBJECTION because she has a meek and quiet spirit? Or,

(2) Does she have a meek and quiet spirit because she is in subjection?

Seek out verses to tell us what a meek and quiet spirit is and also how to put on this inner adornment. Sometimes we women have ideas as to what the inner adorning should be, but our ideas are not SCRIPTURAL.

BACK TO THE BEGINNING

When I was first asked to teach this course, my mind went to the Book of Genesis and to the first wife, EVE. What was there in Eve that God wanted for ADAM and what were the lessons which were for Eve from her CREATOR? These are what I want to know.

The "LAW OF FIRST REFERENCE" is what we should use in discovering God's teaching from His WORDS. The Law of First Reference is the KEY to how God wants us to interpret or understand a doctrine (or teaching).

Whenever we look into the book of Genesis, especially in the creation account, we must glance, at least, at the fact that the Triune God was. He always was—and He was there "*In the beginning God created the heaven and the earth*" (Genesis 1:1) "*by the word of His power*" (Hebrews 1:3b).

Creation took place in six twenty-four-hour days; six days like you and I live every day of our lives, only these six days were the first six days of time and space.

On the sixth day—the day before God rested—animals (creatures, cattle, creeping things, beasts) were created from the ground. Can you imagine the magnitude of beasts coming up from the dust and lumbering around a virgin field? All this holy handiwork--and there was more.

AN INTRA-TRINITARIAN DISCOURSE

The "MORE" was the creation of man and woman. Let us look at Genesis 1:26, where there was an intra-Trinitarian discourse, a pre-creation-of-Adam talk, a conversation that God had with Himself, between the Persons of the Trinity:

> *And God said, "Let us make man in our image, after our likeness; and let them have dominion over the fish of the sea and over the fowl of the air, and over the cattle, and over all the earth, and over every creeping thing that creepeth upon the earth* (Genesis 1:26).

God the FATHER, God the SON, and God THE HOLY SPIRIT said among the Persons of the Godhead, words to this effect:

> *We have made everything except man. It is time NOW to create these ones--these personages who will be like our image and after our likeness, who will be like US.*

THE DICTIONARY DEFINITION OF "IMAGE AND LIKENESS." "Likeness" and "image"—what do these two words mean? Why are they important?

The dictionary says of LIKENESS: *(1) THE STATE OR QUALITY OF BEING LIKE. (2) APPEARANCE: GUISE; SEMBLANCE. (3) A COPY; effigy; portrait. Syn. see RESEMBLANCE.*

The dictionary says concerning IMAGE:

(1) a. AN IMITATION OR LIKENESS OF ANY PERSON OR THING, SCULPTURED, DRAWN, PAINTED, OR THE LIKE; esp., AN IMITATION IN SOLID FORM, AS A SCULPTURED FIGURE; STATUE. b. Hence, form; aspect; likeness; semblance. (2) A COPY or counterpart. (3) A mental representation of anything not actually present to the senses; a picture drawn by the fancy; broadly, a conception; idea. (4) archaic: an illusory appearance; an apparition, (5) A TYPE; as SHE IS THE IMAGE OF DEVOTION. (6) A symbol; a representation, (7) The optical counterpart of an object, produced by a lens, mirror, or other optical system.

THE THEOLOGICAL DEFINITION OF "IMAGE & LIKENESS." Though these are good definitions and we can see some semblance of what we are trying to discover in these passages about the image of God and the likeness of God; theologically the meaning is understood to be PERSONALITY.

THE IMAGE OF GOD = THE PERSONALITY OF GOD

1. the intellect (mind)
2. the sensibility (feelings & emotions)
3. the will

LIKENESS=God is all-knowing, everywhere present, all-powerful. He did not make man thus. God made man in innocency, in His likeness. This is what man lost in sin.

THE WOMAN AT THE WELL

The Lord Jesus told the woman at the well that "*GOD IS A SPIRIT: and they that worship him must worship him in spirit and in truth*" (John 4:24). I tell you this, lest you think that man was created to look like the body of his CREATOR–for God has no body. (This shows us how much Jesus Christ–the second Person of the TRINITY–loved the sinner; to lay aside this beautiful EFFULGENT GLORY to humble Himself and become a man to die for man's sin. Redeeming love–will we ever comprehend it? (Philippians 2:5-8)

EFFULGENT = adj. *Diffusing a flood of resplendent light; radiant.*

THE RESULTANT MEANING: So, we could read this portion of Genesis like this:

> *And GOD THE FATHER, GOD THE SON, AND GOD THE HOLY SPIRIT said among the Persons of the Trinity, "Let us create MAN (meaning male and female) with a mind, with emotions, and with feelings, and with a will like we have (IN OUR IMAGE) and like we are (IN OUR LIKENESS).*

NONE CREATED LIKE MAN AND WOMAN

No animal was made with such personality. No fish or fowl had God-like feelings or a mind patterned after the TRIUNE GOD. No tree had a will to choose or reject its dwelling place—ONLY MAN.

You and I cannot fathom the fellowship in the GARDEN OF EDEN when God walked with the MALE AND FEMALE in the cool of the evening. PERFECT Communion. No hint of hurt or sight of sin. Complete innocence. How could they have wanted for more? Yet, they did.

> *. . . let them have dominion over the fish of the sea, and over the fowl of the air, and over the cattle, and over all the earth, and over every creeping thing that creepeth upon the earth* (Genesis 1:26b).

HAVING DOMINION

Now notice this interesting reading: "LET THEM HAVE DOMINION." Who is this "THEM"? Why, it is ADAM and EVE. She was to have a DOMINATING PLACE over (not ADAM) but over the created things which GOD had previously created that week. She was to be IN CHARGE—WITH ADAM, of all creatures, even the creeping things such as the mouse which today makes her scream in fright. This was to be a JOINT-DOMINION—a joint venture, a universal government. It seems to me, that ADAM was not supposed to rule over EVE, but was to rule WITH HER, in the beginning, before the Fall. In the purpose of God, Eve received her blessings and dignity in ADAM. WHAT CHANGED ALL THIS ARRANGEMENT? SIN!

THE "LIBERATED" WOMAN

It seems to me from this reading, that EVE was a LIBERATED WOMAN; and all of the fuss the "WOMAN'S LIBERATION" makes, will never bring women back to this perfect state, which was in the mind of the TRINITY during their creation week conversation.

True, the blood of Jesus Christ and the acceptance of His sacrifice at Calvary have lifted women above that degraded state she found herself in after the Fall—a state which became worse and worse and lower and lower until in some lands woman was nothing but dirt and the lowest slave. It is because of CALVARY that women have been treated as PEOPLE and have not been cast into the mouths of hungry beasts or the roaring flame to pacify a pagan god. (In many heathen lands where the name of Christ has never been sounded, this "liberation" of woman is not known.)

Husbands who love the Lord Jesus Christ and long to please Him and be doers of the WORD (James 1:22-23), should love their wives as their own flesh and lift them up in their homes (Ephesians 5:28) and in their hearts so that flame of devotion for their mates will light all the space around them like a halo of holiness and love. (See Ephesians 5:8).

> *So God created man in his own image, in the image of God created He him (Adam); male (ADAM) and female (EVE) created He them. (One was created from the dust of the ground, and one was created from the rib of the one created from the dust)* (Genesis 1:27).

SEX IS GOD'S IDEA

Now we have a very interesting account here of God's introducing man and woman to sexual intercourse. If you think I may be stretching it a bit, just contemplate what and how the young couple was to fulfill the

COMMAND of verse 28 of chapter one of Genesis. "*And God blessed them.*"

The GODHEAD blessed—consecrated—ADAM and EVE; pronounced them HOLY; conferred prosperity and happiness on them; guarded them; protected them; praised them; and instructed them in the "ACT OF MARRIAGE."

Oh, to have been so blessed. Would be that Eve had never been deceived by that old SERPENT and had her eyes opened to good and evil, damning every one of us females to become sinners.

It is through no fault of our own that we have been born in sin, any more than we have blue or brown eyes, but we stand or fall in Eve's train, and she has led us down the broad path which leadeth to destruction (Matthew 7:13-14).

But, do not condemn the MOTHER OF ALL LIVING, EVE, for if we had been the one so formed from the RIB of ADAM, would we have stood tall to the beguilement of THAT SNAKE?

> *But I fear, lest by any means, as the serpent beguiled Eve through his subtilty (craftiness), so your minds should be corrupted from the simplicity that is in Christ* (2 Corinthians 11:3).

BE FRUITFUL AND MULTIPLY

After GOD blessed the COUPLE, what did He say to them?

> *BE FRUITFUL, and MULTIPLY and REPLENISH (FILL) the earth* (Genesis 1:28).

Now let's take a fruit tree or a flower. If God would say to the fruit tree, "*BE FRUITFUL and MULTIPLY,*" HE would mean:

"*FRUIT TREE: LET THE WIND BLOW THE POLLEN BACK AND FORTH, LET THE BEES DO THEIR WORK AND HAVE FRUIT ON YOUR TREES. THEN, WHEN THE TIME COMES FOR THE SEEDS TO COME OUT OF THE ROTTED FRUIT ON THE GROUND, BE SURE THERE ARE ENOUGH SEEDS SO THAT MANY OF THE SEEDS WILL BE BURIED INTO THE GROUND AND PRODUCE MORE FRUIT TREES.*"

Notice the SCRIPTURE concerning the trees as to the seed in itself *"and the fruit tree yielding fruit after his kind"* (Genesis 1:11b).

So God said to MAN and WOMAN, be fruitful—have babies—and fill this new earth with your babies. And there is only one way to have babies—that is to have them. GOD blessed the "ACT OF MARRIAGE." He was, and is, all for it!

IT WAS VERY GOOD

At the end of His creation, God saw that, *"It was very good."* Up until Man and Woman were created, GOD always said, *"It is GOOD."* NOW, at the close of CREATION, and before He rested for one whole day, He saw that, *"IT WAS VERY GOOD"* (Genesis 1:31a). Can't you hear Adam respond with a hearty "AMEN, LORD." and Eve laughing like a tinkling bell as Adam held her close to his healing side?

The question is often asked why there were two versions of the CREATION of MAN and WOMAN. This is a good question. The first account of creation in Genesis, Chapter one, gives us the GENERAL PICTURE of creation. The second account gives the reader a fuller, detailed blow by blow description of the making of the Universe and the marvelous miracle of man and his HELPER. Genesis Chapter TWO brings to our attention the HOW, WHY, and WHEN of creation. Aren't we glad that Moses, through the Holy Spirit's out-breathing of inspiration, was used to write the Words which frame the believer's belief in GOD and His creation of the BEGINNING.

THINGS TO DO THIS WEEK

1. **Read, study, and ponder 1 Peter 3:1-6** with the following questions in mind:
   a. Is a wife in SUBJECTION because she has a meek and quiet spirit? or
   b. Does she have a meek and quiet spirit because she is in subjection? Seek out verses to tell us what a meek and quiet spirit and how inner adornment is put on.

2. **Find ways to cancel stress in your life.** There may be some things that you are doing—good things—which should be cut out in your weekly activities because they are causing you to get up-tight, to get out of control, to take time from "HUSBAND-LOVING." If there are such, eliminate them from your life. Test your life for one week without this stressful situation and see if your attitude is better concerning your "HUSBAND-LOVING."

3. **Do not NAG your husband.** It has been said, that if a wife has to say something more than once to her husband, she is nagging. Do you believe this? Maybe you don't, but chances are, your husband does. A husband is not a little boy to his wife; he is her husband. TREAT HIM as such.

4. Read and practice chapter 9, "THE KEY TO FEMININE RESPONSE," from Tim and Beverly LaHaye's book *THE ACT OF MARRIAGE.*

5. **PRAY that God will soften your heart toward the teachings of SCRIPTURE** as regards HUSBAND-LOVING and the price a wife (born-again wife) must pay for success in this endeavor--the price is SUBJECTION to one's husband.

6. Remember the three "s" words in wifeliness and HUSBAND-LOVING. They are:
    a. Subordination
    b. Subjection
    c. Submission

HUSBAND-LOVING LESSON #3

DEAD TO SELF—ALIVE TO SUBJECTION

RESISTING SCRIPTURAL SUBMISSION

How easy it is to resist the teaching of SCRIPTURE in regards to SUBMISSION. Our flesh rises like hair on a frightened dog; we stand against a foe when the word SUBJECTION is mentioned. Why?

It is our old nature rebelling within us, or our old (WO)man not wanting to die to self (Romans 6:11). It is our resurrecting that DEAD (WO)MAN again and pumping carnal life into her. This old nature has been crucified with CHRIST (Galatians 2:20). KEEP IT DEAD.

> *I am crucified with Christ: nevertheless I live; yet not I, but Christ liveth in me: and the life which I now live in the flesh I live by the faith of the Son of God, who loved me, and gave himself for me* (Galatians 2:20).

If the Lord would ask you to climb to the highest mountain for Him, you would get your climbing gear in shape and begin the ascent as soon as possible. If the Lord would ask you to stand on the street corner and pass out gospel tracts, no doubt, you would stand on the windiest day by the busiest corner and distribute literature for the Lord Jesus Christ.

God may require you to climb mountains for Him, or pass out tracts for His glory and the salvation of souls, that's true. But He does not say in the Bible, "Mary, climb a mountain. Joan, stand on a windy corner and pass out tracts." Yes, He DOES tell us to be WITNESSES and He may ask you to do this, it's true. BUT HE DOES COMMAND YOU, as a wife, to be in subjection to your own husband. Question: Are you obeying this clear command of Scripture?

SOMETHING TO REMEMBER— GOD'S GRACE IN SUBJECTION

Remember this, that God does not require a believing wife to do anything without the grace to fulfill that command (2 Corinthians 12:9-10). The Apostle Paul had some kind of infirmity—we are not sure what it was. Some think it had to do with his vision. He prayed that God would remove this affliction which drained him of energy. Remember now, that this was the man whom God used to heal others; but God elected not to heal Paul. In this answer to his prayer—NO—Paul received sufficient grace. He discovered "perfect strength" and Christ's power resting upon him.

> *And he said unto me, My grace is sufficient for thee: for my strength is made perfect in weakness. Most gladly therefore will I rather glory in my infirmities, that the power of Christ may rest upon me. Therefore I take pleasure in infirmities, in reproaches, in necessities, in persecutions, in distresses for Christ's sake: for when I am weak, THEN AM I STRONG* (2 Corinthians 12:9-10).

SUBJECTION LIFTS UP

Remember this also, that God did not give a command to be in subjection to your own husbands in order to degrade the Christian (born-again through faith in Jesus Christ alone) wife. He gives this command to LIFT HER UP, and to win her husband and to have marriage harmony.

This verse in John 12:24 comes to mind, which enforces this principle of dying to self. Jesus is talking:

> *Verily, verily (really, really or in today's vernacular "you better believe.") I say unto you, Except a corn of wheat fall into the ground AND DIE, it abideth alone; but IF IT DIE, it bringeth forth much fruit. He that loveth*

his life shall lose it; . . . If any (WO)man serve me, LET HIM FOLLOW ME; . . . (John 12: 24-26a)

SUBJECTION BRINGS FRUIT

Do you want to bear much fruit in your marriage?—fruit of love, companionship, communion, and sexual fulfillment?

Then get busy for the LORD and put on your SUBMISSION GARMENT. What is that? Why, it is the adorning of your inner (WO)man of the heart with the ornament of a MEEK AND QUIET SPIRIT.

> *But let it be*—(the adorning)—*the hidden man of the heart, in that which is not corruptible, even the ornament of a meek and quiet spirit, which is in the sight of God of great price* (1 Peter 3:4).

OBEDIENCE BEARS FRUIT

Hard words? Yes they are. But they are GOD'S WORDS, breathed into PETER, and he wrote them down for you and me to obey.

> *When we walk with the Lord in the light of His Word, What a glory He sheds on our way. While we do His good will, He abides with us still, And with all who will trust and obey.*
>
> *But we never can prove the delights of His love Until all on the altar we lay, For the favor He shows, and the joy He bestows, Are for them who will trust and obey.*
>
> *Trust and obey, for there's no other way*
> *To be happy in Jesus, but to trust and obey.*
>
> D. B. Towner

NOW LET US TURN TO OUR MARRIAGE MANUAL

Let's get out our magnifying glass with lens focused in on GOD'S CONCERN for woman. That is our concern too, isn't it? If it is not, there must be something wrong with us. Could it be that you are rebelling against the WORDS OF GOD? Or, could it be that you have never been born-again?

MAN, AN INCOMPLETE

It has been such a blessing to me to discover that GOD did not rest until WOMAN WAS CREATED FROM THE SIDE OF ADAM. God looked around and saw everything that He had made and it was GOOD, but He could not pronounce His "GOODNESS" blessing on the "SIXTH-DAY-MAN, (talk about the bionic man) because he was an incomplete creation.

God had created man and breathed into him the breath of life. All of God's creatures were called into being by the WORDS of God's power. He spoke and they were created. But animals (beasts), fowl, and man were created by the "*WORD OF HIS POWER*" from the ground—the dust (Genesis 2:7, 19). Only ADAM had the special "in-breathing" of God. By divine omnipotence, man was formed, all in one powerful creative act--spirit, soul, and body.

MAN NOT EVER A SUB-MAN CREATURE

It is important to note this, for some theistic evolutionists of the neo-evangelical persuasion, theorize that man (ADAM) was an "updated" beast like an ape or baboon whom God decided after thousands of years to breathe HIS breath of life into to make him ADAM. This is FALSE and unscriptural, but taught in many so-called CHRISTIAN COLLEGES. Beware where you send your children.

> *By an act of divine omnipotence man arose from the dust. We cannot say the body was earlier than the soul...but God breathes directly into the nostrils of the one man in the fulness of His personality, the breath of life, that in a manner corresponding to the personality of God, he may become a living soul.* (*Keil and Delitzsch's Commentaries on the Old Testament,* "PENTATEUCH" Vol. I, pp. 79, 80).

MAN—GOD BREATHED

Man was not only a soul, but a soul breathed entirely by God. ADAM'S spirit, soul, and body were created TOGETHER by God. God expired (breathed out) His holy breath into man. Man received HIS breath.

But it is well to note also that the archaic definition of INSPIRE says the following:

INSPIRE: a. to blow or breathe into or upon.

b. to infuse by breathing.

So, in this "inspiration" (archaic), God "inspired" (breathed) into Adam and man became a LIVING SOUL–different from animals.

> *And the LORD GOD* [JEHOVAH GOD], *in the Old Testament is the same "person" as the LORD JESUS CHRIST in the New Testament) formed man of the dust of the ground, and breathed into his nostrils the breath of life; and man became a LIVING SOUL* (Genesis 2: 7).

MAN—A TRIPARTITE BEING

Man is a TRIPARTITE BEING, consisting of "*spirit, soul, and body*" (1 Thessalonians 5:23).

> *The spirit is capable of God-consciousness; the soul is the seat of self-consciousness; the body of sense-consciousness.* (Dr. Pierson, quoted in *GLEANINGS IN GENESIS* by A. W. Pink, pp. 17,18).

THE SCRIPTURE—GOD-BREATHED

It has been a new thought to me, and a double blessing to ponder the Words "GOD-BREATHED" in regard to man's creation and to the inspiration of SCRIPTURES. Both the Holy Writings and Man were "GOD-BREATHED."

> *ALL SCRIPTURE is given by INSPIRATION OF GOD (GOD-BREATHED), and is profitable for doctrine, for reproof, for correction, for instruction in righteousness, that the man of God may be perfect, throughly furnished unto all good works* (2 Timothy 3:16).

This is one of the "3:16" verses that you should be familiar with along with John 3:16, and Genesis 3:16, and others, I'm sure.

You might look in the *Scofield Reference Bible* for an excellent summary and explanation of the doctrine of INSPIRATION (page 1284 in the *Old Scofield*).

THE PURPOSE OF THE SCRIPTURES

I was impressed as I looked up the various meanings of the Words in 2 Timothy 3:16, to see how cutting the SCRIPTURES are as they are applied to the life of a reader—a born-again reader. Notice first, that another term for SCRIPTURES is HOLY WRITINGS, and they are given by being "GOD-BREATHED" and the "HOLY WRITINGS" give gain or advantage for teaching you and me. Besides the advantage or gain or profit of doctrine (teaching), we see that you and I are given the HOLY WRITINGS to censure our faults, to rebuke and to reprimand us. You say, "God gave me the Bible to cut me up?" That's not all, girls; HE breathed out these Words to the apostle Peter to write down in black and white so you and I could be amended, chastised, punished—CORRECTED! You ask, "WHY?" And God responds, so you may be a perfect woman, "that the (WO)man of God may be PERFECT." And that you, as a wife, might be throughly furnished or equipped unto all good works. Now, keep in mind,

GOOD WORKS CANNOT SAVE or get you to heaven, but the believing woman should be a "*PATTERN OF GOOD WORKS*" (Titus 2:7).

Notice that, in these verses, we do not have any mention of the WORDS OF GOD as a comfort (or as a stay in our lives, or a balm for healing, though these truths are taught in other verses). This passage, which deals with the very nature of how the BIBLE came to be, is "*like a hammer which breaketh the rock in pieces*?" (Jeremiah 23:29b)

As a child, my mother taught me Hebrews 4:12, and it is now taking on another facet of light as I think of it in the better understanding of 2 Timothy 3:16-17. Look at verse 15 (2 Tim. 3:15), and see that it was the HOLY SCRIPTURES that Timothy, as a child, had known. No wonder God found a responsive chord in the heart of young Timothy. Are we teaching our children these powerful Words? Are we READING and HEEDING it ourselves? We who claim to love the Lord, do we really love Him? If so, we will read his LETTERS to us—his LOVE-LETTERS. Why not begin this year to READ YOUR BIBLE THROUGH. I have a working plan which I'd be glad to share with you, called "YEARLY BIBLE READING IN ACTION" by D. A. Waite. Ask me about it.

I SAID ALL THAT TO SAY THIS

We are STILL talking about Woman—wife, mother. But, before we can think about woman's creation (for hers was a special creation—weren't they all—but Eve's creation was different from man's or any of the living creatures).

First, we must understand ADAM and his creation and something of the wonder of the CREATOR before we can begin to comprehend WOMAN and all she was meant to be.

MAN CREATED WITH A NEED

God created Adam with a need. God knew what He was doing. He made MAN—every part of him, including his body with the biological equipment to procreate. God made Adam to be strong physically and mentally. He gave Adam needs such as hunger and sexual drives. He made man lonely and unfinished—incomplete. Even the animals which were created and brought to Adam could not satisfy, nor the beautiful Eden, the garden planted by God Himself. God planned the emptiness which Adam had. Only one day old, and man knew he was INCOMPLETE.

> *And the LORD GOD* (Jehovah God) *said, It is not good that the man should be alone. I will make him an HELP MEET* [fit] *for him* (Genesis 2:18a).

MAN CUT FOR COMPLETION

It was on a day like this--the sixth day of CREATION, that God called Adam aside and caused "*a deep sleep to fall upon Adam*" (Genesis 2:21a). Adam did not fight this "deep sleep" for "he slept." During this divine surgery, Eve was formed out of the rib from the first man's side.

How God "closed up the flesh" in Adam's gaping side, I do not know. What laser beam miracle-thread did God use? Or did He just speak the Words? Whatever the method, God had the perfect one and used it. I have often heard and had believed until right now as I write, that the FIRST BLOOD SHED was when the skins were provided for coverings for the sinful, banished husband and wife team of Genesis 3:21. If it were in today's surgery, blood would have been shed when a rib would be removed. But God didn't have to shed Adam's blood.

MAN COMPLETED BY WOMAN

Suddenly the picture of Adam—the first Adam, the one we are talking about here in Genesis, and Eve—the first wife, the one just created in Chapter 2, shine forth as beautiful pictures of the NEW TESTAMENT'S teaching concerning Jesus Christ—the Last Adam—and His Church, THE BRIDE OF CHRIST—all those who have received Jesus Christ as personal Saviour. (Please read Chapter #1 of our *HUSBAND-LOVING LESSONS* [pp. 21-33] for details and instructions on how to be saved). How precious!

No wonder the CREATOR—remember the Triune God is involved here and the LORD GOD (Jehovah God—Jesus Christ) cries out "IT IS VERY GOOD" (Genesis 1:31). These Words ended the sixth day--twenty-four hours. Thus ended CREATION.

A COMPLETED CREATION BROUGHT REST

And with the creating of WOMAN from the side of ADAM, God RESTED. He could not rest until Adam had a wife.

Woman completed Creation. God could not rest until she was created. The WORLD WITHOUT A WOMAN WAS AN INCOMPLETE WORLD. (See how important Eve was to the universe?) It was not until she was created and instructed concerning Sex and Supper (food) that God rested (Genesis 1:28).

God wanted Eve to glorify Him,
to complete Adam, and
to be fruitful and multiply.

Do you have any other reasons for the creating of Eve? If so, list them here:

____
____
____

WIFEHOOD, A DIVINE COMMISSION

GOD CREATED EVE to be:
a wife, and
a mother.

NEVER should we down-grade these DIVINE positions. NEVER should we think or say, "I am JUST a wife." Or, "I am JUST a mother." Eve was commissioned by God to a life of wifehood and motherhood.

On the sixth day, as it began, there were TWO LACKS:

(1) no man to till the ground, and
(2) no woman to complete the man. At the close of the day,

both were taken care of:
(1) man, and
(2) mate.

WOMAN PRODUCES THE ACTION

WOMAN is the action verb to man. He is the subject. He is the nominative and she is the predicate. Woman is to complement, therefore, she is the "subjective complement." Woman is also to complete, calm, console, captivate, caress, cater, charm, civilize, cleave, cohere, comfort, comply, confer, confide, confirm, conform, conjoin, conjugate, conquer, conscript, consent, conserve, consider, consummate, contemplate, converse, coo, coordinate, core, correlate, cradle, cuddle, and cohabit with her husband!

The most wonderful words a wife can hear from her husband's lips should be, "*It is very good.*" Oh to be that kind of wife. And with the help of the Holy Spirit, dwelling within the believer wife, she can be this woman, this wife.

THE DRAMA OF LIFE BEGINS

As we go further into our lessons, we will see that the drama of life began around verse seven of chapter two in Genesis. Here was the starting point of human history. **All history looks back to ADAM and EVE and all prophecy goes forward from this point in time. (The first prophetic statement in Genesis 3:15).**

What a joy to study the lives of our first parents. What a privilege to apply the law of first reference to Eve and plot our paths as WIVES. May God bless us as we seek to surrender to His will. May we not be guilty of falling into the same pitfalls that Eve found herself in.

How many times in her life after she was expelled from the GARDEN, did she wish she had obeyed the Words of God.

TRUST AND OBEY, FOR THERE IS NO OTHER WAY TO BE HAPPY IN JESUS, BUT TO TRUST AND OBEY.

THINGS TO THINK ABOUT AND DO THIS WEEK

1. **Pray that God will soften our heart** toward the teaching of Scriptures concerning submission to one's husband. Pray that we will be more like Jesus Christ and walk in His steps in this area (1 Peter 3:1, 2:21).

2. **Practice your Pubo Coccygeus (P.C.) muscle exercises.**

3. Put item "2 & 3" information to use often this week.

> *Marriage is honorable in all, and the bed (COITUS) in Greek, the marriage bed) undefiled* (Hebrews 13:4a).

4. **BEGIN TO MEMORIZE 1 Peter 3:1-7 from King James Version please.**

5. Add a new "s" word to your list--SURRENDER.
   (1) Subordinate
   (2) Subject
   (3) Submit
   (4) Surrender
   Can you think of any more?

Continue thinking about the meek and quiet spirit in regard to the subjective wife. We will discuss it soon.

Love your husband. Love your enemy. Loving begins in the mind. **SUBMISSION IS AN ATTITUDE**.

(5) **Do not admonish**. What is your attitude here? Don't "BAD-MOUTH" your man.

(6) Can't means won't. Let's cancel the word "can't" from our "HUSBAND-LOVING" vocabulary. How about it?

(7) **Weddings last a day, but marriage is forever**. It's

been sixty-five (as of August 27, 2013) years for me; how long has been your "FOREVER"?

(8) Continue to **FIND WAYS TO CANCEL STRESS IN YOUR LIFE.**

(9) **BECAUSE Marriage is of God, it has to be GOOD.** Think about it.

(10) Take any letter in the alphabet and go through each word in your dictionary, jotting down all words which tell you how to act toward your husband. Look on page 52 [in this LESSON #3], and see what I've done with the letter "c." It will be enlightening to you and a challenge.

(11) QUESTION: **Has there been a definite time in your life that you received Jesus Christ as your Saviour?** If not, what is keeping you from making the most important decision of your life? (Read John 1:12.) I am not asking you if you joined a church or were baptized, but if you are saved from sin.

HUSBAND-LOVING LESSON #4

WINNING BY DYING

TOO LATE FOR LOIS

Let me tell you about a young widow; let's call her Lois. While she and her husband were separated, due to his military career, he died of natural causes. Lois was shocked. Who wouldn't have been?

Death is a dreadful monster, eating into our being, leaving us numb, empty, and perhaps desperately bitter—especially if we have no hope for the deceased soul or no comfort from the Scriptures:

> *(. . . behold, NOW is the accepted time; behold, NOW is the day of salvation)* (2 Corinthians 6:2b).

She looked at me with tears in her beautiful eyes and said, *"Oh, Vonnie, if my husband were only alive today, I would make him a good wife."* (Lois had been led to the Saviour during death's aftershock.)

There is much to the story that I would not reveal, only to say when Lois had a living husband, she was unfaithful to him. When he was away, she was involved with another man. The Lord forgave her of her sin when she accepted the Lord Jesus Christ. She had much guilt connected with her adultery, and his death. Her sincere grief and her recent salvation, made her believe she would be better as a wife if she were only given another chance. But, it was too late.

"Now you say that you would be a good wife, Lois, but how do you really know? Stop torturing yourself with what you could be 'IF.' You had your chance. You didn't love him as you should. You cannot re-do the past. You must be what the Lord wants you to be today." This is some of what I told her.

NOW IS YOUR TIME FOR HUSBAND-LOVING

What is my purpose in telling you this? I want to emphasize to you that it's **NOW** for you and your husband—NOT TOMORROW. Not when he gets a better job, or you have more money, or a bigger house. It's TODAY with you and your husband, not when the children are grown, not when the furniture is paid for, not when he gets that promotion, not when he doesn't work the night shift, not when your surgery is over, not after the Christmas rush. YOUR TIME TO BE A GOOD WIFE IS NOW. . . . This is true, whether you are born-again or not. But so much more should a believer of the Lord Jesus Christ be desirous to be that virtuous, valuable wife of which the SCRIPTURES speak (Proverbs 31:10-31; 1 Corinthians 7; Ephesians 5:22-24; 1 Peter 3:1-6).

OVERLOOK FAULTS AND MERGE PERSONALITIES

The Christian wife must learn to overlook some things in her marriage, about her husband which "rub her the wrong way." She must learn to live under conditions which aren't "perfect" and "story-bookish." **She must realize that she has accepted the proposal of her husband in marriage and that she promised to live with him in sickness and in health and for better or worse.**

When a girl gets married somehow she doesn't think of the "sickness" and the "worse" as she is busily matching brides-maid's outfits with groomsmen's attire. She does not think of the personal inconsistencies and inconsiderations of her groom; only of his handsome features and his outstanding kisses.

When a woman enters marriage, she enters a new room of living. Two households have come together to form another HOME. There will be strains and stresses in pounding together this new building. Customs from two families will clash at times. Ways of doing things will be spotlighted. Words, phrases, punishments, gestures.

Her father may have worked one way, her husband another, producing cultural shock for the bride. His mother may have functioned in a manner so the groom knows his bride is doing everything wrong; thus he continually instructs her how to manage her life. I could go on and on with illustrations of such differences. I am sure you could add to this list fourfold, too. DON'T!

WHAT IS THE HUSBAND-LOVER TO DO?

Remember, we are only concerned in these lessons about the wife's rules found in the BIBLE. (Though there are rules for husbands, we are not the husbands and we are not going to confuse the issues of our responsibility to GOD by being overcome with our mate's failures to follow or their ability to apply God's teaching to themselves.)

First, let's realize that all these petty things—sometimes monstrous differences—are the result of the testing in the Garden of Eden, man's first honeymoon-cottage. There is a TREE OF TESTING in every marriage. God does not want us as women to fail the test—and have miserable marriages. He really doesn't. He wants us to be fruitful and multiply, and fill our cottage with delight. He wants us to have a consuming desire to be good wives, good women, obedient to HIM, and thus obedient to our husbands, submissive to their headship. God wants wives to surrender to their mates and therefore be surrendered.

WHY IS SUBMISSION DIFFICULT?

I have encouraged you to learn a verse of SCRIPTURE found in Romans 6:11. Maybe other teachers on HUSBAND-LOVING use this verse, I do not know. BUT, I feel that if believing women would consider themselves DEAD to the "sin" around them, they can and will have victory in the home. What good is Christian victory in the life of a woman at the grocery store? at the office? (if she is employed outside the home), in the church? What good is all this dying to self and living a life of faith to the outside world, if as soon as she sets her feet into her home, she begins sinning? Where should be our greatest influence?

A SCRIPTURAL WIFE IS A "DEAD" WIFE

Here are some comments on Romans 6:11:

Likewise, reckon	[count on, rely]
ye also yourselves to be dead indeed unto sin	Think how dead a corpse is. You should be insensitive.
The primary reference here is to the SIN NATURE which is IN OURSELVES, not in our husband.	This not only means what we label as BAD SINS, but this means the things and circumstances in your home which cause you to be distraught, over-reactive, un-kind, sulking, sinning as a wife.
BUT ALIVE UNTO GOD	[I think this means, I as a wife, as a mother, as a woman, should be vibrant, radiant, glowing, unto GOD. I do not have to be dead, a dullard, but a beautifully "inner-adorned" wife. (1 Peter 3:4). A SCRIPTURAL WIFE can be "in subjection to her own husband" because she has put herself under GOD; and GOD has set her husband above her as the HEAD.]
through JESUS CHRIST	He is the Second Person of the Trinity. He is the Saviour of the WORLD. He

is the One Who is holding our earth together by "*the WORD of HIS POWER.*" Let's get a fresh and accurate view of JESUS CHRIST. Let's stop thinking of him as a mild man, as a milk-toast person of the GODHEAD, as a helpless, baby-in-a-manger. It is this POWERFUL ONE, GOD THE SON, who can make us ALIVE UNTO GOD, if we just remain DEAD to sin.

our LORD (Romans 6:11).

Is the Lord Jesus CHRIST the LORD of your life? I know you think I am a "harper" on your personal salvation, but you cannot be a GODLY WOMAN, wise unto salvation, if you are not born-again.

That if thou shalt confess with thy mouth the Lord Jesus, and shalt believe in thine heart that God hath raised him from the dead, thou shalt be saved" (Romans 10:9).

For with the heart man believeth unto righteousness; and with the mouth confession is made unto salvation (Romans 10:10).

For whosoever shall call upon the name of the Lord shall be saved (Romans 10:13).

For God so loved the world, that he gave his only begotten Son, that whosoever believeth in him should not perish, but have everlasting life (John 3:16).

TWO ASPECTS OF JESUS' PERSONALITY

(1) JESUS CHRIST AS THE NON-REVILER:

The place of the scripture which he read was this, He was led as a sheep to the slaughter; and like a lamb dumb before his

(2) JESUS CHRIST AS THE ALL-POWERFUL ONE!

(a) The Image of the Invisible God

(b) The Firstborn of all

shearer, so opened he not his mouth: (Acts 8:32, Isaiah 53:7-8).

creation
© The Creator of all things
(d) The One for Whom all things were created
(e) The One Who was before all things (Genesis 1:1; John 1:1).
(f) The Head of the church
(g) The Firstborn from the dead
(h) The One Who is Preeminent over all things
(i) The One in Whom all the fullness of the Godhead dwells bodily (Colossians 1:15-19).

WHICH PATTERN DOES A WIFE FOLLOW?

The BELIEVING WIFE is to pattern her behavior after Jesus' characteristic of being like a "dumb lamb" who opened not His mouth. (See 1 Peter 2:21-3:2; John 1:29).

What do I get from these comparisons of verses? Wives are to follow Jesus Christ's steps as He was like a "dumb lamb" DYING for the guilty, guile-filled sinner. A wife is not supposed to revile, lord it over, or admonish her spouse. SHE is supposed to LIVE THE CHRISTIAN LIFE before him, which is one hundred times more difficult than getting up on Sunday morning, teaching a Sunday School class, or giving HUSBAND-LOVING Lectures.

What you DO speaks so loudly, I can't hear what you SAY.

STIR UP AND WORK OUT

. . . STIR UP the gift of God, which is in thee . . . (2 Timothy 1:6).

Within you is this potential of being a HUSBAND-

LOVER, physically, mentally, emotionally. Stir up this gift and bring the aroma of the SPIRITUAL out in you. BE DEAD TO THE FLESH (Galatians 2:20; 1 Peter 2: 24).

Here's a good question for wives:

> *God forbid. How shall we, THAT ARE DEAD TO SIN, live any longer therein?* (Romans 6:2)

WORK OUT YOUR OWN SALVATION

This passage of GOD'S WORDS have nothing WHATSOEVER to do with getting saved. Nothing you can do can bring salvation to your soul. Jesus Christ did it all. He paid the price at Calvary for your redemption (Ephesians 2:8-9).

Philippians 2:12-13 has to do with "working out the polish" of your life to show that you have been with JESUS.

> *Wherefore, my beloved* [WIVES], *as ye have always obeyed* [Have you obeyed God's commands?] . . . *WORK OUT your own salvation with fear and trembling. For it is God WHICH WORKETH IN YOU both to will* [God's will for your life] *and to* do [obedience--Eve disobeyed God] *of HIS good pleasure* (Philippians 2:12-13).

THE TARNISHED TEAPOT

Think of your marriage as a tarnished silver teapot. "I don't like it," you say. So you get a soft cloth, and plenty of water. You apply TARNISH REMOVER with the cloth and polish and polish, washing and drying the teapot. "*My, doesn't that look nice*!" you say to yourself. Still you are not satisfied and begin to polish some more. Again you polish, wash, and dry. Over and over you see where the tarnish has left imperfections in the craftsman's art. Finally, the teapot is polished to your liking. "*How beautiful*!" you say as you tell your children. The family is thrilled that Mother cared enough to bring out the luster of the silver teapot.

Will that silver teapot stay beautiful without continued care? No. Tomorrow you'll have to polish it again. It will take weekly—if not daily—attention.

This daily attention of polishing your marriage is part of what the Lord means for us women in working out our salvation. We have imperfections—do we ever! We must polish our HUSBAND-LOVING. Soon the whole family will say "Thank you, Mother, that you cared enough for your marriage to work at it, to keep it shining for the LORD and for us."

THE WINNING WIFE IS A DEAD WIFE

Remember the ONLY way a wife can win is to stay dead. (Not "play dead" like a faking dog, but **RECKON herself dead to sin.**)

Take heart if all this seems too hard.

> *FOR IT IS GOD which worketh in you both to will and to do of his good pleasure* (Philippians 2:13).

He will help you polish your tarnished life.

THINK AND DO THIS WEEK

1. **PRAY**, PRAY, PRAY, **YIELD**, YIELD, YIELD . . . to the pricking of the Spirit of God in your life as to HIS WILL for your submissive attitude as a HUSBAND-LOVER.

2. **Memorize ROMANS 6:11.**

   > ***Likewise reckon ye also yourselves to be dead indeed unto sin, but alive unto God through Jesus Christ our Lord*** **(Romans 6:11).**

   Put it above the kitchen sink and yield to the Holy Spirit as He teaches and reaches you through this SCRIPTURE VERSE and through this particular lesson on HUSBAND-LOVING.

3. **BE DEAD to cutting remarks your husband** may make toward you or the children.

4. **ADORN your inner (wo)man** of the heart with a meek and quiet spirit (1 Peter 3:3-5).

5. **DO NOT ADMONISH YOUR MAN** (BY NOW YOU MUST BE VERY AWARE OF THIS SHORTCOMING IN YOURSELF.)

6. **COMPLIMENT YOUR HUSBAND AT LEAST ONCE A DAY—make** it genuine.

7. **ATTEND A BIBLE-BELIEVING, BIBLE-PREACHING CHURCH THIS WEEK.**

8. ANY TIME WOMAN IS CORRUPTED, MAN GOES DOWN.

9. **THROUGH THE WIFE'S WILLINGNESS TO SUBMIT, SHE WINS.**

10. READ GENESIS 1-3, 1 PETER 2-3 this week and meditate upon them.

HUSBAND-LOVING LESSON #5

"HOME SWEETHEART HOME"

HUSBAND-LOVING PAYS

Let me tell you some of the results of our *HUSBAND-LOVING LESSONS*. One of the girls told how she was sitting in a chair reading our lessons—which have written on the cover, in large, bold letters, the words "*HUSBAND-LOVING LESSONS*." Her husband came into the room. He stopped. He looked at the title. Suddenly, a beautiful expression appeared on his face. She said *"I hadn't seen him look so tender for years."*

That husband WAS impressed. His wife cared enough about him to take "lessons" on "LOVING." This woman told me she was going to take her notes and BIBLE and DO what the BIBLE said to change her home and win her man to the LORD. More and more, I am convinced there is a great need for *HUSBAND-LOVING LESSONS* in the local church..

When the girls come into my house on Monday afternoon, they can't wait to get into the WORDS to see what's up for HUSBAND-LOVING. They say. *"We just LOVE this class."* At first, I didn't think too much of it, but now I am beginning to believe them. Why? Because this class is doing a lot for me, too, and I'm the teacher.

Sometimes I tell friends about the class and they look at me like I have my head on crooked, and as if to say "What's the matter with her?" I presume they are thinking I don't know what I am talking about. But, more and more I am CONVINCED of the great need in the LOCAL CHURCH for *HUSBAND-LOVING LESSONS.*

Some women who are resisting the teaching say the class should be called "WIFE-LOVING LESSONS." They feel husbands are not loving their wives as Christ loved the CHURCH. Many husbands treat their spouses mean and like inferiors. I cannot deny many husbands do belittle and are most un-Christ-like and are constantly "cleansing the temple" at home.

I recognize that many husbands are slaves to drink, adulterers, foul-mouthed, two-faced, and they make their homes miserable. But I am not a man to teach such lessons. I firmly believe that if a WIFE does HER PART, the man will come around. It will not happen overnight, but God will honor obedience to His Words.

HOME IS WHERE THE HEART IS

"I never go out at night, unless it is some school function" is what a new Christian wife told me. *"My husband wants me home with him at night,"* she continued, *"and I want to be there." He could be running around with the 'boys' or even drinking or living it up with some woman."*

Now isn't that what the GARDEN OF EDEN was all about in part? Man was home nights and WOMAN wanted to be with him. The beauty of it all is that God blessed this idea and encouraged a helper that was fitting for the man.

Could it be that all these "super-aggressive" churches are making a huge mistake by having church activities every night of the week? When do wife and husband have time to get to know each other? The woman is out to choir practice. lady's meetings, and church visitation (besides prayer meeting). When does the husband have time to be a father and a wife-lover if he is off "winning souls" every night, or at the Deacons' meeting, or taking the young people on a picnic? Just asking.

A few years ago, we were saddened at the plight of an active teacher and soul winner. Everyone thought he was "something" in the witnessing department. While he was doing church work, his wife was having an affair with a neighbor. I certainly do not condone the woman's sinful actions, but if it was his absence which opened the door to such sinful actions, I condemn that absence. What do you think?

PARADISE IS THE PATTERN

The GARDEN OF EDEN was planted by JEHOVAH GOD ("Jehovah" is the name for the Lord Jesus Christ in the Old Testament.)

This EDEN is not the Eden of Assyria (2 Kings 9:12) or Coele-Syria (Amos 1:5). What a beautiful, delightful spot for the honeymoon--a prepared place for a prepared man and his mate.

Eden, which means "DELIGHT," was a proper name for a particular district. The garden was eastward in EDEN. A river flowed out of EDEN (Genesis 2:10) and from this source, the river parted into four other rivers, called PISON (there was gold in them-there-hills, vs. 11), GIHON around the land of Ethiopia (not the CUSH or ETHIOPIA we know today), HIDDEKEL (which is the ancient name for the TIGRIS River). Assyria was on the eastern side of the TIGRIS [Cf., *Keil & Delitzech,* Vol. I, The Pentateuch, in loco]. The fourth river is EUPHRATES (Genesis 2:11-14).

All of this is around the BABYLON area. Look on a map of the Near East in the time of the Assyrian Empire. I think it is very interesting to remember that the Magi, who came to BETHLEHEM to worship the Child Jesus were from the EAST (Matthew 2:2), probably from the same area as EDEN. No one really knows the exact spot of EDEN, because the changes in the earth's topography brought on by the flood, changed everything on earth–including how EDEN was and perhaps even WHERE Eden was.

We are giving some thought to Eden's location because God gave much thought to it, describing its location well. God is interested in our home, and where it is located.

Paradise was, perhaps, like a park filled with *"every tree that is pleasant to the sight, and good for food"* (Genesis 2:9). Can you imagine the beauty of that place? The color, the fragrance, the foliage? Out of the new earth these trees grew and from these trees ADAM and EVE were to eat. No one ate meat until after the flood (Genesis 9:3). All the generations until Noah ate herbs and trees which had their seeds within them. I wonder how many pounds of APRICOT KERNELS Noah put on board the ark?

HEALTH AND HAPPINESS THE VITAMIN WAY

I would like to speak here about vitamins. I am not a doctor but I know from personal experience how much vitamin B Complex has helped me. The vitamin B's are excellent for NERVES. Couple them with Vitamin C and a person can be fortified for stressful situations in one's life (along with spiritual fortification).

There was a time in my life when I was so crabby in the morning and twice as cantankerous at night; when I couldn't stand the wallpaper or the room, etc. Then I began taking the B complexes, and discovered that I could tolerate my life better. Praying didn't help, nor reading the Bible, because my nerves were shot, so to speak. All the Scriptural injunctions in the world didn't help, because I was starving for proper vitamins.

I remember another time when I was at "blood transfusion level" and so anemic that I had to sleep almost all the day. Bible verses couldn't get me going nor clean the house. After building my blood up, I was better, and then my soul and spirit had a good body to work with.

Recently, we have learned that sugar can do much damage to a person's health. We try to limit our intake. Some people are mentally ill because of sugar. Many times eliminating all sugars will produce a brighter, quicker, happier individual. Why don't you consider this, if you are depressed and discouraged, along with Scriptural nutriments?

HONEYMOON PARK HEDGE-AROUND

The GARDEN was a place hedged around. I like to think of the first Home of the first couple in a place protected by the CREATOR and blessed by His presence.

My mind flashes to the book of JOB, where God asked Satan if he had noticed the perfect and upright character of the Patriarch who feared God and shunned evil. Oh, Job had been spied by Satan all right. Probably the Wicked One had tried his best to hit Job with one of his fiery darts. But, try as hard as he could, those burning darts were quenched (Ephesians 6:16).

> *Then Satan answered the LORD and said, Doth Job fear God for nought? Hast not thou made an hedge about him, and about his house, and about all that he hath on every side?* (Job 1:9-10)

I like to think of the Garden of Eden as HEDGED ABOUT with God's protection. Only with God's permission was SATAN permitted in that Honeymoon Park. The entrance of Satan in the body of that Serpent was permitted by God. Adam and Eve were created free moral agents. They were not robots, like a computer. They were not programmed to sin or not to sin. They were Innocent. They had the power of choice. (So do we.)

God placed a *test* in the center of that garden. This Garden home was not different from any other home today. Family after family have *TESTS* in their midst. There was nothing wrong with the tree of the knowledge of good and evil. Often nothing is wrong with a *test* which comes to our lives. It is what we do with that *test* or *temptation* which is right or wrong.

Job did not curse God and die, but, in a sense, Adam and Eve did.

> *. . . for in the day that thou eatest thereof THOU SHALT SURELY DIE* (Genesis 2: 17).

UNINHIBITED INNOCENCE

(We will speak more of the *tes*t in other lessons.) But, now let's go back to the HEDGED-IN-PLACE—the HOME, the place where a man can return after a day's work and shut the door and be alone with his wife and children.

This home where God is welcomed every day, where all was created for man's benefit and pleasure, where there are rules like "thou shalt not . . ." It had the ideal environment (Genesis 2:17).

Adam and Eve were to lead a fulfilled life, not one of blood, sweat, and tears. They were to relish each other's love and work together—he always being the head, and she the subordinate one, he the leader, and she, holding his hand.

Can't you picture them, fresh, and full of vigor, virile, and eager to learn to love? Sometimes they would till the ground together—it was like a game—and, sometimes they romped and played and performed the "act of marriage."

EDEN

In their beautiful innocence, they were free as the animals—making love with abandonment, no inhibitions. No one was there to see them, to make fun of them—only their CREATOR Who approved of them. Had He not said, "It is VERY GOOD"? What affection did not Eve owe to Adam.

What nearness she enjoyed.
What intimacy of communion,
What full participation in all his thoughts.
In all his dignity, and in all his glory, she was entirely one.
He did not rule OVER, but WITH her.
He was lord of the whole creation, and she was one with him.
Yea, as has already been remarked,
She was looked at and blessed IN him.
"The man" was the object;
And as to "the woman;" she was needful to him,
And therefore, she was brought into being.
NOTES ON THE BOOK OF GENESIS by C.H.M., a writer of former years)

A PUZZLE FOR YOU.

Let's remind ourselves that God could not, would not rest until woman was created to complete man. EVE WAS NEEDFUL TO ADAM. **You, my dear reader, are needful to your ADAM.**

"and the LORD GOD said, It IS NOT GOOD that the man. should be alone;"

God is telling you right now, wife, that it is not good for your man to be alone. Oh, Adam could name the animals. He could till the ground. He could harvest the fruit from the trees and bushes. BUT HE WAS ALONE—AND BEING ALONE IS NOT GOOD . . .

How much is your husband without you?

Let's get down to "brass tacks". How often do the two of you make love to each other?

When did you make him feel like the most important man in the world—the ONLY MAN in your world?

"I will make him an help meet [fit] *for him"* (Genesis 2:18).

I think that God is saying that man is part of a puzzle—he needs the OTHER PART. I'm going to make someone to fit his "part" into. Without WOMAN man could exist, but he was incomplete. Without YOU, your husband can exist, but he is incomplete. Do you get the picture?

THE KEY TO THE PUZZLE IS THE LOCK AGAINST ADULTERY

Nevertheless, to avoid fornication, let every man have his own wife, and let every woman have her own husband. Let the husband render unto the wife due benevolence: and likewise also the wife unto the husband. The wife hath not power of her own body, but the husband: and likewise also the husband hath not power of his own body, but the wife. Defraud ye not one the other . . . that Satan tempt you not . . . (1 Corinthians 7:2-5).

Notice the constant emphasis on "OWN husband" and "OWN wife." Doesn't this remind us again of 1 Peter 3:1?

***Ye wives, be in subjection to YOUR OWN HUSBANDS . . .* (1 Peter 3: 1).**

HOME DIVIDENDS

The following are Scripture verses which may help us to be better wives within our EDENS. Let us pray that we will be fortified with "good things" and not yield to the constant presence of the "test" within our HEDGE:

Psalm 101:2 ***I will behave myself wisely in a perfect way. O when wilt thou come unto me? I will walk within my house with a perfect heart.***

Psalm 68:12b *she that tarried at home divided the spoil.*

John 20:10 *Then the disciples went away again unto their own home.* These men had wives and families to go home to. I'm sure you recall Peter's mother-in-law being ill. He couldn't have a mother-in-law without a wife, could he? Or did they do it differently in the New Testament days? (Matthew 8:14; Mark 1:30; Luke 4:38)

Mark 5:19 *Howbeit Jesus suffered him not, but saith unto him, Go home to thy friends, and tell them how great things the Lord hath done for thee, and hath had compassion on thee.* What if no one had been home to talk with? He would have to go someplace else, wouldn't he?

Lamentations 1:20 *Behold, O LORD; for I am in distress: my bowels are troubled; mine heart is turned within me; for I have grievously rebelled: abroad the sword bereaveth, at home there* is as death. When a member of the family sins or is troubled, the whole HOME suffers.

Titus 2:4-5

That they may teach the young women to be sober, to love their husbands [not someone else's husband], *to love their children, To be discreet, chaste, KEEPERS AT HOME, good, obedient to their own husbands, THAT THE WORD OF GOD BE NOT BLASPHEMED.* Do these things, if for no other reason than that the WORDS OF GOD will not be held up in contempt. Oh, Christian wife, if we have failed in any of these areas, and the other areas in this passage, we are making fun of the HOLY WRITINGS—that Book which has been GOD-BREATHED for our correction, instruction, etc. (2 Timothy 3:16-17).

1 Samuel 1:19

And they rose up in the morning early, and worshipped before the LORD, and returned, and came to their house to Ramah: and Elkanah knew Hannah his wife; and the LORD remembered her. Elkanah performed the "act of marriage" with his wife. Where? in a car? at a construction site? in the woods with the robins? No—IN THEIR HOUSE. (But there would be no sin for the married to do such, but it could be public, though, and a little cold).

Joshua 24:15

And if it seem evil unto you to serve the LORD, choose you this day whom ye will serve; whether the gods which your fathers served that were on the other side of the flood, or the gods of the Amorites, in whose land ye dwell: but as for me and MY

HOUSE, we will serve the LORD. The husband should say this. Every Christian woman should long to be a subjective, submissive, subordinate, surrendered spouse, so her husband can take this stand with her. As you yield to God's will in HUSBAND-LOVING, he will yield to God in wife and GOD-LOVING.

Nehemiah 1:6

Let thine ear now be attentive, and thine eyes open, that thou mayest hear the prayer of thy servant, which I pray before thee now, day and night, for the children of Israel thy servants, and confess the sins of the children of Israel, which we have sinned against thee: both I and my father's house have sinned (Nehemiah 1:6). At home is where confession of sin should take place. To each other, and to God.

Psalm 113:9

He maketh the barren woman to keep house, and to be a joyful mother of children. Praise ye the LORD. God can make the childless couple have a good house and a loving home where God is glorified. Precious should be such a home where the two can be one flesh and they can walk with God in the cool of their evenings.

"BE MY LOVE"

Be my love
When shadows fall and evening lengthens,
Be my love, tender, true.

Hear my cries of grief
and do caress me,
Share my thoughts too deep to share with few.

Be my love,
Touch my face with kindness,
Hearken to my inward need.

Give me time,
And strengthen me with smiles and gestures,
Comforting my desperate need.

Be my love,
Though you do not understand me,
Grasp my hand, and hold it to your face;

Feed my heart,
And fill the aching longing
Be my love as well as be my mate.

To my husband
Yvonne S. Waite
April 12, 1974

THINGS TO DO AND THINK ABOUT THIS WEEK

1. **<u>Continue to pray that God will make you yielded</u> to the teaching of the BIBLE concerning being a SUBMISSIVE WIFE.** Some of you are still resisting the Words in this area. I know it is hard. None of us are SARAHS yet; but remember, we are not as old as she was, either. There is hope.

2. Discover a different way to make your home more like EDEN this week.

3. **Clean up your marriage.** Get all that spoiled food out of your refrigerator. Get all that spoiled living out of your marriage.

4. **ATTEND A BIBLE-BELIEVING and BIBLE-PREACH-ING CHURCH THIS WEEK.**

5. CONTINUE READING *THE ACT OF MARRIAGE* by Beverly and Tim LaHaye. What chapter are you on now? Have you begun the P. C. exercises yet? What are you waiting for?

6. **Speaking of the "act of marriage," is three times a week too much to ask?** [As a "bare" minimum?--that's the lowest frequency I could think of.] There are seven days in a week. Three times is like a vacation. There are 52 weeks in a year. 52 x 7 = 365 times. 52 x 3 = 156—doesn't seem like much to me.

7. **Fix yourself up every day—pretty for your husband.** He may notice, he may not, but combine suggestion #7 with suggestion #8, and he'll notice!

8. MAKE LOVE, NOT WAR. In other words, DON'T
   admonish,
   correct, or
   nag.
   Your ADAM married a wife, not a mother.

9. Continue in Genesis, reading and re-reading Chapters 1-3. Read all of 1 Corinthians 7 this week, and if you have commentaries or helpful books, see what they say about the verses.

10. **Hold your husband's hand** as you walk down the street, in the mall, or in church this week. Reach over and take his hand during prayer at church–You want him to miss you in case you die.

HAPPY HUSBAND-LOVING!!

HUSBAND-LOVING LESSON #6

"BE OF GOOD CHEER"

WHAT DOES A WOMAN WANT MOST IN HER LIFE?

I once saw a newspaper ad that said:

> *ZINMAN has more of what woman wants most at 25%~40% off.*

This is what the newspaper ad said. My eyes scanned the words and noticed the women dressed in furs.

> *Save now, pay later with BankAmericard, Master Charge, American Express, or our Zinman NO-INTEREST Layaway Plan,*

the fine print read.

A fur coat? A new car? A diamond ring? Aren't all these "things" invented for her "happiness"? How many times have we "wanted" a new pair of shoes? "I just have to have them." we think, as we anticipate the completion of a new outfit's accessories. Many have the "itch for more," but possessions NEVER satisfy. They are really unimportant to one's lasting happiness.

What does a woman want most in her life? She desires a good and faithful husband. She wants to be happy.

HAPPINESS IS AN ATTITUDE OF THE MIND

Joy is part of the fruit of the Holy Spirit.

PEACE AND JOY ARE TWINS.

BUT the fruit of the Spirit is . . . JOY . . . AGAINST SUCH there is no law (Galatians 5:22).

JOY is not the "ho-ho-ho" of a jolly SANTA CLAUS personality. **JOY** is not the continual making of movement, constant socializing. **JOY** is the result of an inner peace from God—that perfect peace which comes knowing and resting in the fact that one is born-again and one's life is in the hands of the FATHER and NOTHING—no matter how fearful—can touch one who is walking on the path of life guided by the flashlight of GOD'S WORDS (Psalm 119:105).

Peace, I leave with you	Only to you who believe in Jesus Christ as Saviour, for there is no peace to the wicked (Isaiah 48:22).
My peace I give unto you;	[Jesus is talking].
NOT AS THE WORLD giveth, give I unto you	A temporary, superficial peace. Peace is part of the fruit of the Spirit, too, as is joy. (Galatians 5:22).
LET NOT YOUR HEART BE TROUBLED.	Your heart's ATTITUDE should not be faced or set at the dial of TROUBLE or boiling disturbance. This doesn't mean that the daughter of God will not have troubles, or tribulations, or testings. But the Christian woman need not be so swallowed up in that "trouble" that it consumes her being and her "NERVES" conquer her reason. Oh, how easy to write thus. How difficult to practice.
Neither LET it be afraid (John 14:27).	Can it be that you and I LET FEAR take over our thoughts and then, let these fearful thoughts consume our actions?

We must reckon ourselves DEAD indeed to the sin nature and alive UNTO GOD. HOW? "Through JESUS CHRIST, OUR LORD" (Romans 6:11).

"*This is the victory that overcometh the world. EVEN our faith*" (1 John 5:4b).

LET'S DEFINE TERMS—"ATTITUDE"

What should be the **attitude** of the born-again wife and mother (woman)? Is she excluded from heartache because she knows Jesus Christ as her personal Saviour? Is she exempted from friction in the home because she is born-again? No—far from it. Sometimes the woman who is redeemed has more temptations, more conflict, more agony, than the unbelieving slut who stalks the streets.

Let's define the term, "attitude." It means:

1. *Posture; position assumed or studied to serve a purpose; as a threatening ATTITUDE.*
2. *Position or bearing as indicating action, feeling, or mood; as, keep a firm ATTITUDE; hence, the feeling or mood itself; as, a kindly ATTITUDE.*

MAINTAIN AN ATTITUDE OF CHANGE

The Apostle Paul tells Christian women to CHANGE, and NOT to be conformed to the world—this age--the way things are around us, the methods of our neighbor in HUSBAND-LOVING. Don't be like MRS. BLANK. Don't assume her attitude with her husband for your conformity. STOP mimicking your neighbor's husband-loving (Romans 12:2).

Do not make your home patterned after the soap operas' plots or the Hell-doomed daughters at the grocery store.

DO PROVE GOD!

How? By renewing your mind! HERE is attitude again! **CHANGE your attitude! Renew your mind! Put on the mind of CHRIST** (Philippians 2:5). CHANGE YOUR ATTITUDE, Christian wife. **Change your attitude towards HUSBAND-LOVING! Pattern your passion after God's plan of HUSBAND-LOVING!** What do you care if you walk a different path than your neighbor? Does her approval count more with you than the approval of God or the praise of your husband? Think about it.

> *I beseech you therefore, brethren, by the mercies of God, that ye present your bodies a living sacrifice, holy, acceptable unto God, which is your reasonable service* (Romans 12:1).

And be not conformed to this world [including the "world" of husband-loving.]

But be ye transformed by the renewing of your mind. **Change your attitude. Make over your thinking process. Tear down the buildings of your mind and renew (restore to spiritual freshness) your thought processes).**

That YE MAY PROVE what is that good, and acceptable, and perfect will of God (Romans 12:1-2). (I do not believe that we are stretching this verse at all to say that the wife who restores spiritual freshness in her attitude, and the wife who renews her mind from worldliness to Godliness, will be proving by her actions towards her husband what is GOOD and ACCEPTABLE and PERFECT—the will of GOD.

If we, as women, have changed

attitudes, it will reflect in every area of our lives—STARTING with our HUSBAND-LOVING.

MAINTAIN AN ATTITUDE OF CHEER

The Apostle Paul's command. Do you remember the time when the PRISONER Paul was caught in a tempestuous storm which eventually led to shipwreck and despair on the part of the crew and the soldiers? In the midst of the turmoil, Paul stood up and exhorted:

> ***Be of GOOD CHEER;***
> *for there shall be no loss of any man's life among you, but of the ship.*
>
> *Wherefore, sirs,* ***be of GOOD CHEER;***
> *for I believe God,*
> *that it shall be even as it was told me* (Acts 27: 22, 25).

What kind of "cheer" was this? What was Paul exhorting the frightened men in the sinking ship to have? He was telling them to bubble up inside like a boiling pot of hot water with exuberance and happiness, with gladness and radiance, with brightness and rejoicing, with invigoration and exhilaration.

Paul was saying there won't be any loss of life. God has told me—and I believe HIM—all of us will be safe though the ship will fall apart. Everyone be "well boiled"! (**Be of GOOD CHEER.**) (My husband tells me that this is the Greek Word, EUTHUMEIN, which comes from "well" plus "to boil, or to stir up.")

In other words, "Have a good passion within you." Don't work up evil feelings of boiling lust or boiling anger—a bad boil—but bubble up with "good" boiling. All is well.

What a challenge to me as a wife. God is saying to me, *"Do not 'boil up' in lust or in anger. Don't be filled with false cheer, the kind you buy in a bottle. But bubble up; 'boil up' with invigorating brightness. Fill your home with sunshine. Set the emotional pace for the family."*

Christian WIVES	*And be not drunk with wine, wherein is excess; BUT BE FILLED with the Spirit;*
Be of good cheer.	*Speaking to yourselves in psalms and hymns and spiritual songs, singing and making melody in your heart TO THE LORD, giving thanks always for all things unto God and the Father.*
Have a GOOD boil..	***in the name of our Lord Jesus Christ, Submitting yourselves one to another in the fear of God.*** ***Wives, submit yourselves unto your own husbands***
Be a submissive wife.	*AS UNTO THE LORD.* *For the husband is the head of the wife, even as Christ is the Head of the Church and He is the Saviour of the body.*
Be a wife in subjection	*Therefore, as the Church is subject unto Christ,* *So let the wives be to their own husbands in everything* (Ephesians 5:18-23).

THE SON OF GOD'S COMMAND

Jesus Christ told His disciples to BE OF GOOD CHEER and, by extension, he tells born-again women and wives to do the same. Look with me at John 16: 33:

> *These things I have spoken unto you, that in me ye might have peace. In the world ye shall have tribulation: but BE OF GOOD CHEER; I have overcome the world* (John 16:33).

My husband tells me that this word, CHEER (John 16:33) is a different Greek Word for the same English words found in Acts 27. This "cheer" doesn't mean the "good boil" as Paul exhorted his shipmates to have. But Jesus said—if I understand the meaning correctly—*"Wives, I have told you these things, so you'll have peace because you trust me as your Saviour, and I have promised you peace. Oh girls, you'll have troubles, you'll have temptations, things will pile up and there will be family heartaches, but have confidence, be courageous, be filled with assurance, because your Saviour has overcome the world, and you can too. Why? Because I am with you and will strengthen you, and have won the victory over the world."*

BEWARE OF OVER-CONFIDENCE IN YOUR FLESH

Along with telling us to "perk-up," "buck up," "cheer up," "snap out of it," "keep your chin up," etc., there is a warning implied. DO NOT BE OVER-CONFIDENT. Don't be like a swimmer who puts too much confidence in her swimming ability that she forgets the rules of safety and goes too far out into deep water, and gets a cramp and drowns.

What a challenge to be the CHEER MAKER as well as the HOME maker, to stand with CONFIDENCE in our homes as wives, but always aware that our flesh is weak and we who think we stand, be careful lest we fall (1 Corinthians 10:12).

> *Wherefore let him that thinketh he standeth take heed lest he fall. There hath no temptation taken you but such as is common to man: but GOD IS FAITHFUL, who will not suffer you to be tempted above that ye are able; but will with the temptation also make a way to escape, that ye may be able to bear it* (1 Corinthians 10:12-13).

MAINTAIN AN ATTITUDE OF YOUTHFULNESS

The writer of Proverbs advises husbands to REJOICE WITH THE WIFE OF THEIR YOUTH (Proverbs 5:18).

What were we like when our husbands were youths? What kind of exciting young brides were we? **What was there about our personalities which made our husbands want us for their very own possession and not another girl from another town?**

Whatever that attribute was, we still have those original qualities dormant within us. We still have the germs of that youthful lass buried in our minds and bodies. Let's have a resurrection of that youthful girl. We can only do so much with our bodies by dieting, proper rest, and <u>genuine</u> beauty aids [beware of artificial, worldly appearance], but we can return, revive, renew our minds to youthful attitudes now tempered with the wisdom of years and the refreshment of God's WORDS.

AN INTERVIEW WITH MAMIE EISENHOWER

"I have a 19-year-old mind, and an 80-year-old body," said Mamie Eisenhower in a Corley News Service interview with Donna Rosenthal [December 28, 1976, *Camden Courier Post*].

Mrs. Eisenhower declared: *"I try to keep young by learning something new every day . . . "*

She said women today demand too much from their husbands. Wives aren't satisfied and that's why this country is so full of divorces and widows. The article continued*: **"A man should be head of his house.** I don't think WOMEN'S LIB brings happiness, Mamie explained. Women should be happy serving their husbands. Women were made to be second."*

DEAR ABBY HAD AN ANSWER

Years ago, I read a "DEAR ABBY" column in the Camden, New Jersey's *Courier Post*. Though ABBY is not born-again, I observe a good warning in her answer to "WANTED."

> *Dear Wanted: I could be wrong, but consider this: It's possible that this woman you and your sister despise has given your father more happiness, fulfillment, and companionship than he knew in all the years he was married to your mother. It's also possible that your mother may have (perhaps unwittingly) contributed to the collapse of her marriage.*

The answer goes on; but the part I want to emphasize is that this mother may have ***"unwittingly contributed to the collapse of her marriage."*** Of course, I do not believe divorce is Scriptural and I believe that adultery is a heinous sin. This mother could have kept her husband if she would have been a HUSBAND-LOVER of the highest order. What a shame to have all the potential of being an excellent HUSBAND-LOVER and to ignore that potential. Did she nag him? Did she ignore him? Did she fail him sexually? Did she fail to compliment him? Did she make him feel important and needed?

BE A "GOOD THING" WIFE

It is vital to a happy home, not only to "bubble up with good cheer," but also to give out with sexual vitality and vigor. Most normal men want and need sexual companionship. It is the duty of every wife to be this companion, to be this responder and aggressor in things of the body. Read 1 Corinthians 7 again this week.

Do you want to keep your husband? Then be that woman he married. Do you want him to adore you? Then cover him with kisses and caress his person. Let him know that you care more about him, his being, his manliness, than clean socks, dishes, or the evening paper.

One of the girls in our class tells that her husband encouraged her to come to the classes. He doesn't know anything of what we teach, but he just "loves" the title of the lessons. What a precious way to win a man by letting him know you care enough to learn the very best.

May our husbands agree with Proverbs 18:22, and recite in unison:

> *Whoso findeth a wife, findeth a GOOD THING, and obtaineth favor from the Lord* (Proverbs 18:22).

A "FILLIP" FROM MY MOTHER-IN-LAW

My mother-in-law recently sent me this poem which had no title:

It's an art to make something—
a new universe on a rectangle of canvas,
a suit, a dinner, even an entrance.
It's an art to make something happen—
a shopper open her purse, a plant grow,
a prejudice wither, a wound heal.
It's an art to be something—
a good audience, a man's dream, a child's security.
Happily some arts are free of fine arts' stern requirements.
They use your feelings and discoveries—
saffron in rice, linen with velvet,
to add a fillip to the everyday.*
THESE ARE EVERY WOMAN'S ARTS.
(Anonymous)

*Definition of "FILLIP" is "*something serving to rouse or excite; a stimulus.*"

Are you practicing the art of being a "FILLIP" in your home? If not, why not?

THINGS TO THINK ABOUT AND DO THIS WEEK

1. **THINK YOUNG.**
2. **CHANGE YOUR ATTITUDES.** Be a "FILLIP."
3. **SPREAD GOOD CHEER.**
4. BE A "GOOD THING" (Proverbs 18:22).
5. BE PATIENT (**Don't nag.** Bring in your own rubbish cans.)
6. **ELIMINATE STRESS.**
7. FIX YOUR HAIR A NEW WAY.
8. DRESS LIKE A PRINCESS WHILE ADORNING YOUR INNER SELF with a spirit of quietness and meekness.
9. MAKE BREAKFAST FOR YOUR HUSBAND WITH A SMILE.
10. GIVE SEVERAL BACK-RUBS TO THE BODY YOU LOVE. Make your room his private "massage parlor."
11. READ CHAPTER SEVEN "FOR WOMEN ONLY" FROM *THE ACT OF MARRIAGE* by Tim and Beverly LaHaye.
12. ENCOURAGE YOUR HUSBAND TO READ *THE ACT OF MARRIAGE.*
13. **READ AGAIN 1 PETER 2:9-3:17** AND GENESIS 1-3, AND PRAY that the Holy Spirit will guide you in HIS way.

14. MEMORIZE ROMANS 6:11 AND PSALM 101:2 and put them to work as a wife this week. KEEP the old nature IN THE COFFIN.

15. **DON'T SPEND YOUR HUSBAND'S MONEY LIKE WATER.**

16. SURRENDER, SUBMIT, SUBJECT, SUBORDINATE, SANCTIFY YOURSELF.

HUSBAND-LOVING LESSON #7

"A 'DISH' FROM ADAM'S 'SPARE' RIB"

REPORTS FROM THE CLASS

The other day, one of our HUSBAND-LOVERS met me in the SUPER MARKET. She happily said: *"Oh, Vonnie, Vonnie, it's working."* I was thrilled to think that after six Lessons she could see changes in her marriage when she put herself in a subordinate and submissive position with her husband.

Many of the women in our class desire to be good wives which means "SUBMISSIVE WIVES." This SUBMISSION is against their nature; yet they are trusting and believing God to change their marriages.

Let's call one class member, Rose. She said: *"It must be the lessons."* Her husband works shift work and has breakfast at odd hours of the day. Often she has the kitchen all cleaned and he comes in for breakfast. In the past, she has let him make his own. The other morning she got to thinking. She asked herself:

> *If Jesus were here for breakfast, what would I do?*
> *What kind of breakfast would I fix for Jesus*?

She told us that she made the best breakfast with potatoes and everything and her husband was so thankful.

Another class member—let's call her "Kate"—told me that she had not had any contention with her spouse for ten days. How she praised the Lord. *"This isn't like me either."* she related. They went away for several days and I'm sure many precious times of intimate love were theirs—more than three times a week. Why do some women cringe at such a number? I doubt that the husbands are upset—aren't we striving to be "HUSBAND-LOVERS"? Where better to begin such "loving" than in the bedroom? Another member has told me how her marriage is changing because of the class, and how HAPPY she is. Why, her husband has come home for coffee in the morning when he never did this before. They have even had prayer together—a desire of her heart.

Now, don't get me wrong—we in the class are not perfect though we strive to behave in a perfect way and walk within our houses with perfect hearts (Psalm 101:2). We fail and make mistakes. We lose our "cool." Sometimes we "admonish." Sometimes we forget to reckon ourselves dead indeed unto sin, but alive unto God through Jesus Christ (Romans 6:11). Often we fail to keep in the coffin and let the new nature bloom where we are planted. But, we pray to be HUSBAND-LOVERS. Why?

We want happier homes. As some jelly glasses used to say, "HAPPY HOMES GET RID OF BLOOPERS." We have discovered that one of the BIGGEST BLOOPERS in our homes is the woman with the "MRS." in front of her name.

How are you doing out there in READING LAND? We really would like to know if you are applying these HUSBAND-LOVING LESSON PRINCIPLES in your lives. Write us and encourage our hearts with your spiritual progress. I promise not to reveal your names or states, but I would be encouraged to see how God is blessing these lessons. And others might also be blessed to hear how other wives have been helped.

"WOMAN" BUILT FROM MAN

> *And the LORD GOD caused a deep sleep to fall upon ADAM AND HE SLEPT: And He took one of his ribs, and closed up the flesh instead thereof* (Genesis 2:21).

Adam showed no fear or fighting when God "caused" him to sleep deeply. Adam knew the prognosis would be good. Adam willingly "slept" for "completeness."

A "good wife" is the answer, the KEY, to a man's fulfillment. How often you and I miss the best that God would have for us because we forgot that "wife" came from the flesh of man. A child comes from the seed of the man impregnated into a woman and then brought forth from a woman; but, "woman" originally came from the flesh of "man."

As Adam slept, he felt no pain, for he was anaesthetized by God, the Surgeon. And, as the rib was out of Adam's side, the GREAT PHYSICIAN was there–THE LORD GOD (Jehovah GOD–the same Person of the Godhead Who is named JESUS in the New Testament). There was no danger, no doubt that the operation would not be a success. JEHOVAH GOD KNEW WHAT HE WAS DOING.

LIKE BEGETS LIKE

When we discussed this verse the first time in our *HUSBAND-LOVING LESSONS* [p. 50], there was some question as to the number of ribs a man has today. Some of the women thought man had one less rib in the twentieth century because Adam had one removed in EDEN. Others pondered that Adam must have been created with one more rib than men have today.

> *And Adam lived an hundred and thirty years, and begat a son in his own likeness, after his image; not after GOD'S, cf Gen. 1:26 and called his name Seth* (Genesis 5:3).

Here we see that SETH was born [not created like Adam, his father, or "built" from a rib like EVE, his mother] in the image and likeness of his father. Adam could have lost a finger before SETH was born or had a scar on his face from a sharp twig but that did not influence SETH. He was born with all his fingers, with no scars (unless they were birth marks) and with the number of ribs that ADAM originally had.

RIB FACTS FROM THE WORLD BOOK

From the *World Book Encyclopedia*, pp. 296-97, we read the following:

"RIB is anyone of the 24 bones that enclose the chest in the human body. There are 12 ribs on each side of the body. In the back, each rib is connected to the VERTEBRAL COLUMN, or backbone, by small joints, called COSTOVERTEBRAL JOINTS. In the front, the first seven ribs on each side are connected to the

STERNUM, or breastbone. These are called TRUE RIBS. The five others on each side are called false ribs. Three of the false ribs are connected to each other with cartilage. The last two ribs remain free and are known as FLOATING RIBS. The spaces between the ribs, known as INTERCOSTAL SPACES, contain arteries, veins, muscles, and nerves. In mammals, the number of ribs may vary from nine pairs, as in some whales, to 24 pairs, as in two-toed sloths . . ." [Marshall R. Urist (*World Book*, p. 296)].

MAN MINUS A RIB AND PLUS A WOMAN

It is my belief that ADAM went the whole of his life, except for the day he was created—the sixth day, with one less rib than what he was created with. In the place of the rib, there was closed up flesh instead. From that rib, Eve was created. It was the beginning of the human race.

> *And the rib, which the LORD God had taken from man, made* [built] *he a woman, and brought her unto the man* (Genesis 2:22).

LIGHT ON WOMAN'S CREATION FROM KEIL & DELITZSCH

The *Keil & Delitzsch* Commentary stated the following on woman's creation:

> *The woman was created, not of the dust of the earth, but from a rib of Adam, because she was formed for an inseparable unity and fellowship of life with the man, and the mode of her creation was to lay the actual foundation for the moral ordinance of marriage.*
>
> *As the moral idea of the unity of the human race required that man should not be created as a genus or plurality, so the moral relation of the two persons establishing the unity of the race required that man should be created first, and then the woman from the body of the man. By this the priority and superiority of the man, and the dependence of the woman upon the man, are established as an ordinance of divine*

> *creation. This ordinance of God forms the root of that tender love with which the man loves the woman as himself, and by which marriage becomes a type of the fellowship of love and life, which exists between the Lord and His Church* (Ephesians 5:32) (*Keil & Delitzsch*, Vol. I, p. 89).
>
> *If the fact that the woman was formed from a rib, and not from any other part of the man, is significant; all that we can find in this is, that the woman was made to stand as a helpmate by the side of the man, not that there was any allusion to conjugal love as founded in the heart; for the text does not speak of the rib as one which was next to the heart.*
>
> *The Hebrew word is worthy of note here: "from the rib of man God builds the female through whom the human race is to be built up by the male." The design of God in the creation of woman is perceived by Adam as soon as he awakes, when the woman is brought to him by God. Without a revelation from God, he discovers in the woman BONE OF HIS BONES AND FLESH OF HIS FLESH* (*Keil & Delitzsch, Vol. I*, p. 90).

If you and I as wives could fathom the DELIGHT, the FULFILLMENT, and the GRATITUDE TO GOD that ADAM had at the sight of WOMAN, we would each vow before that same LORD GOD to play the ROLE of a BELIEVING WIFE to the thundering applause of our own HUSBAND.

THE "ACT OF MARRIAGE" IS A PRIVATE BUT NECESSARY INTIMACY

Let me say something right here while I am thinking of it. The "ACT OF MARRIAGE" is a personal, private, intimacy which is between one man and one woman—married and approved of God by His blessing on that marriage. My personal opinion is that we should not discuss the details of our sex lives with our friends, no matter how good the friends are. My marriage, your marriage, Mrs. Jones' marriage—all of these marriages—are custom-made. Therefore, no two are alike. It is really no business of my friends what and how I am in the bedroom. The only reason I touch in words on the "marriage bed" (Hebrews 13:4) is that the name of the course is "*HUSBAND-LOVING LESSONS.*" If any wife thinks she is a good wife and fails to perform her duty sexually with her mate, she is flunking the course!

> *Let the husband render unto the wife due benevolence: and likewise also the wife unto the husband. The wife hath not power of her own body, but the husband: and likewise also the husband hath not power of his own body, but the wife.* ***Defraud ye not one the other, except it be with consent for a time,*** *that ye may give yourselves to fasting and prayer; and come together again, that Satan tempt you not for your incontinency* (1 Corinthians 7:3-5.)

When too much note-comparing [unless you are going to a Biblical marriage counselor or Bible-believing Pastor] with one another goes on, this could lead to much personal dissatisfaction with one's self and with one' s mate as well. I always remember what one of my doctors told me when I tried to talk with him about some personal matters concerning my husband and me. He said, *"Does your husband ever complain about you to you? Is he happy with you?"* My answer was that he didn't complain and he was happy with me. The doctor encouraged me to be satisfied with myself because my husband was satisfied with me.

Yet, I as a wife, in my later years, want to be the best wife I can be. I do not want to be over-confident thereby neglecting to be the wife God wants me to be according to HIS MARRIAGE MANUAL. I want to strive to be the BEST I can, but also desire to rest in my husband's love for me. Do you feel the same way?

PRAYER AND CARE NECESSARY TO BE A FAITHFUL "HUSBAND-LOVER"

One of my prayers is that I will always be a faithful wife to my husband. I never want to commit adultery. I must constantly work at my marriage to maintain its

purity. How sad to have fallen into sin, to wreck the precious cleanness of a marriage. I do not want to be that kind of wrecker. Therefore I must pray and take care. I must never put confidence in my flesh, which still houses that old nature (READ Romans 6th Chapter). I want to feed the SPIRITUAL nature within me, not the worldly, fleshly, woman—the carnal nature (Romans 8:6-8, 12, 13). I don't want to teach YOU and then live a lie from what I teach, My prayer is that I bring my body under control, along with my mind, lest I become a "castaway" (1 Corinthians 9:27). This should be your prayer too.

> *But I keep under my body, and bring it into subjection, lest that; by any means, when I have preached to others, I myself should be a castaway* ["disapproved"] (1 Corinthians 9:27).

For this is the WILL OF GOD, Even your sanctification, that ye should abstain	You always want to know God's will? Sanctification: your "holiness, set-apartness" to God. To withhold one's self from participation; to refrain voluntarily from indulgence of appetites. (*Webster's New Collegiate Dictionary*, 1945). The Greek means, "hold yourself completely away from" something.
from fornication;	Illicit sexual intercourse on the part of an unmarried person. Cf. Adultery (*Webster's Dictionary*, 1945).
That every one of you should know how to possess his vessel	This means you and me as wives. Possess: "Taken over." Vessel: A person, regarded, especially in scriptural LANguage, as one into whom something is poured, infused, etc.; as a vessel of grace.
in sanctification	Set aside for a special

purpose—in this case, a holy purpose (Greek meaning).

And honour;
(I Thessalonians 4:3-4)

A price, value, precious thing, dignity, veneration, mark of favor and consideration. In other words; we believing wives should have our bodies taken over for a holy purpose and reckoning it as a valuable, precious possession. Fornication and adultery are immoral acts against our personal private vessel which is not only ours, but more so, our own husband's as in 1 Corinthians 7:1-5.

"BONE OF MY BONE"

Let's get back to our text in Genesis Chapter 2:

> *And Adam said, This is now bone of my bones, and flesh of my flesh; She shall be called WOMAN, BECAUSE she was taken out of MAN* (Genesis 2: 23).

Keil and Delitzsch's comment on this verse, in part, is as follows:

> The words, "THIS IS NOW BONE OF MY BONES" etc., are expressive of joyous astonishment at the suitable helpmate, whose relation to himself he describes in the words, "SHE SHALL BE CALLED WOMAN, FOR SHE IS TAKEN OUT OF MAN." (*Keil & Delitzsch*, Vol. I, page 90).

I like to imagine the wonder in Adam's eyes as he awakened from, the "deep sleep" to discover WOMAN. Was she running through the fields with her hair flying in the balmy breeze? Was she communing with God in the cool of the evening? Or was she lying at Adam's side watching him awaken? I do not know. But, upon awakening, Adam looked at this ONE built from his rib, perhaps touching his side:

> *"And Adam said, This is now BONE OF MY BONES, and flesh of my flesh: she shall be called WOMAN, because she was taken out of Man"* (Genesis 2:23).

"THE COMPLETE MAN"

The following quotation was first given as an introduction to a speech titled, "THE LIBERATED WOMAN," at a MOTHER/DAUGHTER Bicentennial BANQUET at the West Baptist Tabernacle, Vineland, New Jersey.

I would like to dedicate it, at this time; to our third-born son, Richard, and his June bride, Lorraine. May God bless their lives together. It was then published in the June 4, 1975, edition of the *BIBLE FOR TODAY NEWSREPORT* (p. 3), written by yours truly:

> *He stood tall--this creation from the dust of the ground. He who breathed the "breath of' life," faced the sunshine of his first day--eager with anticipation, thrilled with the NEW WORLD about him, telling the animals, tasting the herbs, talking with the TRIUNE, and tracking lonely footprints on the earth's virgin soil. ++ Had any seen such majesty before? Had any known the companionship of the MIGHTY GOD and EVERLASTING FATHER? Who had viewed such paradise? Who had known such innocence? ++ Yet deep within Adam's breast, beat a lonely, unfulfilled heart. And with each beat, a deep yearning burned, an uncontrollable SOMETHING WAS MISSING--as if a part of him were sleeping, still buried in the sands of time from which he had been formed--created. ++ The hues of creation--the greens, the blues, the reds, violet, yellow; orange. The breathtaking sky, the leaping and lumbering beasts by his side, the sunshine warmly tanning his tender skin, the spray of the waterfall on his face, the smell of honeysuckle and the rambling rose, the walking and talking with GOD in the cool of the evenings--all this was his. ++ BUT WHY, oh WHY--this longing within him? This LONELINESS? A lack, a need--how unfair. ++ BUT HIS CREATOR*

KNEW. HE comprehended. For had He not made man? Did He not know his frame? HE knew that it was not good for man to be alone. ++ "Lie down, ADAM, lie down--here, on your home 'turf.'. Do not be afraid. Take my hand--you are not a stranger in PARADISE. Sleep, my son. Sleep deeply.". . . ++ And with a deft hand, GOD took a rib from ADAM'S side, closing the flesh in "the lonely-empty place," leaving a scar as a lifetime memorial to that great awakening DAY. ++ How did God bring "her" unto the man? Was it in the evening breeze, as the red sunset and evening mist formed a halo-glow 'round her head of glory'? Or did ADAM discover his help-meet as she ran towards him with the deer in the clover fields, hair flowing and voice tinkling with laughter? Or did he awaken from his anesthetized sleep, holding his dozing bride close to his wounded side--her hair dampened from her recent creation, her skin pearly-pink, and wet as a newborn? ++ Did MAN ask himself, "What hath God wrought?" as he brushed the ringlets of hair from her unblemished face--his LOVE, his LIFE'S MATE. Or, did his parched lips sound a soft whistle, denoting his masculine approval? Perhaps, he lovingly whispered in her ear, "Bone of my bone, and flesh of my flesh." ++ And as she gazed steadily, unashamedly, at him, did his eyes fill with tears of joy, as his whole being responded to her presence--and with all the passions of his emotion say, "WOMAN."?

"And they were both naked, the man and his wife, and were not ashamed," (Genesis 2:25). (*BFT Newsreport*, "FROM THE TENT DOOR" 6/4/75, p. 3)

THE AGE OF INNOCENCE WAS THEIR JOY

And they were both naked ["stripped"] *the man and his wife and were not ashamed* (Genesis 2: 25).

The reason you and I can't understand the lack of SHAME in ADAM and EVE, the lack of any inferior feeling, pornographic taint, or even human disgust, is because we are living after the

Fall—after sin entered the world. Adam and Eve lived in the period or age (dispensation) of INNOCENCE. Weswho have a sin nature—that which we should reckon dead (Romans 6:11)--do not understand such innocence, such beauty of no filthiness of the flesh. The closest we can understand is the innocence of children (but this is not the same innocence that the ADULT ADAM and EVE possessed in EDEN.) You have all seen toddlers who would go out in the yard bare as they were born, laughing and running, and never feeling one bit of shame as to their clothes-less state. In a small measure, this is how it was with the first couple.

Keil & Delitzsch remarked:

> *Their bodies were sanctified by the spirit which animated them.*
>
> *Shame entered first with sin, which destroyed the normal relation of the spirit to the body, exciting tendencies and lusts which warred against the soul, and turning the sacred ordinance of God into sensual impulses and the lust of the flesh.* (*Keil & Delitzsch, Vol. I*, page 91).

A TEST OF WORLDLINESS

If you, as a born-again wife or woman, discover the
LUST OF THE FLESH,
LUST OF THE EYES,
PRIDE OF LIFE,

*Love not the *world,*
Neither the things that are in the world.
If any man love the world, the love of the FATHER is not in him,

P
R
E
S
E
N
T

For all that is in the world, the lust of the flesh, and the lust of the eyes, and the pride of life, is not of the FATHER, but is of the world.

The LOVE OF THE FATHER is

And the world passeth away,

A-B-S-E-N-T!

and the lust thereof; But he that DOETH the will of God abideth forever (1 John 2:15-17).

Did you pass the test?

The WORLD, I believe, in this verse, means the things about us which bombard our being with all sorts of temptations and entice us away from the FATHER' S love.

> **WORLD (Greek: KOSMOS), Summary: In the sense of the present world system, the ethically bad sense of the word refers to the order or arrangement under which Satan has organized the world of unbelieving mankind upon his cosmic principles of force, greed, selfishness, ambition, and pleasure* (Matthew 4:8-9; John 12:31;. 14:30; 18:36; Ephesians 2:2; 6:12; 1 John 2:15-17). *This world system is imposing and powerful with military might; is often outwardly religious, scientific, cultured, and elegant, but, seething with national and commercial rivalries, and ambitions, is upheld in any real crisis only by armed force, and is dominated by satanic principles.* Cf. Zechariah, 12:14; see Matthew 4:8, note *NEW SCOFIELD BIBLE p.* 1365.

MORE ON LUST

Many times in the Scriptures the word "ADULTERY" is used in connection with spiritual unfaithfulness of Israel or born again believers who unite themselves with the world and feed the flesh, being a friend of the world.

> *Dearly beloved, I beseech you as strangers and pilgrims, abstain from FLESHLY LUSTS, which war against the soul;* (1 Peter 2:11)

> *From whence come wars and fightings among you? come they not hence, even of your lusts that war in your members? Ye lust, and have not: ye kill, and desire to have, and cannot obtain: ye fight and war, yet ye have not, because ye ask not. Ye ask, and receive not, because ye ask amiss, that ye may consume it*

upon your lusts. Ye adulterers and adulteresses, know ye not that the friendship of the world is enmity with God? whosoever therefore will be a friend of the world is the enemy of God (James 4:1-4).

SOME MORE DEFINITIONS

(1) LUST.

noun (as, pleasure, longing)
1. obs. a. Pleasure; liking.
b. inclination; desire.
2. Sensuous desire; bodily appetite; commonly, sexual desire as a degrading passion.
3. Longing or eagerness to enjoy
v. i. To have an eager and esp., an inordinate or sinful desire.
(Webster's Dictionary, 1945)

(2) ADULTERY.
Voluntary sexual intercourse by a married man with another than his wife or by a married woman with another than her husband. Cf. FORNICATION. (*Webster's Dictionary*, 1945)

(3) CONJUGAL
Pertaining to marriage, the married state or matrimonial relations. (*Webster's Dictionary*, 1945)

(4) CONJUGATE.
Yoked or united, esp. in pairs or in marriage; coupled. (*Webster's Dictionary*, 1945)

(5) CORPOREAL.
Of the nature of, consisting of, or pertaining to matter; material; physical. Corporal;
bodily; as man's corporeal frame;
bodily, syn. (*Webster's Dictionary*, 1945)

(6) MONOGAMY.
Single marriage;
specif., one marriage only during life.
cf. deuterogamy , digomy.
b. marriage with but one person at a time—opposed to bigamy and polygamy (*Webster's Dictionary*, 1945).

We will discuss Genesis 2:24 in our next lesson.

THINGS TO THINK ABOUT AND DO THIS WEEK

1. **Plan your work and WORK YOUR PLAN** this week.

2. **PRAY for God's peace** to guard your soul this week (Philippians 4:7).

3. **PROCLAIM verbally to others and your spouse your love for your husband.**

4. **PRAISE your husband often** (Proverbs 31:10-31).

5. PERFUME your person for your husband's pleasure.

6. **PRACTICE the "ACT OF MARRIAGE" often** to your husband's delight. Read Chapter 1, "The Sanctity of Sex" and Chapter 2, "What Lovemaking Means To A Man" from LaHaye's *THE ACT OF MARRIAGE.*

7. **PURSUE every opportunity to show appreciation and affection towards your man** for his sake and to the glory of God.

8. **PERMIT cancellations of your personal plans** if it means being the submissive wife in subordination to your husband.

9. **PLACE yourself in the subjective roll in your marriage** (1 Peter 3:1-6; Ephesians 5: 22-24).

10. PICK attractive clothes and hairdos to adorn your outer "self" while continuing the "inner adornment" of a meek and quiet spirit.

11. POUR him a cold drink of water or a favorite beverage (non-alcoholic) as a surprise treat often.

12. PREACH NOT AT ALL on any subject lest it turn to nagging or admonishing.

13. PUT ON the whole armour of God lest you be hit by the darts of the devil. (Ephesians 6:10-18).

14. **PACE your days to complement your husband's ways.**

15. **PRIORITY #1—READ YOUR BIBLE DAILY.**

16. **PRIORITY #2—STAY IN YOUR COFFIN. Verses to help: Romans 6:11; Psalm 101:2.**

17. PERSONAL QUESTION: Are you "born-again"? (See Chapter 1, pp. 21-33).

HUSBAND–LOVING LESSON #8

THE LEAVING AND CLEAVING PRINCIPLE

LEAVING THE NEST

We have watched the bird learning to fly. We've seen the fluttering parent birds tweeting and twittering near their baby bird, encouraging the young feathers to reach out and take hold of the sky. After much prodding and preaching, the birdling becomes airborne, bringing rejoicing in birdland. Gone are the preceding months of nest-building, egg-sitting, and mouth-feeding. The parent-birds are alone, ready for a soon-approaching SOUTHERN FLIGHT and another nesting period with more egg hatching. THIS cycle is the first lesson in the LEAVING AND CLEAVING PRINCIPLE of life.

Some of us have observed children eager to "fly" on their own; yet parents through pressure and perseverance, have kept the "bird" in the nest and have stunted the growth of their prodigy. When to push from the nest is a big question. If the child leaves home too soon, there can be great damage, which often leads to years of emotional retardation. Yet, if the offspring does not leave the nest early enough, there can be growth-stunting in that maturing process. It is a wise parent, indeed, who can walk according to GOD-given timing, who can give their blessing with a genuine smile as the son or daughter tries his or her wings out in the pathless air.

The greatest test of a mature parent is at the time when the "child" says "*I do*" at the altar. It is then that the parent must step back and let "little" Johnny fly on his own. Yes, parents can be "home" for Christmas visits and special occasions. Parents can be ready with asked advice—only careful not to give too much. Parents are to be back-up-people—so far in the background that Johnny and his bride are able to "fly" without stumbling over the "in-laws" upon every occasion of life. This is a hard procedure for a parent to follow, but it should be one that a parent should discipline himself to adhere to at all costs—even the cost of being lonely.

FLYING ALONE

The newlyweds—no matter what their age—must leave their parents. They must establish new ground-rules of their own. They must not call home every other day for advice or financial aid. It must be established in the minds of the newly-married and their parents that there is a GOD-given rule of LEAVING AND CLEAVING set down, in the WORDS OF GOD. If this separation is not enforced, there can be much damage done to the new marriage which will take years to heal. This is my opinion which is based upon HOLY INSTRUCTION given by God to Moses in the book of Genesis:

> *Therefore shall a man leave his father and his mother, and shall cleave unto his wife: and they shall be one flesh* (Genesis 2:24).

DEFINITIONS

(1) LEAVE: *to desert, forsake*
hence to give up, relinquish
to cease from, stop
to depart, set put,
to cease, desist...
(2) CLEAVE: *to adhere closely*
to stick, cling (Dictionary)

The best illustration I can think of right now for "cleaving" is the baby monkey on the back of its mother. A mate—whether husband or wife—should be like a baby monkey CLINGING to its mother. As a HUSBAND-LOVER, we must "cling" to our husband in spirit and mind and body like a baby monkey on the back of the adult monkey. This is necessary for a SCRIPTURAL MARRIAGE.

It is not two independent individuals walking along the same path, but it is two individuals so close that they are ONE, walking in the same footsteps along the SAME PATH.

THE FIRST "LEAVERS" & "CLEAVERS"

Isn't it strange that the HOLY SPIRIT teaches you and me about leaving father and mother in connection with a man and a woman who never had and never would have a father and mother? Why?

Let's consider some of the answers to that question.

1. Perhaps God wanted Adam and Eve to be ready to give up their own sons and daughters in marriage, without chasing after them.

2. I believe that God wanted to teach you and me to leave our parents when we get married and to CLEAVE to our mates in marriage.

Reflect with me the setting during the LEAVING AND CLEAVING PROCLAMATION. Adam is looking at Eve—he exclaimed "Bone of my Bones, and flesh of my flesh."

Where was he from? The earth, the ground, the place which later God will curse,

> *And unto Adam he said, Because thou hast hearkened unto the voice of thy wife, and hast eaten of the tree, of which I commanded thee, saying, Thou shalt not eat of it: cursed is the ground for thy sake; in sorrow shalt thou eat of it all the days of thy life; Thorns also and thistles shall it bring forth to thee; and thou shalt eat the herb of the field; In the sweat of thy face shalt thou eat bread, till thou return unto the ground; for out of it wast thou taken: for dust thou art, and unto dust shalt thou return* (Genesis 3:17-19).

Loosely speaking, we could say that Adam's mother and father were the GROUND. He was to leave his parents. He NEVER would have returned to his founding DUST if he never would have sinned. In sinning, eventually, Adam died and returned to the DUST.

Eve was not "earthy"; we could say she was "fleshy." *"The first man is of the earth, EARTHY; . . ."* (1 Corinthians 15:47). EVE had a unique standing in all civilization. She was created from the flesh and bone of her husband. [We pointed this out before that all newborn babies come out of their mothers, but NEWLY FORMED EVE came out of a man.] That is why Adam looked at her and named his wife, "WOMAN." Why? Because she *"was taken out of MAN"* (Genesis 2:23). In Genesis 3:20, *"Adam called his wife's name Eve; because she was the mother of all living."*

Though the instruction says "a man" shall leave his father and his mother and cleave unto his wife, by inference, we can assume that a wife is to leave her father and her mother and cling unto her husband.

RESULTS OF "LEAVING" SHOULD BE "CLEAVING"

What are the results of the LEAVING AND CLEAVING PRINCIPLE? One flesh. Remember the puzzle we talked about previously? Remember the unfinished man? Remember woman being the KEY to man's completion—the finishing of the puzzle? This is the one flesh, which God explained to Moses again concerning marriage. [See pp. 69-71 above].

I am sure that it doesn't take too much imagination to expatiate on the word "CLEAVE."

In the Greek language (where this passage is quoted in the New Testament), I am told by my husband, that "cleave" means to be welded or glued. There is a clinging or holding fast implied. The wife and husband are to be so entwined that they appear to be one flesh.

During the actual "ACT OF MARRIAGE," the one flesh indeed is just that. The puzzle parts are locked together, the gluing or welding is complete.

I have before me a bottle of "WELDINGWOOD CONTACT CEMENT." The bottle reads: *"Bonds instantly on contact. Water resistant."* The directions are interesting too:

> *Apply cement to both clean surfaces. Let dry till glossy—fifteen minutes or more. Important: Align surfaces carefully. Adjustment is difficult once contact has been made. Press parts firmly together to affect instant bonding.*

I can't help but think that married couples should use as much caution in their "glue-like" relationships with their mates as they would in following glue instructions in repairing a broken chair or dish.

Some young men and women don't have the difficulty in leaving father and mother, but sad to say, they do not "CLEAVE" to their new mates. Many a young girl is alone while her husband is out busying himself in areas which are not important to strengthening the marriage. Sometimes the young wife is not homemaking in her cottage or apartment, but is gallivanting with "the girls" instead. Could this "wander-lust" be one of our faults as "HUSBAND-LOVERS"? I trust not.

JESUS REINFORCES GOD'S INSTRUCTION ON LEAVING & CLEAVING

Jesus repeated in the Synoptic Gospels God's instruction and exhortation to Moses.

> *And he answered and said unto them, Have ye not read, that he which made them at the beginning made them male and female, And said, For this cause shall a man leave father and mother, and shall cleave to his wife: and they twain shall be one flesh? Wherefore they are no more twain, but ONE FLESH. What therefore God hath JOINED TOGETHER, let not man put asunder* (Matthew 19:4-6).

> *And Jesus answered and said unto them, For the hardness of your heart he wrote you this precept. But from the beginning of the creation God made them male and female. For this cause shall a man leave his father and mother, and cleave to his wife; And they twain shall be one flesh: so then they are no more twain, but one flesh. What therefore God hath joined*

together, let not man put asunder. (Mark 10:5-9).

These passages show us that Jesus Christ was in full agreement with the teachings of God to Moses in that a man should leave his father and mother and CLEAVE unto his wife. (By inference, we are taking that this Scripture also teaches that a woman leaves her family and clings to the man as well.)

Because a woman was made from man, her place is that of a complement to that husband—helping him, fitting in with him, and responding to his needs.

I used to fight this position myself. It was very hard to be the one who draws alongside and be the complimenter like the salt and pepper to a vegetable or the fancy tie to a plain suit of clothes. But, as the years go by, I really don't care that much anymore. I do not know if I have become more submissive or less independent. I know one thing is that I have felt better physically and therefore it has been easier to die to self because I do not have to struggle to have strength to walk or just to exist.

As I'm writing this lesson, I am recovering from an illness—perhaps the flu—and memories have flooded my being of those years when I was not well, but very anemic because of various physical complications. I think the Lord has permitted me these recent weeks of weakness to remind me of the difficulty that a wife can have in physical fatigue. She cannot be the responder and complimenter that she longs to be because there isn't the physical ability within her being. Some husbands become kinder and more tender during illnesses while others became harsh and dictatorial. Here again, we must as tailor-made "HUSBAND-LOVERS" tend to our OWN HUSBANDS, not the kind one across the street or the quiet one in the hardware store.

> *Wives SUBMIT yourselves unto YOUR OWN HUSBANDS AS UNTO THE LORD* (Ephesians 5: 22).

> *. . . ye wives be in SUBJECTION to YOUR OWN HUSBANDS* (1 Peter 3: 1).

CAN A WIFE CLEAVE TO AN ALCOHOLIC HUSBAND?

What do we do with the problem which one wife has told me in her life? She is not well, in fact, may die within the year unless the LORD steps in invigorating her with miracle health. Her husband is an alcoholic. They are young parents in their early thirties with three children. Because of her physical problems, she is not supposed to have any more children, according to her doctor. Her husband doesn't want to "kill" her in child-birth, so he doesn't touch her sexually. How can she be a Scriptural wife?

It is easy for me to pen words to "help" her, but will MY words help? No. I do not have this home situation. I have never had to live with a drinker of anything but milk. Personally, I have not walked in her shoes. But GOD is the same GOD of her problems as of mine. The WORDS of GOD have spoken from the pen of the writers for her too. The writings are inspired by the Holy Spirit and they instruct; they correct; they edify. The same principles set forth for one wife CAN WORK as well for another wife.

Yesterday, I was talking with a woman who said she was an alcoholic—doesn't drink at the present time. She said that to be hollered at for her drinking, to be hated for the way she was when drunk just compounded the problem. She was not proud of her intoxicated state. She had a desperate problem, and was handling it through liquor. Wrong way, but her way. To be told her faults and to be despised because of her inebriated condition, did not help her need.

One of the girls in our class was helpful in discussing husbands who go to the "tap room." She said that the Lord is teaching her to be just as happy to have him home if he is drunk or if he is sober. She said that she greets him at the door with the same enthusiasm and the same cheer as if he were not tipsy. She said she used to sleep in another room when he was drunk, but now she stays where she belongs—by his side. I am sure that the LORD will bless this woman and some day her desire that her husband be saved will come to pass because she has learned to love THE MAN (her own husband) and to be dead to the sin in his life and the sin it stirs up in her life.

> *Likewise reckon ye also yourselves to be dead indeed unto sin, but alive unto God through Jesus Christ our Lord. Let not sin therefore reign in your mortal body, that ye should obey it in the lusts thereof* (Romans 6:11-12).

It is just as wrong for a wife to "sin" by being upset with her drinking husband—or any kind of sinning in her husband—as it is for the husband to sin in the first place. In fact, if the husband is not born-again [See pp. 23-28 above], he is living a sinful life because he is living like his father, the devil (John 8:41, 44). The unsaved husband is living according to his sinful nature and a wife should not be amazed at the fruit of that sinful nature.

If a man is an alcoholic, it could be that he has low blood sugar (hypoglycemia) and is drinking in a desperation (unknown to him) to raise his blood-sugar-level in his brain. He should have a five to six-hour glucose-tolerance-test and have it read by a doctor who agrees with the premises found in *BODY MIND AND SUGAR* by E. M. Abrahamson, M.D. and A. W. Phezet. There is a chapter called "Alcohol & Alcoholics" on page 151, and a discussion on ALCOHOLISM on page 180.

CLEAVING IS AN ATTITUDE AND DEMANDS ACTION

It is the Christian wife who should manifest the spiritual nature—the spiritual fruit. [See "A SCRIPTURAL WIFE IS A 'DEAD' WIFE" on pp. 58-59, above].

What are some things a woman can do towards her man to show him that she is CLEAVING unto him only?

1. **She can thank him** for marrying her.

2. **She can compliment** his person—tell him how handsome he is to her (and ask God to help her mean it. As we say something, we begin to believe it ourselves, if we don't already.)

3. **She can thank him** for supporting her and the children.

4. **She can thank him profusely for helping around the house**, even if it is only lifting the paper from the chair to the floor.

5. **She can ask his opinion concerning anything** and many things, and show respect and honor to that opinion.

6. **She can greet him at the door** with a welcoming kiss and hug.

7. **She can make herself attractive,** not necessarily spending a lot of money in the process.

8. **She can woo him** sexually in any manner that works for her and him.

9. If sexual restrictions are placed upon her by a physician due to health reasons, she can read and discover (if she doesn't already know) how to satisfy his physical needs anyhow.

10. **She can NEVER refuse him sexually** (cf. 1 Corinthians 7:3-4), except by common consent, and then not for many days, and only for fasting and praying (1 Corinthians 7:5).

A marriage is like a magnet—it should attract positively towards the mate, and negatively away from the parents from which the couple have come. I don't mean that there should be unkindness towards the mother and father, but if the parents do not let go of the child who is married, sometimes this appears to be unkindness. **It is the wise parent who doesn't insist upon "running" by remote control the newly-married children.** Do not insist that the bride spend holidays, birthdays, etc. with the home family. In fact, **encourage independence**. Encourage the newlyweds to go to their own doctors and dentists and so forth of their own choices, wherever they might be living rather than to keep on going to their "family" physicians. It doesn't mean that a parent isn't standing by to aid, but it does mean that a parent isn't like a prompter in a play, ready to jump out at the first burp or error.

WHAT ABOUT ELDERLY OR ILL PARENTS?

The question has come up in class concerning elderly parents. Where should they stay in their need? Should they go to a rest home? Should they live with the married children?

We read in the Scriptures that a man who doesn't take care of his family is worse than an infidel:

> *But if any provide not for his own, and specially for those of his own house, he hath denied the faith, and is worse than an infidel* (1 Timothy 5:8).

> *But if any widow have children or nephews, let them learn first to shew piety at home, and to requite their parents: for that is good and acceptable before God* (1 Timothy 5:4).

The Words of God commands that the believer have respect and honor towards his or her parents. We are to "HONOR" our father and mother. The commandment to do so is written right before "Thou shalt not kill" (Exodus 20:13).

> *Honour thy father and thy mother: that thy days may be long upon the land which the LORD thy God giveth thee* (Exodus 20:12).

> [Jesus said]*: For God commanded, saying, Honour thy father and mother: and, He that curseth father or mother, let him die the death* (Matthew 15:4).

> *For Moses said, Honour thy father and thy mother; and, Whoso curseth father or mother, let him die the death:* (Mark 7:10)

> *Children, obey your parents in the Lord: for this is right. Honour thy father and mother; (which is the first commandment with promise;) That it may be well with thee, and thou mayest live long on the earth*

(Ephesians 6:1-3).

When parents need the children to help support them, there is a definite need for the children to do so. If a mother, for instance, cannot earn a living in her widowhood, or if a father is too old to work, or if parents are in need of shelter, home, and food, it would be absolutely UN-Christ-like and inhumane NOT to take in the parents and provide a welcome home for them. Most children would want it so.

PARENTS LIVING WITH CHILDREN WALK UNDER NEW HOUSE RULES

It is also true that married children living with parents walk under the OLD HOUSE RULES. Primarily the LEAVING AND CLEAVING PRINCIPLE is an attitude of mind and heart. [Though I really believe with all my heart that the new family and the old family should not live together in the beginning of the marriage especially, if ever.]

If it becomes necessary for a mother to live with her children, there should always be impressed upon that mother and her children that the attitude of LEAVING AND CLEAVING prevails. It is to the husband that the wife should go for consolation and advice, not to the mother. It is in the wife that the husband should find solace in times of distress or happiness, not in the mother.

House rules should be written up in order that no misunderstandings erupt as to who is the head of the house and that the attitude of LEAVING AND CLEAVING PREVAIL. I believe, if it is necessary for two families to merge, there can be happiness as long as the man of the house is the head and the wife of the house is the mistress of that home.

Because of the LEAVING AND CLEAVING PRINCIPLE, many a woman who finds herself alone with her children cannot return to her mother and father's house with ease. The young woman with young children has to put herself again under her parent's authority when she dwells under their roof. This causes much heartache, no matter how much the young woman loves her parents. **My personal opinion is that it is best for a**

woman or a man who has had a home of his own, to maintain his own home, even if it be a poor dwelling, for he or she would be the mistress or master of that home. What do you think?

> *Genesis 2:24 are the words of Moses, written to bring out the truth embodied in the fact recorded as a divinely appointed result, to exhibit marriage as the deepest corporeal and spiritual unity of man and woman, and to hold up monogamy before the eyes of the people of Israel as the form of marriage ordained by God. But as the words of Moses, they are the utterance of divine revelation; and Christ could quote them, therefore, as the Words of God (Matthew 15:4). By the leaving of father and mother, which applies to the woman as well as to the man, the conjugal union is shown to be a spiritual oneness, a vital communion of heart as well as of body, in which it finds its consummation. This union is of a totally different nature from that of parents and children; hence marriage between parents and children is entirely opposed to the ordinance of God. Marriage itself, notwithstanding the fact that it demands the leaving of father and mother, is a holy appointment of God; hence celibacy is not a higher or holier state, and the relation of the sexes for a pure and holy man is a pure and holy relation.* (p. 91, of *Biblical Commentary on the Old Testament* by C. F. Keil, D.D., and F. Delitzsch, D.D.).

CONCLUSION

In closing, let us reflect on the two-pronged fork that we find with the LEAVING AND CLEAVING PRINCIPLE. As a married person, especially newly married, we should encourage a COMPLETE LEAVING of parents and a surrendered CLEAVING to our mates. As a parent, we should encourage the pushing of a newly married child out of the nest and the cutting of all apron strings so their baby marriage can develop and grow without retardation from doting mothers and checkbooks of the fathers.

THINGS TO THINK ABOUT AND DO THIS WEEK

1. **Continue to pray** that you will be toward your husband:
    a. submissive
    b. subjective
    c. subordinate
    d. surrendered
    e. sexually oriented

2. Review *HUSBAND-LOVING LESSONS* #1-7. Ask the Lord to refresh your mind and attitude how a Christian wife should act.

3. Review the Scriptures to make us HUSBAND-LOVERS supreme.

4. **Read what LOVE-MAKING MEANS TO A WOMAN**, Chapter 3, page 33, from *THE ACT OF MARRIAGE*. Share this chapter with your husband, but if he is not interested, don't be surprised or hurt.

5. ATTEND a BIBLE-BELIEVING and preaching church this week.

6. READ your BIBLE DAILY.

7. Make a list of actions which you can do to be a better wife.

8. **Make a list of attitudes which you can change to be a better wife.**

God bless you as you seek to serve the Lord Jesus Christ in your home through HUSBAND-LOVING.

HUSBAND-LOVING LESSON #9

PARDON ME, BUT DO I DETECT

A POWER FAILURE?

1 Corinthians 7:1-5

Let us turn to 1 Corinthians 7, looking at every verse, applying the WORDS OF GOD to our heart and life.

Before cutting into the meat of the passage, and answering the Corinthians' questions, "Is it all right, Paul, NOT to marry?" or "Is it okay not to have sex with a woman?" Let's think about the group of people to whom the apostle Paul was writing.

The Corinth of Paul's time was a NEW CORINTH which was re-built by Julius Caesar upon the crushed wastelands of an old Corinth, destroyed hundreds of years before.

BACKGROUND DATA ON CORINTH OF THE NEW TESTAMENT

Corinth was situated on a tableland 200 feet above the sea on an isthmus connecting the lower peninsula of Greece with the mainland. Behind the city to its SOUTH, rose a Gibraltar-like rock 2,000 feet high called the "Acrocorinthus." "The city of the two seas" had two harbors, Cenchreas on the eastern sea and Lechaeum on the western. Aristides called the city "a palace of Neptune." Others spoke of it as the "eye of Greece," or the "capital and grace of Greece." [Facts taken from *The First Epistle to the Corinthians*, Introduction, p. 11, by R. C. H. Lenski.]

The apostle Paul spent 18 months in Corinth—at first this was not his intention. It was the hub of commerce and its harbors berthed ships from almost every country in the world. The streets were filled with visitors swelling the 600,000 to 700,000 populous of that pagan metropolis [Cf. *International Standard Bible Encyclopedia* (ISBE), "Corinth"].

There was no act too vile nor deed too degrading for the Corinthian citizens:

> *At night the city was made hideous by the brawls and lewd songs of drunken revelry. In the daytime, its markets and squares swarmed with Jewish peddlers, foreign traders, sailors, soldiers, athletes in training, boxers, wrestlers, charioteers, racing-men, betting-men, courtesans, slaves, idlers and parasites of every description.*
>
> *The corrupting worship of Aphrodite, with its hordes of HIERODOULOI* ["temple-slaves"], *was dominant, and all over the Greek-Roman world, "to behave as a Corinthian" was a proverbial synonym for leading a low, shameless and immoral life. Very naturally, such a polluted and idolatrous environment accounts for much that has to be recorded of the semi-pagan and imperfect life of many of the early converts.*
>
> *Paul was the founder of the church in Corinth. Entering the city with anxiety, and yet with almost anxious hopefulness, he determined to know nothing among its people "save Jesus Christ and Him crucified"* (1 Corinthians 2:2). *Undoubtedly, he was conscious that the mission of the cross here approached its crisis. IF IT COULD ABIDE HERE, IT COULD ABIDE ANYWHERE.*
>
> *. . . The converts were drawn largely but not entirely from the lower or servile classes* (I Corinthians 1:26; 7:21); *they included Crispus and Sosthenes, rulers of the synagogue, Gaius, and Stephanas with his household, "the firstfruits of Achaia:* (1 Corinthians 16:15). *He regarded himself joyfully as the father of this community* (1 Corinthians 4:14,15) *every member of which seemed to him LIKE HIS OWN CHILD* [p. 713, *I.S.B.E., op. cit.*].

I am quoting directly from my source books so you can get the full flavor of the wickedness in Corinth; that place where Paul won souls to Jesus Christ and established a church. It was in this city with such a foul background that the grace of God worked in the lives of believers snatched from pagan idolatry and practices. "*Where sin abounded, grace did much more abound*" (Romans 5:20b).

Continuing to read on from *The Interpretation of St. Paul's First and Second Epistle to the Corinthians* by R. C. H. Lenski, pp. 12-13:

> *Corinth was a wicked city even as larger cities in the empire went at this period. The very term "CORINTHIAN" meant profligate, and the verb "to Corinthianize" meant to have intercourse with prostitutes. The temple of Venus in the old city boasted that a THOUSAND FEMALE SLAVES were kept there who were FREE to strangers. Venus worship was a mark of the new city likewise although we have no account of the females connected with the new temple. NON CUIVIS HOMINI CONTINGIT ADIRE CORINTHUM ("It is not every man's lot to go to Corinth.")--from Horace--became a proverb which was translated also into Greek. Money was freely spent for sinful pleasures. Paul wrote his description of pagan vice, Romans 1:18-32 in Corinth. One of the chief attractions was the Isthmian games, the custody of which was restored to the new city. Greeks and Romans flocked to these contests, and the mobs came in crowds; but the effect of these spectacles was degrading.*
>
> *Corinth was never famous for its philosophers; the name of not one outstanding Corinthian philosopher is known to us. Its boast was trade and the arts. Corinthian brass became famous, and Corinthian capitals and pillars are still known in architecture. While philosophical and speculative ideas were undoubtedly current in Corinth, we should go wrong if we thought that the members of this congregation were swayed by philosophical considerations because Corinth was located in Greece. The puffed-up people whom Paul scores in Corinth, and the few doubters*

> *there who made free with the resurrection were no better than many superficial scientists and philosophers of modern times.* [Cf. Lenski, *op. cit.*, pp. 12-13].

TEN QUESTIONS ANSWERED IN 1 CORINTHIANS

1 Corinthians is a very practical book. From the pagan background of these new believers, we can see that there were many problems for the Christians, which they didn't know how to handle SCRIPTURALLY.

Some of the questions on Paul's mind were:

1. Whom should you follow? Paul, Apollos, Cephas, or the Lord Jesus Christ? This causes church splits. (1 Corinthians 1:10-12).
2. Why is fornication among you? It is the worst kind—incest. (1 Corinthians 5:1). And the whole lot of you Christians are indifferent to the sinful business and live as if nothing wrong were going on in your midst. Why?
3. Why are you Christians going to pagan judges to solve your legal problems? (1 Corinthians 6:1-8).
4. What harm is there in eating meat offered to idols? (1 Corinthians 8).
5. What part does a woman play in public worship? (1 Corinthians 11), and what about her hair length?
6. What about some regulations concerning CHURCH SUPPERS and the COMMUNION table? (1 Corinthians 11:17-34).
7. Why are you ignorant concerning spiritual gifts? (1 Corinthians 12-14).
8. What importance does the RESURRECTION doctrine have for you? (1 Corinthians 15).
9. What are you doing with your tithes and offerings? (1 Corinthians 16).
10. Why is it necessary to marry if you don't want to? (1 Corinthians 7) and if a mate leaves, can you re-marry?

TO MARRY OR NOT TO MARRY?—THAT IS THE QUESTION (1 Corinthians 7:1-5)

It is about this last question that we HUSBAND-LOVERS are interested at this point in our learning.

In our class period, we touched on this chapter for two weeks. It was interesting that on the second week, we had two unmarried women in class—one never had been married, and the other a widow. I wondered, as I looked into their faces, what I would be saying to help them from the WORDS; but, as we dug into the Chapter, we found much comfort from the Scriptures for the unmarried woman as well as the married.

It is my opinion that a woman who has the "gift of God" to be single can have a blessed, full-life. She can be victorious—if she is born-again—and she can walk life's path with purpose and joy. God's promises are for the unmarried as well as for the married. The joy of serving the Lord Jesus Christ and daily witnessing for HIM can be as great a challenge for the single woman as for the married. May God grant you His sufficient GRACE in living with the Lord exclusively in an unmarried vocation, if this is the state to which God has presently called you.

PAUL PAINTS MARRIAGE AS A PICTURE OF JESUS CHRIST & HIS CHURCH

As we open 1 Corinthians 7, let us not forget two facts: (1) That Paul, who is writing here, has written to the Christians from the corrupt Corinthian community; and (2) That he has written with great praise concerning the pleasure of marriage and its fulfillment in other passages.

He has used human marriage as the picture of Christ's perfect relationships with His BRIDE, the Church (the blood-washed SAINTS).

For the husband is the head of the wife, even as Christ is the head of the church . . . (Ephesians 5:23a-b) *Husbands, love your wives, even as Christ also loved the church, and gave himself for it; That he might present it to himself a glorious church, not having spot, or wrinkle, or any such thing; but that it should be holy and without blemish. So ought men to love their wives as their own bodies. He that loveth his wife loveth himself. For no man ever yet hated his own flesh; but nourisheth and cherisheth it, even as the LORD THE CHURCH: For this cause shall a man leave his father and mother, and shall be joined unto his wife, and they two shall be one flesh. This is a great mystery: but I speak concerning Christ and the church. Nevertheless let every one of you in particular so love his wife even as himself; and the wife see that she reverence her husband* (Ephesians 5:25-33).

1 CORINTHIANS 7--VERSE BY VERSE: IS IT OKAY NOT TO MARRY?

BIBLE VERSES	COMMENTARY ON THE VERSES
Now concerning the things whereof ye wrote unto me: It is good for a man not to touch a woman (1 Corinthians 7:1).	Paul is saying, "You've written me especially concerning marriage questions. You are saying to me--Is it okay, Paul, if we don't want to get married? Is there nothing immoral for a man NOT to have sexual relations with a woman?" This is a refreshing question, indeed, for twenty-first century man. In this day, when being a virgin is looked down upon, we wish more Christians would ask such a question.

PRIVATE OWNERSHIP PREVENTS SIN

Nevertheless, to avoid fornication, let every man have his own wife, and let	But, Christian brother or sister, to keep away from having sexual intercourse with the opposite sex in a promiscuous manner, you should have your own

every woman have her own husband (1 Corinthians 7:2).

mate. "Fornication" is performing the sex act between unmarried people (or when one is unmarried it is "fornication" for that person). Adultery, on the other hand, is between married people who are not married to each other (or when one party is married, it is "adultery" for that person).

Likewise, ye wives, be in subjection to your own husbands (1 Peter 3:1).

Marriage is another case of PRIVATE OWNERSHIP—one wife to one man is the ratio. A man is to have his OWN wife and a woman is to have her OWN husband, just like Adam and Eve. Adam said: "*Bone of my bone and flesh of my flesh.*" She was HIS WOMAN. And today, HUSBAND-LOVER, you are your husband's EXCLUSIVE WOMAN.

Wives, submit yourselves unto your own husbands, AS UNTO THE LORD (Ephesians 5:22).

Once again I will restate: too many wives have the "roving eye," looking at other men, other husbands, and forget their personal, individual HUSBAND-LOVING assignment is their OWN man.

THE MUTUAL DUTY BETWEEN MATES

Let the husband render unto the wife due benevolence: and likewise also the wife unto the husband (1 Corinthians 7:3).

A husband has many duties to his wife. The paramount duty and privilege in this verse is satisfying his wife sexually. A woman is a sexual person as well as a man, and she has sexual needs. It is the duty of each husband to fulfill the sexual needs of his wife.

Then a wife has a duty to perform towards her man—that of giving herself to her mate in God's given way for the "act of marriage."

Somehow, some way, couples get this simple, sexual, biological urge and need all mixed up in their thinking. Sex is natural and a God-ordained privilege and need. It is the spouse's duty NOT to withhold her body from her partner's. If she does so (or if he does so), this is sin.

A WIFE HAS NO "AUTHORITY" OVER HER BODY

The wife hath not power of her own body, but the husband: and likewise also the husband hath not power of his own body, but the wife (1 Corinthians 7:4)

This word, "power," is the word "authority" and my husband tells me that this GREEK Word is the same word for "POWER" found in John 1:12. (Not the word, "Power" found in Romans 1: 16, which means the "dynamite" of God.)

Jesus Christ was a Jew. He came to His own people, the Jews, but they rejected Him. So the Lord Jesus Christ the Son of God turned to you and me (Gentiles).

So, as many as genuinely receive the Lord Jesus Christ—the Gift of God—have "*eternal life through Jesus Christ our Lord*" (Romans 6:23)—to that person (you and me) the Lord Jesus Christ has given the "AUTHORITY" to become the daughters of God.

The Lord Jesus Christ has given us the AUTHORITY—the power—to be children of God.

This same "authority" word is the kind of TAKEOVER, the kind of CONTROL, the kind of POWER, which MY husband has over MY body. It is the kind of authority your husband has over your body. It is the kind of power that you have over your husband's body.

Know ye not that your bodies are the members of Christ? shall I then take the members of Christ, and make them the members of an harlot? God forbid (1 Corinthians 6:15).

What? know ye not that he which is joined to an harlot is one body? for two, saith he, shall be one flesh (1 Corinthians 6:16).

Flee fornication. Every sin that a man doeth is without the body; but he that committeth fornication sinneth against his own body.

What? know ye not that your body is the temple of the Holy Ghost which is in you, which ye have of God, and ye are not your own? (1 Corinthians 6:17-19).

When I was married, I was twenty-one years old. My body was mine. (It was also the temple of the Holy Spirit, for I was saved. 1 Corinthians 6:19). BUT, when I married D. A. WAITE, this body was mine, but HE had authority over it. My husband has the power over it. It is HIS body—though it is MY body—to do with what and how he wants to do with it sexually.

This is a strong statement, but it is what Paul is saying.

He is saying that your husband's body is yours, girls. When you want his body sexually, you should be able to have it because he no longer has authority over his body; YOU DO.

Your body is your husband's—not to be given to any other man. Another man has NO AUTHORITY over your body. When your husband wants you sexually, he should have you, because you are his body.

CO-SUBMISSION RESULTS IN YIELDING TO "BODY AUTHORITY"

For ye are bought with a price: therefore glorify God in your body, and in your spirit, which are God's (1 Corinthians 6:20).

Now here is a precious truth found in verse 4 of 1 Corinthians 7. It is the truth of submission to one another.

We have learned from 1 Peter 3:1 that a wife should be in subjection "to her own husband." This is her duty and is something a Christian wife should willingly do in order to win her husband by her behavior to the Lord as Saviour. (1 Peter 3:1). Wives are to submit to their OWN HUSBANDS as unto the Lord (Ephesians 5:22).

Some "WOMEN-LIBBERS" are teaching today—even in so-called "evangelical" circles—about husbands submitting to their wives. I suppose they have reference to verses like Ephesians 5:21. "*Submitting yourselves one to another in the fear of God.*" Christian people should be speaking in spiritual things like giving of thanks, spiritual songs, singing and making melodies in the heart. All of this is a result of being Spirit-filled, not taken over in body and mind and spirit with wine as a drunken person, but taken over by the HOLY SPIRIT (Ephesians 5:18-9).

It is a dangerous doctrine to teach women that their husbands should be submissive to them. It is a dangerous position. A wife is ALWAYS to be in submission to her husband—this is the rule. The only exceptions would be in such

matters as being told to murder or to go out and commit adultery or to do anything contrary to God's Words—matters against the moral law of God.

The wife hath not power of her own body, but the husband: and likewise also the husband hath not power of his own body, but the wife (1 Corinthians 7:4).

Here in 1 Corinthians 7:4, we see co-submission. It is beautiful and thrills my heart.

It is when a woman gives her body over to the man who has "power" of her body (her own husband) that she submits to him.

It is when a man gives his body to the woman who has "power" over his body (his own wife), that he submits to her.

This is why adultery is such a sin. For a mate is submitting to the wrong "authority," a false authority, a sinful authority. What shame!

You want your husband to be submissive to you? Then ask for his body. That is the only time that I've found in my study on HUSBAND-LOVING that a wife has a "submissive" husband.

Think about it. And practice it. Then you will find that you will also have a HAPPY HUSBAND.

"DEPRIVING" ONE ANOTHER LEADS TO SATANIC TEMPTATIONS

Defraud ye not one the other, except it be

Up to this point, all of Paul's counsel to us HUSBAND-LOVERS and our mates *with consent for a time, that ye may give yourselves to fasting and prayer; and come together again, that Satan tempt you not for your incontinency* (1 Corinthians 7:5).

has been positive. Now we have a NEGATIVE COMMAND.

Don't you dare cheat one another of the "act of marriage." Don't deprive your mate of sex.

Well, you can deprive your husband of HIS RIGHT if BOTH of you agree to have a sexual truce or reprieve for devotions (religious reasons).

We will continue 1 Corinthians 7 in future lessons.

IF you have mutually agreed to take "time out" for fasting and prayer, okay. But, DON'T FAST and PRAY too long—you will not only fall over in a faint from weakness, but in that weakened physical condition, SATAN will tempt you with unrestrained passions in your sexual appetite. Satan tempted Jesus in a hungered condition. We who are not sinless (as He was and is) are not able to withstand such buffeting as Jesus was (Matthew 4: 2-3).

Let me ask you a question. How long can you go without food? Also, even in your most spiritual mountain-top experiences, how long do you pray?

Likewise, ye wives, be in subjection to your own husbands; that, if any obey not the word, they also may without the word be won by the conversation of the wives; While they behold your chaste

I have a sneaking suspicion that none of you go long without food. So I say, with boldness, that none of you should go too many days without sex with your own husbands. Why? Lest lewd behavior replace your chaste manner of living. This "NOT DEPRIVING" one another goes both for HUSBANDS and WIVES.

What guilt would hang upon your head

conversation coupled with fear (1 Peter 3:1-2).

if your husband should be unfaithful because you were selfish and did not recognize that he had authority (power) over your body—that your body was no longer yours, but his.

While you are off on a woman's retreat, your husband could be committing adultery with your best friend. Think about it.

IS "THREE" YOUR MAGIC NUMBER?

In our lessons we have encouraged wives to "make love" and not war with their mates. A target number has been set up as THREE TIMES A WEEK for the "ACT OF MARRIAGE" with your own husband. We have discussed that sex is an all-important factor in HUSBAND-LOVING and without the exercise of this God-given ability, a woman is NOT a good "HUSBAND-LOVER."

In grasping for a number such as "three," I used several criteria.

First of all, I determined:

(1) That there were seven days to a week.
(2) Half of seven is 3 & ½.
(3) Could a person go without food for 3 ½ days?
(4) Could she? Should she? Would she?
(5) Determining an average age of married couples.
(6) Determining various sexual appetites.
(7) Reading a few statistics.

In view of all the above considerations, I conjured up the goal of "THREE TIMES A WEEK" as a minimum HUSBAND-LOVING requirement, with no criticism for higher achievers.

I have been criticized for this—believe it or not. To be truthful, I scratch my head in disbelief to think that born-again women are so naive to think their husbands would not be pleased—yes DELIGHTED—with such wifely behavior. One happy wife told me "DOUBLE OR NOTHING."

QUOTES FROM KINSEY

Let me quote from *KINSEY'S SEXUAL BEHAVIOR IN THE HUMAN FEMALE.* Excuse the frankness, but how else can we learn?

> *Frequency of Experience.* *The average (active median) frequencies of marital coitus in the sample had begun at nearly three (2.8) per week for the females who were married in their late teens. They had dropped to 2.2 per week by thirty years of age, to 1.5 per week by forty years of age, to 1.0 per week by fifty years of age, and to once in about twelve days by age sixty. These figures are closely comparable to the frequencies indicated by the males in the sample. We have already noted that studies of paired spouses indicate that females estimate the frequencies of their marital coitus a bit higher than males estimate them, evidently because some females object to the frequencies of coitus and therefore overestimate the amount they are actually having. Males, on the other hand often wish that they were having coitus more frequently and consequently may underestimate the amount they actually have* [underlining is mine].
>
> *. . . the day-by-day calendars which we have on some hundreds of cases of married females and males show a remarkable regularity in the occurrence of marital coitus. There are of course, periods of illness, periods of menstruation or pregnancy, periods when the spouses are separated, and other interruptions in the regular sequence of coital rates. But, by and large, coitus in marriage occurs with a regularity which is not equaled by any other type of sexual activity in the female, although it may be matched by the masturbatory, coital, and sometimes homosexual activity of the male. This suggests that it is the male rather than the female partner who is chiefly responsible for the regularity of marital coitus.*

Individual Variation In Frequency. The individual variation in the frequencies of marital coitus had been considerable. This had undoubtedly depended on differences in the interests and capacities of the individual females, but it had also depended on the great variation which exists in the interest and capacities of the male spouses.

The most common frequencies in the sample had been close to the median frequencies. They lay between two and four times per week for the younger age groups, but had dropped to about once a week by age forty. In the younger groups, only a few individuals had had coitus less often than once in two weeks. The number of those who were having such low rates of contact had increased in the older age groups, and the percentages with such a low rate had begun to dominate by the middle forties. My question here is the following: Do you consider yourself YOUNG or OLD? Do you want a young and vibrant marriage, or an OLD and FEEBLE ONE? Can you THINK YOUNG?

The maximum frequencies in all of the age groups had extended considerably beyond the median or modal values. Some 14 percent of the married females in the sample had had marital coitus with frequencies of SEVEN OR MORE PER WEEK during their late teens. By thirty years of age, it was only 5 percent, and by forty years of age it was only 3 percent who were having coitus with average frequencies of seven or more per week. However, in each age group, from the youngest to age forty, there were some individuals who were having coitus in their marriages on an average of four times a day, every day in the week.

By fifty-five years of age there were only two individuals in the sample who were having coitus as frequently as seven or eight times per week, and none who were having it more frequently. [pp. 348-352 of *Sexual Behavior in the Human Female*, by the Kinsey Report.]

DEFINITION:
Coitus: *"Sexual intercourse, coition."*

QUOTES FROM LAHAYE

Now let us quote from *THE ACT OF MARRIAGE—The Beauty of Sexual Love* by Tim and Beverly LaHaye:

> *The Sexual Numbers Game. No study of sexual response would be complete without considering the frequency of intercourse. As REDBOOK says, "When it comes to making love, Americans seem particularly preoccupied with numbers." We have already observed that frequency is dependent upon many things—age, health, immediate pressures (business, social, family, financial), resentment, guilt, inability to communicate about sex, and a host of other things. Both surveys, however, indicate that frequency is not nearly so important as satisfaction. We are convinced that it is much more important to bring sexual satisfaction to your partner with almost every lovemaking experience than it is to run a bedroom marathon.*
>
> *There is no set "normal frequency" pattern. Each couple should find the frequency level at which they feel comfortable and enjoy each other. Even that level will vary at times. However, both our survey and REDBOOK'S indicate that most wives in their late thirties and forties desire more lovemaking than they receive. Most husbands would be advised to leave their vocational problems at the plant or office so that they may spend more time loving and enjoying their wives.*

LaHaye then gives the following summary:

> *We are quite satisfied that our survey has established that over the long years of matrimony, Christians do indeed experience a mutually enjoyable love relationship and that they engage in the act of marriage more frequently and with greater satisfaction than do non-Christians in our society. This will not really come as a surprise to those who know and obey*

biblical principles, because the Scriptural keys to happiness require that we learn and obey the principles of God.

It is a sad paradox that so many of those who have rejected or neglected God in their pursuit of sexual freedom and happiness often live miserable lives, whereas the Christian, whom they tend to despise or ridicule as being too "straight," enjoys the things the non-Christian is seeking. It is our prayer that many who have not previously considered Jesus Christ will begin to realize the fact that He does make a difference in one's life. (*The ACT OF MARRIAGE*, by Tim and Beverly LaHaye, pp. 214-217, from the Chapter on "Sex Survey Report"].

ANOTHER ANSWER AS TO FREQUENCY

In LaHaye's book, on page 252, under "FREQUENCY," in answer to a question "How often does an average couple make love?" the answer is something like this. People are not "average" and it is difficult to publish "an average." Much depends upon the individual's temperament, jobs, bedroom privacy, etc.

Dr. Wheat's survey involving five thousand couples, come up with a computer's average of TWO TO THREE TIMES A WEEK.

Dr. Herbert J. Miles' survey of young couples tabulated 3.3 days or about twice a week.

A *PARADE MAGAZINE* reported once a week among six thousand modern executives of all ages with pressured jobs.

LaHaye's survey from Christians (born-again believers) who attended his seminars showed "ABOUT THREE TIMES A WEEK over the entire period of marriage" as "average."

The author goes on to say that "*whatever brings enjoyment and fulfillment to the two of you is 'average' for you.*"

A WORD OF WARNING FOR "LOW AVERAGE" WIVES

I would like to add this one word of Warning in letting up on an active "several times a week" love life with your husband.

While you may be satisfied with less than the "average" Christian couple's average over your whole married span—THREE TIMES PER WEEK—your HUSBAND MAY WANT MORE. By the way, LaHaye and I agree and I didn't take a survey—I just read the Bible and have been married a few years. He may never tell you. But he may commit adultery to get his quota in, as many, many men in the world do daily. Think about it. You may want each "encounter" to be a "special occasion," but he may want just plain "meat and potatoes" and could wander to another "restaurant" while you're buying the candles.

DEATH RETURNS THE "AUTHORITY" OF ONE'S BODY TO ONESELF

While writing this particular lesson, we have heard of the sudden, unexpected death of a dear neighbor—a HUSBAND-LOVER'S mate. Now this woman is no longer a HUSBAND-LOVER. Her body has been returned to herself now. Now she has had the "power," the "authority" rights to her body returned to her. She has been reverted by the death of her mate to the unmarried, private ownership of her person.

What if death should stalk your house tonight? What if you should awaken to the sound of your husband's last breath and moan? What if he should pass into eternity? What if your body's "due" (1 Corinthians 7:3) was suddenly returned to you? How would you feel about the kind of sex life you surrendered to him? Your HUSBAND-LOVING days would be over. (That is, unless and until you re-married in the Lord.)

No one made you get married. No one stood with a gun at your head, I am sure, and said: "You must wed." You did it yourself. You accepted the challenge of marriage.

ARE YOU A CHICKEN HUSBAND-LOVER?

If you are born-again, you must walk as a believing wife in submission to your mate. This is the only happy way. But more than happiness, it is the Scriptural way.

Why do women insist upon their own WILLFULNESS? What are you afraid of? The only thing that could possibly happen if you follow our HUSBAND-LOVING RULES is the decreasing of yourself, and the increasing of your husband's love and devotion to you. Are you too “CHICKEN” to try?

THINGS TO DO AND THINK ABOUT THIS WEEK

1. **Have you started to nag or admonish your husband again?** If so, stop it.

2. **Have you forgotten to yield to the will of God concerning subjection? It so, BEGIN.**

3. **Have you neglected to pursue your man sexually?** If that’s true, go after him.

4. Did you slip into the old pattern of thinking, forgetting YOU married a MAN. If you have, change your thinking.

5. Read “SEX EDUCATION” (Chapter 4) in *THE ACT OF MARRIAGE* by LaHaye.

6. Memorize Romans 6:11 and get in your coffin. Memorize Psalm 101:2 and watch your walk when you are out of it.

7. **Pray that the Lord will make you willing** to be a SCRIPTURAL, surrendered, subordinate, submissive, subjective, sexually aggressive, sanctified and separated HUSBAND-LOVER.

8. Read 1 Corinthians 6:13-7:40; Ephesians 5:22-24; 1 Peter 2:9-3:6; Genesis 2. **Don't get HUNG-UP on the husband’s part. This is NOT your concern.**

9. Read your Bible daily, pray often, seek Christian fellowship in a BIBLE-preaching church.

10. **Eliminate unnecessary stress in your life.** This takes self-discipline and courage.

HUSBAND-LOVING LESSON #10

TO STAY, OR NOT TO STAY—THAT IS THE QUESTION!

> *An unprecedented rise in broken marriages among older men and women is causing concern among their children and puzzling social workers.*
>
> *In 1974, the number of divorced and separated Americans 45 years and older was 4.4 million, nearly twice as many as 10 years earlier.*
>
> *This is a much more rapid rate of increase than among younger couples, whose marital problems, until recently, held the spotlight.*
>
> *As a result of the increase in divorces among older people, ecologists are devoting more attention to the ramifications of the trend--focusing not only on the parted couples, but also on their families.*
>
> *. . . The impact of these divorces on children could affect the family structure for generations.* (From *U.S. NEWS & WORLD REPORT*, December 20, 1976, p. 56).

Let us continue in our study of 1 Corinthians, Chapter Seven—though there is much more to say on the preceding verses, and, as the Lord extends our class sessions together, we will return to the first five verses often. Always remember that it is within these verses that either much delight or dilemma is found between husband and wife. It is either "defrauding" one another, or "delighting" one another.

PAUL'S WORDS ARE AUTHORITATIVE ON MARRIAGE

But I speak this by permission, and not of commandment (1 Corinthians 7:6).

If you notice in this portion of Scripture, Paul often says words of this kind. What does he mean? Is he telling us that some things he writes are from the Lord and other things are only his personal idea?

No, I do not believe so. Paul is saying: "There are portions of Scripture that we CAN READ WHICH SAY 'SO AND SO,' but THERE IS NEW teachings from God which the Holy Spirit is giving me to write unto you." The apostle tells us that what he is writing is what the Lord has given him permission (authority) to write.

SINGLENESS IS A "GIFT OF GOD"

For I would that all men were even as I myself. But every man hath his proper gift of God, one after this manner, and another after that (1 Corinthians 7:7).

"I wish (says Paul) that everyone was like I am—UNMARRIED (whether NEVER married, or, as in Paul's case, I believe, a WIDOWER staying UN-MARRIED and not REMARRYING)." To remain unmarried is a gift from God.

Some Christians have one gift and some have another. You may have the gift of "helps" or the gift of "singing" or being a "teacher" but not "the GIFT of being "unmarried."

It is not necessary to assume that Paul had never been married. Marriage was regarded as a DUTY among the JEWS. A man was considered to have sinned if he had reached the age of twenty without marrying. The Mishna (if accurate) fixed the age of marriage at seventeen or eighteen, and the Babylonish Jews as early as fourteen. A rabbinical precept declared that a Jew who has not a wife is not a man. It is not certain, but most probable that Saul was a member of the Sanhedrin (Acts 26:10). If so, he must have been married, as marriage was a condition of membership. From verse 8, it is plausibly inferred that he classed himself among widowers. [*Word Studies in the New Testament* by Vincent, pp. 218-219.]

It is NECESSARY for us to understand the three types of "unmarried" folk Jesus was talking about and Paul knew about.

But he [Jesus] *said unto them, All men cannot receive this saying, save they to whom it is given* [that of remaining unmarried.]

1. Some people are born with some physical limitation within their bodies that causes them not only, not to be able to parent children, but also that cause them not to have matured sexually so that <u>they have no ability to have intercourse</u>—to put it bluntly.

For there are some eunuchs, which were so born from their mother's womb: and there are some eunuchs, which were made eunuchs of men: and there be eunuchs, which have made themselves eunuchs for the kingdom of heaven's

2. Some people have had an operation or have been mutilated (Such as a man who has had his male organ cut off as a torture method). I usually think of a Eunuch as a man. Remember the CHAMBERLAINS in the book of Esther who were the "keepers" of the women (Esther 2:3)? These "men" were EUNUCHS (castrated males).

sake. He that is able to receive it, let him receive it (Matthew 19:11-12).

But the younger widows refuse: [supported by the church for church work] *for when they have begun to wax wanton against Christ, they will marry;* (1 Timothy 5:11).

And withal they learn to be idle, wandering about from house to house; and not only idle, but tattlers also and busybodies, speaking things which they ought not.
I will therefore that the younger women marry, [Paul is writing here] *bear children, guide the house, give none occasion to the adversary to speak reproachfully. For some are already turned aside after Satan.* (1 Timothy 5:13-15).

A bishop [the minister, or pastor of a Bible-believing church] *then must be blameless, the husband of one wife, vigilant, sober, of good behaviour, given to hospitality, apt to teach;* (1 Timothy 3:2).

3. Some people for "the kingdom of heaven's sake" have decided they can serve the Lord in a fuller way—without sin, without burning up sexually inside of themselves, without constantly falling into sexual sin of one kind or another. Some of these SPECIALLY CALLED individuals may have been married before, but now either through death or their mate's departing accept this as a "gift of God" and live and serve the Lord Jesus Christ in all purity of mind and body.

This unmarried state is not a requirement for Christian service. It is not a must for a pastor or a missionary. In fact, it is often much better for a preacher to be married. [Paul has much to say about requirements for the ministry in other portions of the Scripture.]

MARRIAGE VERSUS SPONTANEOUS COMBUSTION

I say therefore to the unmarried and widows, It is good for them if they abide even as I. But if they cannot contain, let them marry: for it is better to marry than to burn (1 Corinthians 7:8-9).

Paul says something like this to those single women and WIDOWS: *"It is GOOD if you can stay unmarried. BUT, if you cannot possess that part of the fruit of the Spirit called TEMPERANCE, or "self control'* (Galatians 5:22-23)*; if you cannot restrain yourself; or check your passion like one would check their coat at a public dining room and forget about it during the evening meal; you better go find a man and get married and 'get with it' sexually. Why? You are not a woman who exercises restraint as to the refraining from sexual intercourse with one to whom you are <u>not</u> married."*

Come, let us take our fill of love until the morning: let us solace ourselves with loves.

For the goodman [husband] *is not at home, he is gone a long journey:*

He hath taken a bag of money with him, and will come home at the day appointed.

With her much fair speech she caused him to yield, with the flattering of her lips she forced him.

Sad to say, many so-called "born-again" women rush into "affairs" making messes of their lives, searing their consciences. What sad women they are—some are fallen "HUSBAND-LOVERS" who spit in the face of God and laugh at the shock in the eyes of their families, ignoring the grief they have caused, thinking, "I can get away with it. None will know."

<u>Paul continues</u> to tell us that it is better to get married <u>than to burn</u>. Burn what? Burn the rubbish? Burn the coals in the fireplace?

<u>Vincent</u> tells me that *"to burn" is continuous present: to burn ON;*

continuance in unsatisfied desire [p. 219, *WORD STUDIES IN THE NEW TESTAMENT*].

He goeth after her straightway, as an ox goeth to the slaughter, or as a fool to the correction of the stocks; (Proverbs 7:18-22).

Both you and I know that a fire which is burning and smoldering, will soon erupt and burn the house down. Sometimes costly fires are caused by SPONTANEOUS COMBUSTION. This is the "picture" of why it is "better to marry than to burn."

Paul has not said that celibacy is BETTER than marriage, though he has justified it and expressed his own personal preference for it. [p. 126, *Word Pictures in the New Testament*, A. T. Robertson]

Have we not power [no right] *to lead about a sister, a wife, as well as other apostles, and as the brethren of the Lord, and Cephas?* [This is Simon Peter whom some say was the first Pope, which he was not, but some say that he was so] (1 Corinthians 9:5).

If Paul wanted to marry as the other apostles had, he was free to do so, (1 Corinthians 9:5), but he had a "gift from God" and that was sex-control (self-control).

> *This charismatic gift of sexual self control is valuable also in the married state, for it frees from all temptation (last clause of verse 5). The fact that in this state such control does not mean avoidance of all legitimate sex contact verse 3 places beyond question.* (p. 281, R. C. H. Lenski, *op. cit.*)
> . . . *This does not mean that a strong inclination toward marriage is one of God's charismatic gifts for the simple reason that no grace and no special gift of grace is needed for*

And he arose out of the synagogue, and entered into Simon's house. And Simon's wife's mother was taken with a great fever; and they besought him for her (Luke 4:38).

that, the constitution of our nature suffices entirely. What Paul means is that one Christian has a special gift from God in one direction, another in an entirely different direction. Grace works in all manner of directions as Paul shows in 1 Corinthians 12.8, etc. (Lenski, *op. cit.*, p. 282)

Paul expressed the WISH that all men and women had the "gift of God" to live alone; but God distributes this "gift" as HE chooses—there is not a clash between Paul's "wish" and God's distribution of the gift.

> *Many other gifts besides sexual self-control are so fruitful and so lovely in themselves that we might well wish them for all Christians, yea, all men, and yet we know in regard to our wish, as Paul knew regarding his wish, that it must remain unfulfilled.* (Lenski, op. cit. p. 282).

> *Certain things had to be said and to be understood, and Paul says them in the right way. The purity of his mind is reflected in every word and expression. This is the model for preaching and Christian discussion.* (Lenski, *The Interpretation of St. Paul's First and Second Epistle to the Corinthians,* Wartburg Press, Columbus, Ohio, p. 282)

MARRIAGE "DEPARTURE RULES" FOR BELIEVERS

And unto the married I command, yet not I, but the Lord, Let not the wife depart from her husband: (1 Corinthians 7:10)

For this cause shall a man leave his father and mother, and cleave to his wife; And they twain [two] *shall be one flesh: so then they are no more twain, but one flesh. What therefore God hath joined together, let not man put asunder* (Mark 10:7-9).

And he saith unto them, Whosoever shall put away his wife, and marry another, committeth adultery against her. And if a woman shall put away her husband, and be married to another, she committeth adultery (Mark 10:11-12).

But and if she depart, let her remain unmarried, or be reconciled to her husband: and let not the husband put away his wife (1 Corinthians

What could be plainer? Hey, Lady, DON'T LEAVE YOUR HUSBAND. . . God says so; this is not man's idea. Where does the LORD command that a wife depart not from her husband? Think. That's right.

Jesus told the disciples all about the "leaving and cleaving principle" [See HUSBAND-LOVING LESSON #8 (pp. 105-117) and make it a part of your married thought-pattern.]

Paul is just enforcing what the Christians there at Corinth already knew from the Scriptures and from the teaching of Jesus Christ. (See Genesis 2:23-24). Paul wrote the people at Ephesus the same thing in Ephesians 5:31: *"For this cause* [because believers are members of Christ's body when they accept Him as personal Saviour] *shall a man leave his father and mother and shall be joined unto his wife, and they two shall be one flesh."* Marriage is a picture of Christ and His Church.

Sometimes women do strange things, don't they? Sometimes they say, "I can't stand this marriage anymore. I can't stand his yelling, his arrogance, his dominating way, I'm leaving." So, off she goes, leaving behind all of her "life's work"—her children, her home, her

7:11).

husband, her reputation.

Now if a woman has left her husband, she has two choices:

REMAIN UNMARRIED

1. Never, never, never remarry. Never, never become "one flesh" with another man. (Are you thinking, "Oh, I didn't think that applied here!")

RECONCILE TO HER HUSBAND

2. Be friendly again with her husband. Bring herself back in harmony with her mate. Settle her differences. Adjust herself to him and his needs. Re-unite in a quiet submission under his headship as her husband once again.

They say unto him, Why did Moses then command to give a writing of divorcement, and to put her away? He [Jesus] *saith unto them, Moses because of the hardness of your hearts suffered you to put away your wives: but from the beginning it was not so* (Matthew 19:7-8).

Here's something Paul has for husbands. "DON'T DIVORCE YOUR WIFE!" (This is NEW TESTAMENT TEACHING.) It is much stronger than the Old Testament. It allowed divorce because of the hardness of the hearts of the Israelites. Today we Christians are under grace and have a higher standard than those under the law (See Deuteronomy 24:1-4).

MARRIAGE "DEPARTURE RULES" FOR "MIXED" MARRIAGES

But to the rest speak I, not the Lord: If any brother hath a wife that believeth not, and she be pleased to dwell with

Up to this point, Paul has been speaking to believing wives married to believing husbands and believing husbands married to believing wives.

him, let him not put her away.

And the woman which hath an husband that believeth not, and if he be pleased to dwell with her, let her not leave him (1 Corinthians 7:12-13).

This, of course, is how a marriage should be. It is wrong for a Christian woman to be "yoked" up with an unbelieving man. This is the UNEQUAL YOKE spoken of in 2 Corinthians 6:14. A born-again woman should never even consider marrying an unsaved young man, no matter how wonderful he may be. In fact, she should never even consider DATING him or going out with him. See our NOTES on what it means to be "born-again" on pp. 23-27 above.

Be ye not unequally yoked together with unbelievers: for what fellowship hath righteousness with unrighteousness? and what communion hath light with darkness? (2 Corinthians 6:14)

But if you find yourself in this state of an unequal yoke due to ignorance or defiance of the WORDS of God [or, if both of you were unsaved when you married, and now one of you is saved and the other is unsaved], Paul has a few words for you now.

You Christian women who are married to an unsaved husband, do you know what the Lord is telling Paul to instruct you to do? He is saying: "Wife, if your husband is happy living with you, if this gives him personal pleasure, don't you dare leave him."

Paul continues: "I will tell you why you better not pick up your suitcase and go, because your presence in the house makes that house a very special place."

For the unbelieving husband is sanctified by the wife, and the unbelieving wife is sanctified by the husband: else were your children unclean; but now are they holy (1 Corinthians 7:14).

You're asking how can your presence make your home (with your unsaved husband, your drinking husband, your adulterer husband, your foul-mouthed husband) a "holy" home?

How can God say that your "dwelling" together with your kind, clean, good-providing, unsaved husband is right?

But ye are a chosen generation, a royal priesthood, an holy nation, a peculiar people; that ye should shew forth the praises of him who hath called you out of darkness into his marvelous light: (1 Peter 2:9)

There may be many reasons that an unbelieving husband should continue "husbanding" the believing wife. Verse 14 of 1 Corinthians says one of the reasons is that the Christian wife's salvation has made her a chosen person, a princess of God, a set apart person. She has been called forth to show the praises of the Lord Jesus Christ.

As obedient children [daughters], *not fashioning yourselves according to the former lusts in your ignorance:*

You, wife, as a Holy person, have brought the HOLY Spirit into that home of yours. Your presence in your home brings the presence of Jesus Christ within you. When you shut the bedroom door, you and your husband are locked up together WITH THE LORD.

But as he which hath called you is holy, so be ye holy in all manner of conversation [life];

Whether your husband knows it or not, he is a very special person, because he is married to a BELIEVER.

Because it is written, Be ye holy; for I am holy (1 Peter 1:14-16).

What a challenge to us as Christian wives. What a job cut out for us. Here again is the responsibility thrust upon us wives to walk the submissive walk of a believing wife, letting our behavior and our inner dress of a meek and quiet spirit wrap our lives like a glowing shawl of faith.

Forasmuch as ye know that ye were not redeemed with corruptible things, as silver and gold, from your vain conversation received by tradition from your

Have you slipped into the nagging habit? Have you taken on the "mother attitude" instead of the "lover attitude" with your husband?

fathers; But with the precious blood of Christ, as of a lamb without blemish and without spot: (1 Peter 1:18-19)

Likewise, ye wives, be in subjection to your own husbands; that, if any obey not the word, they also may without the word be won by the conversation of the wives; (1 Peter 3:1).

Have you joined your husband in his drinking? Have you failed to be a pure Christian in deed and word in the home, without lording that purity as a blue ribbon holder, waiting for stars in your crown?

HOLY CHILDREN NEED HOLY HOMES

. . . ELSE WERE YOUR CHILDREN UNCLEAN; but now are they holy. (1 Corinthians 7:14b)

Now thanks be unto God, which always causeth us to triumph in Christ, and maketh manifest the savour of his knowledge by us in every place.

For we are unto God a sweet savour of Christ, in them that are saved, and in them that perish: [your family] (2 Corinthians 2:14-15)

You and your unsaved husband have precious children. These offspring are the product of your love, your sexual love. Your "babies" are in this world because, you and your husband are "one flesh."

Because of you, believing wife, and mother, your children are exposed to the gospel. They can come to know Jesus Christ as Lord and Saviour because someone (that's you) cares and prays for them and lives before them in a Godly way.

By the way, do you live before your children in a godly way? Do you strive for more holiness within? Do you read the Bible and pray daily for continued fellowship? Do you attend a Bible-believing church and take your children with you, encouraging your husband to attend (if this doesn't make him mad at you)?

Do you live so that your family—the ones who are blessed because you as a born-again person dwell with them in your home—can smell the fragrance of Christ in your life?

IF DEPARTURE COMES—BE PEACEFUL

But if the unbelieving depart, let him depart. A brother or a sister is not under bondage in such cases: but God hath called us to peace (1 Corinthians 7:15).

NOW some unbelieving husbands may depart, perhaps for another woman [could it be that the present wife was not giving him his "due" of verse 3?], or because he just can't stand this Christian wife. He doesn't want the sanctified atmosphere that a Christian woman is supposed to bring.

If it be possible, as much as lieth in you, live peaceably with all men (Romans 12:18).

The wife is bound by the law as long as her husband liveth; but if her husband be dead, she is at liberty to be married to whom she will; only in the Lord (1 Corinthians 7:39).

For the woman which hath an husband is bound by the law to her husband so long as he liveth; but if the husband be dead, she is loosed from the law of her husband.

So then if, while her

If the unbeliever flees or departs, the Christian wife is left at home. She must remain in this lonely state, but she is not under slavery to make him come back to her. She must learn to live in peace and not bicker back and forth with him. God has called her to peace. This, too, is part of the fruit of the Holy Spirit (Galatians 5:22-23).

Is this what you want, believing wife? For your husband to flee—depart—or would you, by your submission to him want to make "home" so precious that he'll want to stay, even though you love Jesus Christ with all of your heart and he does not, yet?

William J. Hopewell, Jr., D.D., in his booklet (p. 21, *MARRIAGE AND DIVORCE*—available from the B.F.T. for $8.00 plus $5.00 S & H) says on this passage, 1 Corinthians 7:15:

husband liveth, she be married to another man, she shall be called an adulteress: but if her husband be dead, she is free from that law; so that she is no adulteress, though she be married to another man (Romans 7:2-3).

Using the context, then, to interpret the specific meaning of the word, "bondage" in verse fifteen means that a brother or sister is not bound to live together with the deserter. He or she is free to keep loyal worship to God minus the unbelieving dominance of his or her unsaved partner. But again, there is no evidence in the context for divorce or for remarriage.

To say that this "not under bondage" means that the marriage is dissolved, is to say that the marriage is now divided, the couple being no longer one flesh, but two separate entities as they were before marriage. That directly contradicts all the teaching in the Word that marriage is permanent and indissoluble. To say that "not under bondage" means a person is free from his old marriage and able to remarry opposes the context as well, for Paul is admonishing every man to abide in his present status (Hopewell, *op. cit.*, p. 21).

A WINNING WIFE IS A WILLING "HUSBAND-LOVER"

For what knowest thou, O wife, whether thou shalt save thy husband? or how knowest thou, O man, whether thou shalt save thy wife? (1 Corinthians 7:16)

"Wife," (Paul is saying), "how do you know that by dwelling with your husband, by submitting to his "lordship" in your marriage (1 Peter 3: 6) by not constantly correcting him, by not mothering over him like a hen, by

> sexually fulfilling him as his "lover," by being a "super-duper" HUSBAND-LOVER, HOW DO YOU KNOW that your living with that unsaved man, may not bring him to JESUS CHRIST?"

Just the other day, we renewed an acquaintance with—let's call her Mrs. Fullbright. To our surprise she told us, *"Since I've seen you last, I have been divorced."* What was the story? *"My husband fell in love with his secretary and they married six years ago."* I couldn't help but wonder what kind of a "HUSBAND-LOVER" she was. Did she wish she had lowered her pride and tried every trick of the HUSBAND-LOVING trade to keep that man? Maybe she did. Maybe nothing she could have done would have kept him. But, in the lonely times, in the hollowness of her empty heart, does she wish she had tried harder?

THINGS TO THINK ABOUT AND DO THIS WEEK

1. **You married a man.** Don't expect his reactions to be that of a woman.

2. Your man may NEVER change.

3. You as a HUSBAND-LOVER must change.
   a. **Change your ATTITUDE.**
   b. Change your nagging to NO NAGGING."
   c. Change your marriage motivation.
   d. **Change your "won't" to "WILL."**
   e. Change your "want to" to "WHAT EVER YOU SAY, DEAR."
   f. CHANGE your underwear daily.
   g. Change your clothes, buy some new ones or get some acceptable ones.
   h. Change your perfume.
   i. Change your furniture around in the house.
   j. Change the way you clean the house to keeping it

better.

k. Change your Bible reading habits–to better ones.

l. **Change your mind about "not loving your husband" to thinking he's "MR. WONDERFUL."**

4. Read your HUSBAND-LOVING notes. Keep up to date and review.

5. REVIEW, REVIEW, REVIEW:
   LESSON #1 THE CHALLENGE OF SUBMISSION"
   LESSON #2 "BACK TO THE BEGINNINGS"
   LESSON #3 "DEAD TO SELF-ALIVE TO SUBJECTION"

6. Read Chapter 5 of *THE ACT OF MARRIAGE* about "THE ART OF LOVEMAKING," from Tim and Beverly LaHaye's book. You can read portions of this book or the whole book to your husband, or he may read it himself. (He may not though.)

7. Purchase the book by Wm. J. Hopewell, Jr., D.D. called *MARRIAGE AND DIVORCE* ($8.00 from B. F. T plus $5.00 S & H).

8. **Read 1 Peter 2:21—3:6.**

HUSBAND-LOVING LESSON #11

BLOOM WHERE YOU ARE PLANTED

Several years ago, my Mother and Dad sent me a gospel tract which was entitled "BLOOM WHERE YOU ARE PLANTED." I don't remember too much about the content, but that title has never left me.

This is the intent of this admonition: *God has put me in a certain soil. Your soil may be different from mine. You may have more sunshine in your garden than I have. You may have prettier colors than I have, but my soil is just that--MY SOIL. God has planted me in it and I dare not walk away from that holy ground!*

What a challenge to me as a wife and a mother. Oh, don't fool yourself. There have been plenty of times when I've wanted to run away from my old dirt. The humus across the street, across the state, in somebody else's flower box looked so much better than mine.

But God said to me, "BLOOM where YOU are planted. I want you there to grow in grace for me."

This is what the Lord is telling us as HUSBAND-LOVERS:

> *There you are, girl, in that soil, and it's all yours. That husband you married is YOURS, Lady, and no one else's. Don't run away from him; don't push him out of the house; just love him and obey the blooming rules.*

You say, "You don't *know* the man I married." I don't need to. God tells us in His Words,

> *Brethren, let every man, wherein he is called, therein abide with God* (1 Corinthians 7:24).

Now let us return to our text of 1 Corinthians 7 and see what else the Holy Spirit will show us. Please have a prayerful spirit as you study and a burdened heart towards obedience.

STAY IN YOUR OWN CLAY

But as God hath distributed to every man, as the Lord hath called every one, so let him walk. And so ordain I in all churches (1 Corinthians 7:17).

Here the verse is saying, "Where did God save your soul?" There? In that situation? With that wife? With THAT husband? Okay, stay there. This is what Paul preached in all his churches which he established under the Lord's blessing.

Is any man called being circumcised? let him not become uncircumcised. Is any called in uncircumcision? let him not be circumcised. Circumcision is nothing, and uncircumcision is nothing, but the keeping of the commandments of God (1 Corinthians 7:18-19).

If the Lord saved your soul and you were circumcised (he's talking to men, of course, here)--stay in that condition. Even if you were saved being uncircumcised, don't run to the nearest doctor and have the operation performed on your person. All circumcision is the obeying of the commandment of God for the Israelite who was under the law of Moses, not resting in the grace of God (John 1:17).

For the law was given by Moses, but grace and truth came by Jesus Christ (John 1:17).

Let every man abide in the same calling wherein he was called. Art thou called being a servant? care not for it:

What is Paul telling us in these four verses? He's saying to you women, if you were saved as a slave, don't be upset that you still have that occupation. Remember, you are really free. (John 8: 32, 36). Your spirit is free and liberated by the precious blood of Jesus Christ *but if thou mayest be made free, use it rather. For he that is called in the Lord, being a servant, is the Lord's freeman: likewise also he that is called, being free, is Christ's servant.*

Ye are bought with a price; be not ye the servants of men.

Brethren, let every man, wherein he is called, therein abide with God (1 Corinthians 7:20-24).

which has washed you from your filth of sin.

If you were born-again and a free woman, praise the Lord, but you really aren't free, you know. You are a servant of the Lord God.

So, no matter what your status, you are purchased with a price (1 Peter 1:18-19) and you must serve the ONE Who bought you.

I like what Dr. William Hopewell says concerning verses 20, 24, and 26 of this chapter 7:

"*The context surrounding 1 Corinthians 7 is that of persecution against believers causing much unhappiness and pain in their lives at that time. Paul's whole exhortation is that in whatever state they were, 'FREEZE'! They were to remain as they were in order not to increase the pain of persecution upon them. 'Let every man abide in the same calling wherein he is called' (v. 20). 'Brethren, let every man, wherein he is called, therein abide with God'* (v. 24). 'I suppose therefore, that this is good for the present distress'" (v. 26). (Hopewell, *op. cit., MARRIAGE & DIVORCE*).

TO MARRY OR NOT TO MARRY WAS THE QUESTION

Now concerning

Once again the apostle Paul is telling you that nothing is written down in the Scriptures from the Lord on this subject, *virgins I have no commandment of the Lord: yet I give my judgment, as one that hath obtained mercy of the Lord to be faithful* (1 Corinthians 7:25).

but he has his thoughts on the matter and he must be faithful to what the Lord has given to him on this teaching concerning virgins. What he DOES say, however, is written under the guidance of God the Holy Spirit, and these words are therefore INSPIRED OF GOD, and are not to be treated as though they were not.

Now, you readers know the definition of a VIRGIN is *"an unmarried woman, esp. a girl; One who has not had sexual intercourse."* (*Webster's New Collegiate Dictionary*, 1947).

I suppose therefore that this is good for the PRESENT DISTRESS, I say, that it is good for a man so to be (1 Corinthians 7:26).

Don't forget the conditions in corrupt Corinth. Don't forget the kind of lives these Corinthians were brought out from when they were converted to Jesus Christ.

Paul may be saying here: "It's really better because of the oppressing, poor life you lead, and the exceedingly corrupt and lustful neighborhood about you, that men and women should not get married."

Art thou bound unto a wife? seek not to be loosed. Art thou loosed from a wife? seek not a wife (1 Corinthians 7:27).

"Hey there, Christian," Paul advises, "If you are married, that's where it is. If you are unmarried, foot-loose and fancy free." As Dr. Hopewell says, "FREEZE"!

But and if thou marry,

It's not a sin to marry—far from it. Some of your daughters have married. They're certainly not sinning. But, I'll tell you one thing, they are going to have plenty of trouble. Marriage brings trouble and little ones. Oh, how Paul wanted to spare *thou hast not sinned; and if a virgin marry, she hath not sinned. Nevertheless such shall have trouble in the flesh: but I spare you* (1 Corinthians 7:28).

these "virgins" the pain and tears which accompanies the kisses and hugs of marriage. This is not to knock marriage, but it is just to be honest about the facts of life.

THE DIFFERENCE BETWEEN EARTH'S AND HEAVEN'S SOIL

But this I say, brethren, the time is short: it remaineth, that both they that have wives be as though they had none;

And they that weep, as though they wept not; and they that rejoice, as though they rejoiced not; and they that buy, as though they possessed not;

And they that use this world, as not abusing it: for the fashion of this world passeth away (1 Corinthians 7:29-31).

"The time is short." Paul was looking for the rapture of the Church, when Christ would take the saved ones home to heaven (1 Thessalonians 4:13-18). The present distress would then be over. Believers would be with the Lord Jesus Christ in GLORY. Those who were married on earth would have no mates in heaven (Mark 12:25) in the same sense as on earth, at least. Those that cried on earth would have their tears wiped away by God (Revelation 21:4). Those who rejoice and have pleasure with their wives and families would be thrust into a new environment with different priorities. Those that were filled with the business of the world – buying and selling—would be in a place where it was too late to possess new davenports, curtains, cars, or lawnmowers. Those who were caught up in the world's "buzz" would be the same as those who led a docile role. Why? The fashion of this world would pass away. The world and its glow are only transitory.

MARRIAGE MAKES FOR EARTHLY-MINDEDNESS

But I would have you without carefulness [anxiety]. *He that is unmarried careth for the things that belong to the Lord, how he may please the Lord:*

"How I long that you be without anxiety, Corinthian friends in the Lord," Paul was saying. If you are single, your whole care, your whole thought, your whole life, can be zoned in on the Lord Jesus Christ. WHEN YOU WAKE UP IN THE MORNING, YOUR FIRST THOUGHTS can be, "I must run over to the church and teach my Bible class." Or, "Mrs. Smith is in the hospital; I must take her a word of cheer about the Lord Jesus Christ."

But he that is married careth for the things that are of the world, how he may please his wife (1 Corinthians 7:32-33).

But if you are married, your first thought in the morning might be: "I must make the living so my family can eat and be clothed," or, "I wonder how baby is doing after her high temperature."

THE UNMARRIED ONE HAS NO HUSBAND TO PLEASE

There is difference also between a wife and a virgin. The unmarried woman careth for the things of the Lord, that she may be holy both in body and in spirit: but she that is married careth for the things of the world, how she may please her husband (1 Corinthians 7:34).

In case you never read it in a book, ladies, there is a difference between a wife and a virgin. Both are female—one has had sexual intercourse, the other has not. But there is more of a difference.

The virgin can care for one of two things. She can either care about herself—be in love with number one, herself; or she can make the Lord Jesus Christ #1 in her life and devote that life to His service wherever she is or whatever she is doing.

She can dedicate her body and her spirit to the LORD.

But the married woman—that's another story. She can't read her Bible all the time, nor pray when she longs to talk to the Father always. Why? The children are calling her name or her husband wants a button sewn on his shirt or the sewer has just backed up all over the bathroom floor and company is coming to supper.

Then, when the married woman finally gets a few minutes to sit down and read the paper or the Bible or write a letter to her mother, MR. HUSBAND says, "Let's go to bed." Looking at the clock, she discovers that it's only nine-thirty.

THE UNMARRIED ONE HAS NO DIVIDED LOYALTIES

And this I speak for your own profit; not that I may cast a snare upon you, but for that which is comely, and that ye may attend upon the Lord without distraction (1 Corinthians 7:35).

Paul's whole concern was whether the Corinthian believers would commit sexual sins or not. Of course, he didn't want them to (cf. 1 Corinthians 7:1-2); but his yearning for them was their spiritual growth and service. He longed for them to serve the LIVING LORD, not to be distracted with earthly affairs like Martha (Luke 10:40) who had divided loyalties. Martha was burdened with making lunch instead of complete absorption in spiritual matters. His purpose in warning them of the pitfalls in marriage was not to lasso them like a cowboy and make them remain virgins. He just was constrained to tell them the facts about life. Certainly, it would be a "distraction" if you were constantly "burning" in lust for some man, hence you should seek a husband, and go on serving the Lord (1 Corinthians 7:2).

WHAT IS A FATHER TO DO?

But if any man think that he behaveth himself uncomely toward his virgin, if she pass the flower of her age, and need so require, let him do what he will, he sinneth not: let them marry.

Nevertheless he that standeth stedfast in his heart, having no necessity, but hath power over his own will, and hath so decreed in his heart that he will keep his virgin, doeth well.

So then he that giveth her in marriage doeth well; but he that giveth her not in marriage doeth better (1 Corinthians 7:36-38).

This passage is talking with Daddies. Fathers in those days arranged husbands for their daughters. It was bothering some of the fathers because their believing Corinthian daughters were getting up in years. [They were all of twenty years of age.] Some men didn't think because of the times and seasons that their daughters should be thrown into matrimony. These fathers thought that their girls were mature enough and not "hot" sexually [What father really knows?], and that they could have the "gift" of spinsterhood. Some dads were firm in this position; others were wavering; yet many knew that their offspring would "burn" with unfilled passion if they didn't find a husband for them.

Paul is settling down their distraught hearts by saying, "Either way you go, boys, is fine with the Lord." [Cf. Lenski's *Commentary* on this, *op. cit.*].

Right here I would like to interject a personal feeling. We have a twenty-year-old daughter. She is beautiful—of course I'd say that—and has a glowing personality. It would have been wonderful to have had her graduate from college, but she found her man. We approve of him 100%, and trust her judgement completely that he is the one for her. Therefore, with his whole blessing, her father has given her in marriage with no regrets.

As parents, we must be very careful not to thwart the LORD'S leading in our children's lives. It is God who is leading them. We are just the parents. We must trust HIS ways with them, and believe that all we have instilled within their lives and hearts as they grew up in the home will manifest itself in obedience to God's commands for them. This doesn't mean, however, that we are not to give them wise counsel, as needed, or if needed.

DEATH BREAKS THE MARRIAGE BOND

The wife is bound by the law as long as her husband liveth; but if her husband be dead, she is at liberty to be married to whom she will; only in the Lord (1 Corinthians 7:39).

Paul may not have wanted to put a woman in a noose, but she certainly puts herself in one by chaining herself to one man for the length of his life. If, per chance, he outlives her, the "bondage" to her mate is the entire length of her life.

Life is a long time to be bound to a person whom we don't like. That is why one must be sure before diving into the sea of matrimony, because once a woman is in the drink, she swims, and swims, and swims.

Be ye not unequally yoked together with unbelievers: for what fellowship hath righteousness with unrighteousness? and what communion hath

The liberty, the return of her "body power" [see Lesson #9, pp. 119-138], the becoming her own person again, is not hers until the death of her spouse.

light with darkness?

And what concord hath Christ with Belial? or what part hath he that believeth with an infidel? (2 Corinthians 6:14-15)

Wherefore come out from among them, and be ye separate, saith the Lord, and touch not the unclean thing; and I will receive you, (2 Corinthians 6:17)

Then, no longer is she bound to the man. She is freed to be a girl again and capture another husband.

"ONLY IN THE LORD" is the writer's way of warning. CHRISTIAN WOMAN, DON'T BE UNEQUALLY YOKED TO AN UNBELIEVING HUSBAND.

"WHEN YOU ARE SINGLE YOUR POCKETS WILL JINGLE."

But she is happier if she so abide, after my judgment: and I think also that I have the Spirit of God (1 Corinthians 7:40).

Paul is convinced that his judgment is excellent. He feels that these young virgins, who the fathers are worried about, would be far happier if they didn't get married at all.

But, Paul, try to tell a young girl this. Women in love do not believe you. Such unromantic reasoning, they say.

This afternoon I was hunting for a frozen salad recipe in my cook books when I chanced upon the following poem. The poem rebuked me because just this noon I failed a children-loving and a husband-loving test.

"THE GREATEST TEST"

Help me to walk so close to Thee
That those who know me best can see
I live as Godly as I pray
And Christ is real from day to day.
I see some once a day, or year
To them I blameless might appear;
'Tis easy to be kind and sweet
To people whom we seldom meet;
But in my home are those who see
Too many times the worst in me.
My hymns of praise were best unsung
If HE does not control my tongue
When I am vexed and sorely tried.
And my impatience cannot hide.
May no one stumble over me
Because Thy love they failed to see;
But give me, Lord, a life that sings
Of victory over little things.
Give me Thy calm for every fear
Thy peace for every falling tear;
Make mine, O Lord, through calm and strife
A gracious and unselfish life;
Help me with those who know me best
For Jesus sake, to stand the test.

Barbara C. Ryberg

THINGS TO DO AND THINK ABOUT THIS WEEK

1. **Let's pray more for definite things,** naming them and writing the requests on paper. If it is only five minutes of real praying a day, let's try it.

2. **Let's eliminate more of the unnecessary things in our lives** which turn us to shrews and screaming mothers. We may have to give up something we really

enjoy in order to be a better person.

3. Let's **stop admonishing our husbands**.

4. **Let's be consistent in our church attendance.** Of course, the church should be a separated, Bible-believing church.

5. **Read Proverbs 31:10-31.**

6. **Learn Psalm 101:2:**

   "I will behave myself wisely in a perfect way...
   I will walk within my house with a perfect heart."

7. Learn 1 John 4:4 *"Greater is He that is in you, than he that is in the world."*

8. Read "FOR MEN ONLY" (p. 82) from *THE ACT OF MARRIAGE* by Tim and Beverly LaHaye.

HAPPY "BLOOM-DAY" TO YOU!

HUSBAND-LOVING LESSON #12

KNOW YOUR ENEMY

There was a time when the military made a special point to inform the troops—Army, Navy, Air Force and Marines—all about the enemies of our country, the UNITED STATES OF AMERICA. Our fighting men were instructed concerning the foe in every area and in the smallest detail. What did the enemy look like? How did he talk? What were his tactics and what were his beliefs? How did he dress? How did he walk?

One day the U. S. Government didn't think this admonishment with the flashing warnings against the COMMUNIST enemy needed to be waved in front of the eyes of our fighting men. What happened? The men in uniform took a "soft" attitude toward the enemy, and toward the end of 1960, and the beginning of 1961, the spirit of VICTORY died, bringing in the "NO WIN" POLICY of "policing" instead of "conquering." A vivid example "phantom" was the Vietnam conflict. If a strong ANTI-COMMUNIST position had been maintained, and the smell of the fires of victory had been burning in the hearts and on the hearths at the home front, HISTORY would portray a fighting force which knew its enemy and had CONQUERED it, rather than the sad story of seeing ALL of NORTH VIETNAM handed over to the COMMUNIST MONSTERS for torture, brutality, and liquidation.

You and I as HUSBAND-LOVERS MUST KNOW OUR ENEMIES. Is he tall? Is he short? Is he friendly or mean? Is he ghost-like or in bodily form? Does he curse or does he praise? Is he dark or is he light? Does he splash about calling attention to himself, or does he slink into our lives? WHAT IS HIS NAME?

Let us look in the third chapter of the book of GENESIS and catch a glimpse of THE ENEMY. <u>See that third word in the first verse</u>?

> *Now the SERPENT* [the shining one] *was more subtil than any beast of the field which the LORD God had made. And he said unto the woman, Yea, hath God said, Ye shall not eat of every tree of the garden?* (Genesis 3:1a).

INTRODUCING THE DECEIVER

Ladies, let me introduce to you your enemy. I know you cannot miss him as he walks proudly around your EDEN. See how tall he stands? The sun's reflection is caught in the precious gems which adorn his person. Isn't he the shining one? How polished is his speech. His words flow like honey from his beautiful mouth. His suave manner and his subtle thoughts win and woo many who forget he is their enemy and fail to resist his persuasive prevarication. **One might be deceived and think he is an angel of LIGHT instead of the chief ruler of DARKNESS. His name is Satan, the DEVIL, a dealer in dirty deeds.**

> Satan is a person of dignity, created perfect, a cherubim, vested with great authority [Pettingill, see below] and the TOPSTONE of the primal creation [F. C. Jennings from Chafer's *Theology*.]

Satan is not all-powerful (omnipotent) though powerful.

Satan is not all-knowing (omniscient) though he is knowledgeable.

Satan is not everywhere present (omnipresent) though he gets around this world swiftly.

Lewis Sperry Chafer wrote in *MAJOR BIBLE THEMES* that:

> *"Satan's power is increased by innumerable hosts of demons who do his will and serve him."*

It is through the wicked spirits that Satan is in touch with the whole earth.

William Pettingill, in his *BIBLE DOCTRINE PRIMER*, declares that Satan is a REAL BEING and is mentioned by the name of SATAN 66 times and by the name DEVIL 34 times. He has many other names also.

He has PERSONAL NAMES
Performs PERSONAL ACTS
Has PERSONAL PLANNING & PLOTTING
WITH PERSONAL REASONING & SCHEMING

PRIDE GOETH BEFORE A FALL

The CRIME of SATAN was PRIDE. Let us never forget that. Over and over in reference books, the verse found in 1 Timothy 3:6 is quoted. Because of its importance to scholarly men, I think we should look at it and apply it to our lives in our EDENS (our homes) and in our HUSBAND-LOVING. The context is speaking of qualifications of a Pastor of a church.

Not a novice, lest being lifted up with pride he fall into the condemnation of the DEVIL (1 Timothy 3:6).

This minister should not be a NOVICE—a recent convert, one who has not been tried and tested like the tempering of steel for a bridge. Why shouldn't he be a person who is like an apprentice or one who is new in Christian work? Why shouldn't he be as one who runs "hot and cold" with the Lord? Why? Because PRIDE could grab hold of his heart. Pride could lift him like a lofty balloon and float him to the sky.

"Oh, don't you preach like an angel?" a sweet parishioner will coo. Larger and larger his balloon of pride will expand until "pop." the NOVICE crashes to the ground, splattering his testimony and altering his life.

> *With that befogging of mind which pride engenders, it is possible so to be misguided as to undertake the very opposite line of action from that which infinite wisdom has dictated.* (*Systematic Theology* by Lewis Sperry Chafer, VOL. II, p. 64).

This is what happened to Satan, created Lucifer. He was a novice compared to the eternal state of the GODHEAD.

LUCIFER, the "*son of the morning,*" (Isaiah 14:12) was the highest being created among the creatures of God. He was on duty and in command on the MOUNT OF GOD and the guard of God's HOLINESS.

> *He walked in unbroken relation to divine holiness.* (Chafer, *op. cit.*, II, p. 42).

What caused the demotion of the "son of the morning"—the transformation of the ARCHANGEL to the ARCHFIEND of the fallen angels? (Chafer, *op. cit.*, II, p. 34).

> *He became the embodiment of evil and wholly void of good . . . Satan is a living personification of deception* (Chafer, *op. cit.*, II, p. 35).

LUCIFER—PERFECT IN BEAUTY

In our classes we studied briefly the two passages which set forth Lucifer and his greatness and beauty [Ezekiel 28:11-17; and Isaiah 14:12-14], and because of this beauty and wisdom, his balloon of pride was popped and he fell from his authoritative position among the Cherubims (the plural of Cherub, as spelled in the KJB) and will someday be cast into the pit of Hell, chained forever with his fellow fiends who dared defy God and follow this base fellow.

There is a mention of the "king of Tyre" but there is more than an "earthly king" here. There is a "power" and a creation higher than a "worldly" throne and personality.

God's Words come to the prophet in tears and grief.

Son of man, take up a lamentation upon the king of Tyrus, and say unto him, Thus saith the Lord GOD; Thou sealest up the sum, full of wisdom, and perfect in beauty (Ezekiel 28:12).

Thou hast been in Eden the garden of God; every precious stone was thy covering, the sardius,

Satan (the fallen Lucifer) had within his person and personality perfection in beauty and wisdom. It is true, Satan had been in EDEN. It doesn't matter which EDEN you think this was for he was there, no matter. He is the PRINCE OF THE POWER OF THE AIR. That's the air where the birds and the planes and space ships fly around.

He had the best "outfit" of any creation of God. Such jewels are only mentioned in two other places in Scripture according to Chafer:

(1) The high priest's breastplate

topaz, and the diamond, the beryl, the onyx, and the jasper, the sapphire, the emerald, and the carbuncle, and gold: the workmanship of thy tabrets and of thy pipes was prepared in thee in the day that thou wast created (Ezekiel 28:13).

(Exodus 28:17-21); and

(2) In the NEW JERUSALEM (Revelation 21).

What a handsome sight! The trouble was LUCIFER knew it and he didn't take any pride-depressant!

His vocal chords were unique. He seemed to have his own personal ALLEN ORGAN without the need of computer cards. How he could praise the LORD! But, alas, his praise turned to prater and self-pride.

LUCIFER—CORRUPTED IN CRIME

Thou art the anointed cherub that covereth; and I have set thee so: thou wast upon the holy mountain of God; thou hast walked up and down in the midst of the stones of fire (Ezekiel 28:14).

As some think that the Cherubims protected and watched over the MERCY SEAT and the presence and GLORY of God in the tabernacle, so LUCIFER held the same post upon the HOLY MOUNTAIN--the site of GOD'S throne in the third heaven.

Up and down among this HOLY PRESENCE walked the BRIGHT AND SHINING ONE [LUCIFER]. He was free to roam.

> *. . . the stones of fire may be the manifestation of that consuming fire which Jehovah is. In such a case, this declaration would suggest that the first estate of this angel was one in which he walked in unbroken relation to divine holiness.* (Chafer, *op. cit.*, II, p. 42).

Thou wast perfect in thy ways from the day that thou wast created, till iniquity was found in thee (Ezekiel 28:15).

> *Through the degenerating power of sin, Satan as did ADAM, became an entirely different being from that which God created* (Chafer, *op. cit.*, II, p. 44).

The "iniquities" of Satan are many. Before any of the "*I wills*" of Isaiah 14 were voiced from that mouth and vocal cords created for praises of God, Lucifer developed "secret sin." He said in his heart:

(1) *I will ascend into heaven,*

(2) *I will exalt my throne above the stars of God* [the other angels].

(3) *I will SIT also upon the mount of the congregation, in "the sides of the NORTH"*: (Psalm 48:2). He wanted to sit on the very throne of the HOLY ONE in the NORTH—perhaps Jerusalem).

(4) *I will ascend above the heights of the clouds*; [perhaps the third heaven],

(5) *I will be like the MOST HIGH* (Isaiah 14:12-17).

> *By his sin he lost his original holiness and heavenly standing, but he retains his wisdom, and he has turned his surpassing abilities into ways of evil and his understanding has been prostituted to the level of lies, deception, snares and wiles.* (Chafer, *op. cit.*, II, p. 44).

SATAN—THE PIED-PIPER PRINCE

It would be foolish for me to attempt to do a study on this portion of Scripture, or on the whole teaching on SATANOLOGY. I am far from an expert.

Lucifer, with his winning ways, skillfully wooed disgruntled angelic creatures into rebellion against GOD. This pride-filled Cherub trafficked among the HOSTS, slandering THE MOST HIGH, conscripting a mutinous army, but he was not "pulling the wool" over God's eyes.

The power of Satan and his fallen fiends is limited. They cannot do anything outside of the permissive will of God. Notice how he, after his fall, had access to God's presence and "dickered" with God concerning JOB's life and health. (Job 1:6—2:8). He is constantly "accusing the brethren" [the born-again ones]:

> *for the accuser of our brethren is cast down,*
> *which accused them before our God day and night.*
> (Revelation 12: 10b)

He is the PRINCE OF THE POWER OF THE AIR, the SPIRIT that now worketh in the children of disobedience (Ephesians 2:2). See also John 11:31; 14:30; and 16:11.

SATAN—PRESENTLY A POWER PERSON

Lewis Sperry Chafer, in his book, *MAJOR BIBLE THEMES*, says:

> *Though morally fallen and NOW JUDGED in the cross, Satan has not lost his position, and he has lost but little of his power. His power both as to personal strength and authority is disclosed in two forms:*
>
> *1. HIS PERSONAL STRENGTH. His personal strength cannot be estimated. According to his own declaration which Christ did not deny, he has power over kingdoms of this world, which kingdoms he said were delivered unto him, and which power he bestows on whom he will* (Luke 4:6). *It is said of him that he had the power of death* (Hebrews 2:14), *but that power has been surrendered to Christ* (Revelation 1:18). *Satan had the power over sickness in the case of Job* (Job 2:7), *and was able to sift Peter as wheat in a sieve* (Luke 22:31; 1 Corinthians 5:5). *Likewise, Satan is said to have weakened the nations, to have made the earth to tremble, to have shaken kingdoms, to have made the earth a wilderness, destroying the cities thereof, and not to have opened the house of his prisoners* (Isaiah 14:12-17). *Against the power of Satan even Michael the archangel durst not contest* (Jude 1: 9)*; but there is victory for the child of God through the power of the Spirit and the blood of Christ* (Eph. 6:10-12; 1 John 4:4; Rev. 12:11).

Satan's power and authority are exercised always and only within the permissive will of God.

> *2. SATAN IS AIDED BY DEMONS. Satan's power is increased by the innumerable host of demons who do his will and serve him. Though he is not omnipresent, omnipotent, nor omniscient, through the wicked spirits he is in touch with the whole earth. (Chafer, MAJOR BIBLE THEMES,* "Satan: His Personality and Power," pp. 120-121).

SATAN HATES HUSBAND-LOVERS

There is coming a time—during the GREAT TRIBULATION —that the DEVIL will be cast out of HEAVEN for good. His mischief will be limited to EARTH. During the thousand-year millennial reign of Christ, the EVIL ONE will be chained for a 1,000 years, released, and then finally thrown into the Lake of Fire for eternal punishment and doom (Revelation 12:7-12; Isaiah 14:12; Luke 10:18; Revelation 20:1-3, 7; Revelation 20:10).

No wonder this evil PRINCE is prowling around like a roaring, devouring lion, seeking his prey. (1 Peter 5:8). He is fighting a lost cause. He was defeated at Calvary (Hebrews 2:14-15; John 16:11; Colossians 2:14-15) but refuses to accept defeat.

Satan and his demons [or devils] want to keep the unsaved [prisoners] bound, and the CHRISTIAN defeated with unbelief and pride. He passes as an "ANGEL OF LIGHT" with a false beam covering his wicked, darkened inner being (2 Corinthians 11:14).

Oh, Christian wife, we must know our ENEMY and beware of his crafty wiles. We must not become a lover of the evil world system of which Satan is the PRINCE (1 John 2:15-17). We must beware of falling into the SNARE of the devil—what a hunter is that fallen angel! His fields are full of traps.

> *Lest he fall [speaking again of the NOVICE] into reproach and the snare of the devil* (1 Timothy 3: 7).

> *And that they may recover themselves out of the snare of the devil, who are taken captive by him at his will* (2 Timothy 2:26).

There is a positive and negative response to Christian living which every woman who wants to be a HUSBAND-LOVER should be made aware of. Satan does not want us to have VICTORY when it comes to being a good wife. Satan does not want us to submit to the teaching of God concerning the subject. If we go on the broad way of WIFEHOOD, we will have a marriage which will end in destruction, but if we take the narrow, non-women's liberation path, we will have happy husbands.

SATAN HATES GOD'S BOOK. Do not listen to the perversion of Scripture which SATAN is mis-quoting and which so-called "CHRISTIAN" WOMEN'S LIBBERS are "adding to" God's Words just as the Serpent and EVE did in the Garden of Eden (See Genesis 3:1-3).

Satan is still trying to de-throne God and update HIS WORDS.

Take the positive route in Christian living.

> *SUBMIT yourselves therefore to God. RESIST the DEVIL, and he will flee from you* (James 4:7).

RESIST SATAN'S WORK IN YOUR EDEN

Dr. Chafer has an interesting quote concerning Lucifer which brings to mind ADAM and EVE (whom we are going to be studying in the next lesson). But more than reminding me of the first man and wife, it compels me to think of my position as a HUSBAND-LOVER.

> *The essential evil character of sin here, as everywhere, is an unwillingness on the part of the creature to abide in the precise position in which he [she] has been placed by the creator.* (Chafer, Theology, *op. cit.*, II, p. 49).

You are placed in your EDEN—your home—with your ADAM—your husband. There are RULES in the

SCRIPTURE concerning you as a wife. There is fruit you can eat and there is fruit forbidden (Genesis 2:16-17). TEMPTATION through people, places, and things—instigated by the evil spirits—will be in your way to fail in HUSBAND-LOVING. BE FOREARMED AGAINST the SNARE-SETTER! Resist his attacks on your HOME and he will flee (James 4:7).

SOME THINGS TO DO AND REMEMBER IN HUSBAND-LOVING

1. **Are your ATTITUDES still rooted in the past?**
   a. Are you still responding to the hard things and difficult situations in your marriage in the OLD WAY and with the OLD ATTITUDES? (Learn to live Philippians 3:13-14)

2. ATTITUDE IS THE MIND'S PAINT BRUSH.
   a. It can color a situation gloomy or gray, or cheerful and gay [happy].

3. You may be disappointed, but **do not be discouraged**. Discouragement is the Devil's own tool.

4. **Learn by heart 1 John 4:4** and put it on a card where you'll see it often during the day:

   > *Greater is he that is in you* [God the Father, God the Son, and God the Holy Spirit] *than he that is in the world* [Satan]. [This is for born-again wives only.]

5. Read "FOR WOMEN ONLY" in *THE ACT OF MARRIAGE* by LaHaye, p. 90.

6. **Observe daily feminine hygiene.** MITCHUMS DEODORANT is very good for checking perspiration—but first be sure to use soap and water in all areas. Bathe or shower daily.

7. **Are you overweight?** Have you been practicing your PuboCoccygeus (P.C.) muscles?

8. Read Genesis 3 again in preparing for future lessons.

9. How about your prayer life? Try talking with God in a sweet communion without constantly asking Him for something. Keep resisting Satan by loving your husband with a supportive attitude.

HUSBAND-LOVING LESSON #13 THE SMILING SERPENT SAYS HI!

HUSBAND-LOVING LESSONS DISCOURAGE BANTERING

"How dare you make a decision without consulting me first?" This is what a young wife said to her husband upon learning that he had promised to meet someone at seven o'clock in the evening. *"I can't make it by that time!"* she continued. The husband quietly looked at her and said, *"I promised."*

All of this banter between this young father and mother was before my eyes and those of others. Would it not have been better for her to quietly, privately remind him that he didn't get home from work until 6:45 and that the baby sitter wouldn't be there that early? Couldn't she have spoken to her husband in a mannerly, tactful way? Or, would it not have been better for her to think, *"How can he make it by that time? Oh, well, he knows his schedule. I'll just trust my husband's judgment in the matter."*

HUSBAND-LOVING LESSONS HELP WITH BITTERNESS AND BAD ATTITUDES

How prone we are to react to present situations because of past circumstances and memories. Our attitudes are still rooted in the past. We must pull up those roots of discord and bitterness (Hebrews 12:15). We must, as women who are redeemed by the precious blood of the Lord Jesus Christ (1 Peter 1:18-19), transplant our attitudes into the soil of *"reaching forth unto those things which are* *before . . .*" (Philippians 3:13-14).

As a full-fledged HUSBAND-LOVER, we see a PRIZE before our eyes. Born-again wives have a "high calling" from God in Christ Jesus. One of the PRIZES of taking up your cross and following the Lord Jesus Christ is being a "wife" approved of God (2 Timothy 2:15). **Wives MUST "divide" the Words of God rightly. We must see in the SCRIPTURES God's commands for us. And does He have them? This is the problem with marriages today. Women are forsaking the SCRIPTURES. Women are running away from the WORDS OF GOD and making messes of their lives**, of their marriages, and of their children's lives—to say nothing of the heartbreak and disruption in their husbands' lives.

HUSBAND-LOVING LESSONS ARE NOT SEX TECHNIQUE LESSONS

I am at a loss to understand the STRANGE SILENCES, the peculiar glances the hidden snickers, when one of our HUSBAND-LOVERS innocently mentioned that she was going to "HUSBAND-LOVING CLASSES." One woman is said to have commented, *"The idea of teaching husband-loving. I never thought I'd see the day when someone would teach how to love a husband."* She is also said to have mentioned the surprise at someone teaching sex to a group of women.

Well, first of all, let me set something straight. I am NOT teaching SEX to women. But, even if I were, may I ask you, what is wrong with teaching SEX to women? If I should ask a medical doctor to come into our class—and I very well might some day—to teach us about our bodies, about contraceptive methods, etc. etc., would a cry of amazement be uttered from the Ladies Aid Society? Probably not. But, because I—a laywoman, a wife—dare to mention the word "SEX" or the "ACT OF MARRIAGE," freely but with discretion to a group of girls who desperately want to be good wives, some dare to criticize.

HUSBAND-LOVING LESSONS PRACTICALLY APPLY SCRIPTURES TO THE LIFE

Is the Bible a practical Book, or isn't it? Answer that question. If you say it is not practical, well, just stop reading it, girls. If it is just a Book to put on a shelf and carry under your arms on Sunday and prayer meeting night and to be read at funerals, just stick it on the bottom shelf with the family scrapbooks. But, IF you say it is a PRACTICAL BOOK, then let's practice what we read and what is preached from that Book.
When I was in Bible School [Moody Bible Institute in Chicago, Illinois], we had one very practical course. It was called PERSONAL EVANGELISM. We as students were TAUGHT how to lead souls to the Lord Jesus Christ and we put our lessons to the test. We were taught how to pick children up for Sunday School—and did it. We were taught how to do jail work and we DID it. We were taught how to go into hospitals and visit the sick, and we DID it. etc. etc.

This HUSBAND-LOVING COURSE is an ACTION course. We read the WORDS—we apply the WORDS—and we DO the WORDS (James 1:22-23). What good are all the soul-winning courses and lessons, if one never tried to win a soul to the Lord Jesus Christ? What good is all the SCRIPTURE on the ways of a wife, if a wife refuses to act upon the knowledge of those WORDS?

A GOOD WIFE IS A DOER OF THE WORDS

But be ye doers of the word, and not hearers only, DECEIVING YOUR OWN SELVES (James 1:22).

If you do not follow the WORDS of GOD—THE RULES OF THE WIFE--the whole world knows you are a bad wife. YOU are the ONLY one who is fooled. Poor masquerading you!

For IF any [wife] *be a hearer of the WORD, and NOT a DOER,* [s]*he is like unto a*

The wife who reads in [hears from] the Bible that she should SUBMIT and OBEY her husband (Ephesians 5:22, 24; 1 Peter 3:1-6); the wife who reads (hears) that she should RENDER

[wo]*man beholding* [her] *his natural face in a glass: For* [s]*he beholdeth himself, and goeth* [her] *his way, and STRAIGHTWAY* [immediately] *FORGETTETH what manner of* [wo]*man* [s]*he was.* (James 1:23-24)

(discharge a sexual obligation) unto her own husband "*his due*"—not some other man's (1 Corinthians 7:3, 5; Hebrews 13:4). A wife who is NOT a DOER of that WORD, is like a woman who sees dirt on her face and walks away from the mirror, not bothering to wash her face. Not only does a wife who ignores the will of the LORD for her from the Book, walk away from that INSTRUCTION, but she forgets THE INSTRUCTION and carries on with life as if she didn't have a DIRTY FACE, or a disobedient heart.

In time, as you read these lessons, you will find that a good husband-lover's marriage is like a city built on three hills. One mountain is SUBMISSION the second is SEX and the third is SCRIPTURE. Without ALL THREE, SUBMISSION, SEX, and SCRIPTURE, marriage fails and falls, and cannot be considered a good Bible-based marriage.

A GOOD WIFE IS A HAPPY WIFE, "DOING" THE WORD

But whoso LOOKETH into the perfect law of liberty, and continueth therein, [s]*he being not a forgetful hearer, BUT A DOER OF THE WORK, THIS* [WO] *man shall be blessed in his* [her] *deed* (James 1:25).

BLESSED (happy) is the woman who walks not among the ungodly counselors or stands in the streets of the woman-libber street people, or sits in the chair as the scorner of GOD'S royal commands (See Psalm 1:1).

Her children arise up, and call her blessed [happy]; *HER HUSBAND also, and HE PRAISETH HER. Favour is deceitful, and BEAUTY is VAIN: but a woman that FEARETH THE LORD, she shall be praised* (Proverbs 31:28, 30)

This HAPPY wife is a true daughter of SARAH, respecting and admiring her husband (1 Peter 3:5-6), not becoming "all of a flutter" over anything her husband is or does. This "happy" wife is adorned "inwardly" with a "meek and quiet spirit" (1 Peter 3:3-4).

Now let us turn to GENESIS, Chapter Three, and see how the first WOMAN, the FIRST wife, responded to the WORDS of God. We will discover, if we do not know already, if EVE was a DOER of the WORDS OF GOD or just a hearer. Will the MOTHER OF ALL LIVING look in the mirror and see a dirty face and walk away from that TRUTH, or will she respond to the dirt and do something about it?

ACT 1—ADAM & EVE—HAPPY AND IN LOVE

How long Adam and Eve lived in their first home—EDEN—in innocence and tranquility, we do not know. How long they romped with the roe and lion, laughing at the antics of the monkey and the bear, God doesn't say. Those days are hidden from the history books and unwritten on the pages of earthly tablets.

The love which Adam and Eve shared, the intimate details of their tender embrace, the meeting of their eyes in love and devotion, their precious private moments, have evaporated into the ether dome of eternity past.

ACT II—ENTER THE TEMPTER IN A SERPENT COSTUME

One fact we know is that the SERPENT spoke. And on that very day—that day of crafty, cunning conversation,—God ceased to talk with man in the cool of the evening. Creation groaned and the world was turned around. Sin flew into the new-born world and built a nest in the midst of man's being, never to fly away again—until the Lord Jesus Christ Himself returns.

ACT II—SCENE #1: THE SERPENT SPEAKS—THE LINGERING WOMAN LOOKS & LISTENS

Now the serpent was more subtil than any beast of the field which the LORD God [Jehovah God] *had made* (Genesis 3:1).

How many days it has been since fallen LUCIFER—SATAN—had taken his abode within the body of the SERPENT, we do not know. The beautiful CREATURE was formed with other beasts from the dust of baby earth by the will of God (Genesis 2:19-20; 1:24-25).

It was into this subtle, rare, tenuous, mentally acute creation that the DECEIVER deigned to dwell. The serpent's natural instincts—its insights and perceptions, its analytical abilities offered the ACCUSER OF THE BRETHREN a body from which to sting ADAM and EVE with subtle poisons of unbelief and insidious disobedience. What a shrewd reptile.

Here we have the FALLEN LUCIFER, (Hebrew, HELEL, "*shining one*") embodied in the serpent. Can't you see it now? PRIDE, robed in the dazzling dress of an exquisite CREATURE—an angel of light? (2 Corinthians 11:14).

Dr. William Pettingill wrote:

> *Satan's favorite arena is in the realm of education and religion. He cares not HOW CULTURED MEN MAY BECOME, nor HOW*

> *RELIGIOUS, if only they do not know and obey God* [Underlining mine]. (*Bible Doctrine Primer*, Wm. Pettingill, D.D., page 27).

For a brief study on SATAN, refer to Chapter 12, "KNOW YOUR ENEMY" from *HUSBAND-LOVING LESSONS*, page 167.

I wonder how many previous conversations Eve had with the SERPENT. Could they have talked about common things? Had they dialogued before? Had such palaver become common with THE SHINING ONE? Had he so softened her resistance to the UNUSUAL--a talking creature--that Satan could NOW strike with the venom of the PERVERTED WORDS?

We have many questions. Much is unknown. The imagination darts in all directions, but I must rest upon the advice of Dr. L. S. Chafer to *"respect the silences of GOD."*

ACT II—SCENE #2: THE SERPENT & EVE DIALOGUE—ADAM SILENTLY STANDING NEAR

And he [the Serpent/ Satan] *said unto the woman, Yea, hath God said, Ye shall not eat of every tree of the garden?* (Genesis 3:1b)

Not to ADAM--the husband--who was standing with her (cf. Genesis 3:6c), did the SHINING ONE smile and speak; but to the WOMAN, the WEAKER VESSEL (1 Peter 3:7) did he apply his wiles.

Not to the HUSBAND--the MAN who was formed from the "DUST of the ground"--(Genesis 2:7) did the WICKED ONE scheme or not at the One who gave him a name [Adam] did he hiss (Genesis 2:20).

This PERSONIFICATION of EVIL, the SERPENT, stood by the TREE and glowed—oozing light (2 Corinthians 11:14) and coating his words with the candy of deceit.
Did his coat dazzle Eve's eyes as he stood tall, reflecting the sunlight? Were his vocal tones as pearls dropping from his lips?

With an assiduously saccharine smile, be asked, "*YEA HATH GOD SAID*?"

Keil and Delitzsch *Volume I*, The Pentateuch, *BIBLICAL COMMENTARY OF THE OLD TESTAMENT*, page 94] wrote that the SERPENT is saying:

> *Hath God indeed said, "YE shall not eat of ALL the trees of the garden?" or "Is it REALLY the fact that God has prohibited you from eating of ALL the trees of the garden?" In other words, "YE SHALL NOT EAT OF ANY TREE?"*

Casting all your care upon him [God]; *for he careth for you. Be sober, be vigilant; BECAUSE your adversary THE DEVIL, as a ROARING LION, walketh about, SEEKING whom* [INCLUDING WIVES] *he may devour:*

Whom resist stedfast in

What is the DEVIL doing? He is going about as a "wolf in sheep's clothing," snarling DOUBT in Eve's ear. He is asking Eve a question to provoke her thinking. He is DIALOGING with her. Watch him as he works. He will make a statement and then Eve will make a comment. They both will give a little ground to each other. Notice Eve does not "RESIST" any of his statements with FAITH. By the time their "detente" is accomplished, EVE will have lost *the faith,* [*faith cometh by hearing and hearing by the WORD of God*] *(1 Peter 5:7-9;Romans 10:17).*

everything and SATAN will have captured Adam's HELP MEET [*fitting or suitable*]. Therefore, the BEGUILER will be one step nearer to trapping ADAM.

Is it too far-fetched to consider this temptation coming upon Eve due to her refusing her husband sexually? (1 Corinthians 7:5, see above, pp. 271-275). Had it been several days—perhaps a week or more—that ADAM and EVE had not performed the "act of marriage"? This is one of the "silences of God." We do not know why the serpent chose that moment to tempt Eve.

DEFRAUD YE NOT one the other, except it be with consent for a time, that ye may give yourselves to fasting and prayer; and COME TOGETHER AGAIN, THAT SATAN TEMPT YOU NOT for your incontinency [lack of self-control] (1 Corinthians 7:5).

Satan has other means to make one who fellowships with God fall besides promiscuous sex.

Cursing and blaspheming God
Bowing to carved images
Killing
Stealing
Lying
Coveting
Getting angry over little things
Etc., etc.

Notice his wiles. Satan works from without to within, which is the reverse of the DIVINE operations. God begins HIS WORK in man's heart, and the change wrought there reacts and transforms the outward life. [Cf. Arthur W. Pink, *Gleanings in Genesis*, p. 37].

Instead of commanding the SERPENT as Jesus did, "*Get thee BEHIND ME, SATAN*" (Luke 4:8), Eve began her unholy confab.

Seeds of DOUBT, UNBELIEF, AND PRIDE were rooting in her heart which was beating excitedly because of the intellectual stimulation of this conversation.

ACT II—SCENE #3: EVE, LOOKING AT THE SERPENT, NOT SEEING THE "WAY OF ESCAPE"

It was as if an imaginary line had been drawn on the ground in the GARDEN OF EDEN. A line which said, *"WHO IS ON THE LORD'S SIDE?"* At this point in our study, EVE is picking up one foot, ready to step over to SATAN'S SIDE, ready to turn her back on Paradise and her PROVIDING Creator, ready to sell her soul for a MESS OF POTTAGE (Hebrews, 12:16).

But there was still time for her to RESIST THE DEVIL. He would have fled from her FAITH. (James 4:7). She could have looked for the WAY of ESCAPE (1 Corinthians 10:13) and taken it!

How often in our living, in our homes—our GARDENS of EDEN—does the TEMPTER come to us in some beautiful, familiar form. How often our spirits are low—perhaps our husbands have spoken unkindly to us, or our children's demands have over-pressured our minds, and the TEMPTER'S assistants have asked, *"Hath GOD SAID?"*

With some ridiculous PERVERSION of the WORDS of GOD, Satan tempts us. Our hearts beat wildly with the new sounds to our ears. Our lusts are stirred and our pride is lifted up (1 John 2:16). Take care. What goes up must come down. HUSBAND-LOVERS, beware. Don't fail, don't fall. Take the "way of escape"!

THINGS TO THINK ABOUT AND DO THIS WEEK

1. **Consider going with your husband on a week-end together—without the children.** If you can't manage a whole week-end, just go away for one day and overnight into the next day. You will he surprised what this special time ALONE with your husband and AWAY from the every day cares of life and business will do for both of you. The longer you are together, the more you'll forget the HOME CARES and be wrapped up in each other. IMPORTANT. BE alone. Don't go to a conference or visiting married children or brothers or sisters. The purpose is a HONEYMOON. How many other people were on your FIRST honeymoon?

2. **How about going out together for a "date"** such as a "dinner date" or a concert or even walking through the Mall holding hands?

3. **Holding Hands is important.** Remember how you used to love to hold HIS hand when you were going together?

4. Sitting close in the car STILL can be fun. Have you tried it lately wearing a seat belt?

5. **Meet HIM at the door** with a hug and a kiss, making HIM feel very important and special. Isn't he?

6. **Comb your hair and LOOK PRETTY when he is around the house** (Other women where he works are doing this.) ALWAYS make HIM feel that you CARE enough for HIM to take time to look good FOR HIM—even when you are washing the dishes.

7. **COMPLIMENT HIM**—"How strong you are." or "You look especially nice today, dear." or "Thank you so much for fixing the bathroom faucets." BE SINCERE. You will be, because YOU WANT TO BE THE BEST WIFE HE HAS.

The way to a man's heart is not by way of the STOMACH. A woman told me that if she were teaching HUSBAND-LOVING, she would teach cooking. What do you think? If you are of the "cooking" school, beware lest the cooking go to your stomach (and legs, and arms, and face, etc.) rather than to HIS.

8. *". . . to seek for an efficient cause of sin is like attempting to see darkness, or hear silence"* [From Augustine (350-430), as quoted in Chafer's *Theology, Vol. II*, p. 213].

9. The trouble with men is not EXTERNAL but INTERNAL. What he (she) needs most is not a new BERTH but a new BIRTH. [Cf. *Gleanings in Genesis*, by Arthur Pink, Chapter 4, p. 34].

10. 1 Peter's kind of submission *"requires an aggressive, active submission"* (Jay Adams).

11. A new "S" word for our HUSBAND-LOVING is **"SUPPORTIVE."** How good to back up our husbands in what they are doing. In their jobs—do we support them?
    a. In their heartaches, are we supporting their grief?
    b. In their happiness, are we rejoicing with them?
    c. In their decisions, do we encourage and support? Or, are we taking our nightgowns and sleeping on the couch?
    d. **Subordinate** –
    e. Submissive –
    f. Subjective –
    g. Surrendered –
    h. Sexually aggressive –
    i. Sanctified ["holy" like Sarah in 1 Peter 3--separated unto God]
    j. SUPPORTIVE!!

12. Read again the first Three Chapters of Genesis. Ask the Lord to reveal to you the areas in your life where SATAN is deceiving you. Confess this sin and turn from it--going on

in victorious HUSBAND-LOVING!

13. Read and ponder "The Unfulfilled Woman" (Chapter 8) of *THE ACT OF MARRIAGE* by Tim and Beverly LaHaye.

14. Are you doing your P.C. exercises?

HUSBAND-LOVING LESSON #14

DISOBEDIENCE OR DESTINY?

DESTINY and FATE. What part do these words and their meanings have in the lives of believing women? Is it right for a blood-washed CHRISTIAN to speak of her destiny or her fate? Is it SCRIPTURAL for me to say, concerning my life and the good and the bad which have touched it, that is my DESTINY—that is my fate?

Do you know what my first reaction is to these words and what they connote in my imagination? The immediate reaction is NO, NO, a thousand times NO!! I am a CHRISTIAN WOMAN and have been redeemed from my sin. Eternal life is mine. I have been bought with a price. My life is not a chance, like a car raffled off at a bazaar. I am a PERSON. GOD has a PLAN FOR ME, not some indirect blowing of a whim of FATE or LUCK.

We CANNOT be like that blonde movie star with the "'girl next door face" driving up and down the avenue in a convertible, gleefully singing, "Qué será será; whatever will be will be, etc." (All the while, her personal life off the silver screen is falling apart and running contrary to the wholesome character she is portraying).

There are several words which should never be found in the CHRISTIAN (born-again) WOMAN'S vocabulary. "DESTINY and FATE" are two, and LUCK and DIVORCE are others. Can you think of more forbidden words?

DEFINITIONS. Let's look in good old Merriam Webster for some definitions.

FATE "that principle, or determining cause or will, by which things in general are supposed to come to be as they are or events to happen as they do; DESTINY.

That which is DESTINED or DECREED; appointed lot.

Ultimate lot; final outcome, specif. ruin; disaster, death.

(cap) Greek and Roman relig. The goddess, or one of the goddesses, of fate OF DESTINY; esp. pl. FATA pl. of fatum, the three goddesses supposed to determine the course of human life. They are CLOTHO (Spinner), who spins the thread of life; LACHESIS (Disposer of Lots), who determines its length, and ATROPOS (Inflexible) who cuts it off. Syn. CHANCE; LOT, FORTUNE.

DESTINY "That to which any person or thing is DESTINED; lot; DOOM.

The predetermined course of events often conceived as a restless power or agency; FATE.

(cap) the goddess of DESTINY, pl. the three FATES. syn. DESTINY, FATE, DOOM

DESTINY stresses the idea of what is irrevocable; FATE, <u>the idea of fixed or ruthless, often blind, necessity</u>; DOOM, that of final, esp. UNHAPPY or CALAMITOUS, AWARD OF fate."

CIRCUMSTANCES OF LIFE CAN BRING YOU TO THE CROSS

You may say, *"So many unhappy things have happened in my life. Things which I had no control over; things which have just pushed their way into my years which, if I could have helped, I would have never entertained."*

Tragedy, death, illness, wayward children, calamity, sorrow may stalk you. If you are unsaved, why blame FATE? Why throw up your hands and sit in a chair and let the world go by? Perhaps God has permitted these heartaches and hardships to cover your soul in order to draw you to Himself. Has HE spared your life from malignancy or death? Has He left you numb with pain or paralyzed—yet alive?

> *The Lord is not slack concerning His promise,*
> *as some men count slackness,*
> *but IS LONGSUFFERING towards us,*
> *NOT WILLING THAT ANY* [That means you, girl.] *should perish, but that*
> *ALL SHOULD COME TO R E P E N T A N C E . . .*
> (2 Peter 3:9)

> *That IF thou shalt CONFESS WITH THY MOUTH*
> *the Lord Jesus* [not do any works or be good or go to church]
> *and shalt BELIEVE* [where?] *IN THINE HEART* [not in thy head]
> *that God HATH raised Him from the dead,*
> *thou SHALT BE SAVED.*

> *For with the heart man believeth UNTO RIGHTEOUSNESS:*
> *and with the MOUTH CONFESSION is made unto salvation*
> (Romans 10:9-10).

Oh, SINNER, stop blaming the circumstances of your life, for the situation that you find yourself in today. Forget your past horrors, your past griefs. Let these former things pass away and permit the SPIRIT OF GOD to do a work of grace in your life. Let the FATHER draw you to the SON. It is the DEVIL you are to resist, not the *"still small voice"* of God beckoning you to COME.

> *All that the FATHER giveth me shall come to me; and him that cometh to me I will in no wise cast out.*
>
> *No man can come to me, except the FATHER, which hath sent me, draw him . . .* (John 6:37, 44)

The storms and strifes of your life are sad, indeed, and I would be the last person not to weep when you weep and laugh when you laugh. But DON'T say "what will be, will be" and blindly accept a pagan FATE or DESTINY. Believe right now you can do something to turn your life around. You can accept THE LORD JESUS CHRIST as your Saviour and rejoice.

NO DESTINY OR FATE MOVED ADAM & EVE TO EAT

Let us now turn to the book of Genesis and see how DESTINY and FATE did not play a role in the life of Adam and his HUSBAND-LOVER, Eve. What was the sin which plunged mankind into condemnation? (John 3:18). You're right. DISOBEDIENCE and UNBELIEF.

> *. . . While the truth that God foreknew, the oncoming reality of sin does not constitute a beginning, in the sense that it presents no enactment of sin, His foreknowledge does enter largely into this phrase of the doctrine of sin. That form of Dualism which contends that two opposing principles—good and evil—have existed from all eternity, and that they are both primary and essential—the one as fully as the other—CANNOT BE RECEIVED. A digression at this point into either the ancient or the more modern dualistic philosophies is uncalled for. Suffice it to say that, while in the permissive will of God there has arisen a kingdom of darkness into which are gathered fallen angels and fallen human beings and which sets itself against God, that kingdom has not existed forever and its end is clearly predicted when it shalt have wrought that which was in view when it was divinely permitted to run its course. In other words, the Bible*

> *assigns to evil a transitory character—recording its beginning, its course, and its end. SIN IN ANTICIPATION AND SIN IN ACTION ARE TWO WIDELY DIFFERENT IDEAS and no more can be asserted regarding the eternal aspect of evil than that God foreknew and permitted it . . .* (Lewis Sperry Chafer, *Systematic Theology, Volume II*, p. 236).

We will notice as we study Genesis 3:2-6, that God did not make Adam and Eve sin. They did it freely after discussion with one another, but not discussion with God. God had spoken, "Thou shalt not eat." but they preferred Satan's enticement: "Thou shalt be as gods."

EVE was the WOMAN-LIBBER of the "Eden Century." She went ahead in her own willful way, never asking her husband's advice, deliberately contradicting the WORDS of her CREATOR. God did not make them to sin. HE did not create them to sin. But HE knew they would, because HE was God. But He created them capable of standing the test if they chose to pass it.

I, as a mother, have often seen my toddling child fall and get hurt. I have not wanted that child to be injured, but knowing he was only a baby and foreknowing his weakness and inexperience in walking, I knew he would fall. This was not FATE or DESTINY, but just the child being a new walking baby, and his mother knowing the same.

> *When God pronounced judgement upon ADAM, He did not say I AM PARTLY TO BLAME SINCE I CREATED YOU. The blame rested on Adam ALONE. (Eph. 2: 3), and the ORIGINAL SIN with all its fruitage is never linked to God in ANY way* (Chafer, *op. cit., Vol. I*, p. 237).

EVE KNEW THE WORD, BUT ADDED TO IT

And the woman said unto the serpent, We may eat of the fruit of the trees of the garden: But of the fruit of the tree which is in

The pages of HISTORY would have been altered if Eve would have looked at the SERPENT with HOLY BOLDNESS and commanded,

> *Get thee behind me,*

the midst of the garden, God hath said, YE SHALL NOT EAT OF IT, neither shall ye touch it, LEST YE DIE (Genesis 3:2-3).

> *Satan: thou art an offence unto me: for thou savourest not the things that be of God,* . . . Matthew 16:23

But she did not refute him, nor rebuke him. She did not RESIST. So the BEAST stayed and played on her lusts—her pride, her flesh, and her eyes. (1 John 2:16).

Resist the devil, and he will flee from you. (James 4:7).

The dialogue progressed.

The SERPENT'S "Hath God said?" was resounding in Eve's mind. Always with insidious tactics the TEMPTER asks questions to cause doubt and disbelief. Always, with cunning-serpent-like ways, SATAN casts doubt upon the TRIUNE GOD'S authority. In other words, the SERPENT was saying, "God doesn't know what He is talking about, EVE." Or, "God doesn't mean what He says. He's just talking through His hat."

Yea, hath God said, (Genesis 3:1b)

Instead of defending her CREATOR and FRIEND by saying *"Yea, LET GOD BE TRUE, but every man a liar . . ."* (Romans 3:4a), she ADDED to the WORDS OF GOD.

"Oh, you beautiful CREATURE you. It's so stimulating to talk with you— such a delight. ADAM NEVER tickles my ears with such intellectualism. And When GOD fellowships with us, He is so NEGATIVE." These could have been the words of EVE as her thoughts were ascending the throne of PRIDE (Proverbs 16:18).

Pride goeth before destruction, and an haughty spirit before a fall (Proverbs 16:18).

"You're mistaken, sir," EVE might have cooed to the SERPENT. *"God has given us permission to eat of the fruit of ANY of the* trees *in our GARDEN-HOME."*

"But, there is one tree—that ordinary-looking one over there, God has forbidden us to eat OR EVEN TOUCH," Eve lied—acting older than her days and wiser than her innocence. You see, HUSBAND-LOVERS, God never told the first couple not to TOUCH the tree or its fruit, ONLY not to EAT of it.

Perhaps leaning closer to his attractive ear, Eve might have whispered: *"And you know what? God told ADAM and me that if we eat even one tiny bite of that 'NO-NO,' we would die."* Can you imagine that?

For as [s]*he thinketh in his heart, so is* [s]*he:* (Proverbs 23:7a)

Perhaps as she said the word, "DIE," she wondered what "die" was. Was it fun? Was it like tilling the ground? Or was it a place outside EDEN? Death was an unknown quantity, an unheard of pasture. NO creature or thing had experienced it. Could it really be that it was not real, but only a ploy which GOD was using to restrain EVE from having a good time? After all, what was there to do for fun in the GARDEN? Why should she be deprived of what was really hers? A worldly spirit was sprouting within her being. This was innocence yearning to be set free--milk curdling to cheese--REBELLION–beginning in the heart (See Proverbs 23:7).

> *Hence, in Eve's case, the form of her reply evidenced the fact that she had admitted in her heart the serpent's crafty inquiry. Instead of adhering strictly to the exact words of God, she actually added to it.*
>
> *Now, either to add to or take from God's WORD proves very clearly that HIS WORD is NOT DWELLING in my heart: or GOVERNING my conscience. If a man is finding his enjoyment in OBEDIENCE, If he is living by every WORD that proceedeth out of the mouth of Jehovah, he will assuredly be acquainted with, and fully alive to HIS WORD. . . .* ©. H. Mackintosh, *NOTES ON THE BOOK OF GENESIS*, p. 34).

EVE BELIEVED THE SERPENT, THUS CALLING GOD A LIAR

And the SERPENT SAID unto the woman, YE SHALL NOT SURELY DIE (Genesis 3:4).

Ye are of your father the DEVIL, and the lusts of your father ye will do. He was a murderer from the beginning, and abode not in the truth, because there is NO TRUTH IN HIM. When he speaketh a lie, he speaketh of his own: for he is a liar, and the

What is SATAN doing here? Isn't he calling God a liar? With a bright smile on his face, dressed in his "spiritual" robe of false religion (2 Corinthians 11:14), the FATHER OF LIES (John 8:44) contradicts the WORDS of the HOLY GOD.

Keil and Delitzsch say that the SERPENT is saying to Eve, *"You will positively not die."* A boldfaced lie from the inventor of prevarication.

> *That is to say, it is not because the fruit of the tree will injure you that God has forbidden you to eat it, but from ill-*

father of it (John 8:44).

For God [ELOHIM] *doth know that in the day ye eat thereof, then your eyes shall be opened, and ye shall be as gods* [ELOHIM], *knowing good and evil. Genesis 3:5*

will and envy, because He does not wish you to be like HIMSELF . . . , a truly satanic double entendre, in which certain agreement between truth and untruth is secured. By eating the fruit, man DID obtain the knowledge of good and evil, and in this respect became like God (vers. 7 and 22). This was the truth which covered the falsehood 'ye shall not die,' and turned the whole statement into a lie, exhibiting its author as the father of lies, who abides not in the truth (John 8:44). *For the knowledge of good and evil, which man obtains by going into evil, is as far removed from the true likeness of God, which he would have attained by avoiding it, as the imaginary liberty of a sinner, which leads into bondage to sin and ends in death, is from the true liberty of a life of fellowship with God.* (Keil and Delitzsch, "The Pentateuch," Vol. I, p. 95 of *BIBLICAL COMMENTARY ON THE OLD TESTAMENT*)

Satan was trying to make God seem like a distant BEING to EVE. Instead of calling him a closer name such as the LORD GOD, Satan used the more distant name, "ELOHIM." He used the more general and indefinite name to obscure the personality of the living God, thus exaggerating the prohibition to refrain from swallowing the fruit. (cf., *Keil and Delitzsch, op. cit.*].

We should observe that in reality man did not originate sin. It was recommended by SATAN, and ADOPTED by man. (L. S. Chafer, *Major Bible Themes*, p. 134)

EVE SAW THE FRUIT, ATE, AND GAVE TO ADAM

And WHEN the woman saw that the tree was good for food, and that it was pleasant to the EYES, and a tree to be desired to make one wise, she took of the fruit thereof, and did eat, and GAVE ALSO UNTO HER HUSBAND with her; and he did eat (Genesis 3:6).

Suddenly this very tree which was always part of the GARDEN of EDEN; this very tree which Adam and Eve had cultivated many times, probably; this very tree that had never bothered EVE before, became the BIGGEST CHALLENGE in the world to her.

Evidently, for the first time she looked at it, not with the trusting eyes of an obedient creation of God, but with the lustful eyes of a DOUBTER.

"Why, that tree IS good for food." She might have thought. *"I have never seen such beautiful foliage in my life. See that perfect shape of the branches and the way the bark is formed."* The more she gazed, the greater her greed. How she wanted to be wise. What was good? What was evil? Eve had no idea. Why, only God knew those things. Oh, to be like God and know the difference.

But I fear, lest by any means, as the SERPENT BEGUILED EVE through his subtilty, so your minds should be corrupted from the simplicity that is in Christ (2 Corinthians 11:3).

> The inner cravings of her own being responded to the temptation from without and she yielded to evil, and thus repudiated God. (L. S. Chafer, *Theology, Volume II*, p.210).

And Eve ate. The SERPENT had beguiled and deceived her. But his MISSION OF EVIL was not over. Did he watch? Would ADAM lower his principles and disobey also?

Was Adam standing near Eve during her TEMPTATION? Verse 6 says: "*She gave also unto her husband WITH HER.*" It seems from that reading that he was standing with her during the whole diabolic dialogue, though it could also mean that Adam ate "along with her" in addition. It appears that he saw Eve concede point after point in her match with the DEVIL until she yielded to her ENEMY.

For ADAM was FIRST FORMED, then Eve.

She ate. *"Hmmm, not bad.* " Holding the fruit out to ADAM, looking so adorable and cute, he fell to her coquettish ways. Thus ADAM succumbed to sin.

And ADAM was NOT DECEIVED, BUT the woman being deceived was in the transgression (1 Timothy 2:13-14).

And with that morsel of fruit, ADAM bid farewell to freedom and said hello to condemnation and endless guilt.

Why did ADAM, who knew full well the consequences of eating that fruit, go ahead and partake? Was he so blind to the WORDS of GOD and its consequences that he failed to heed those WORDS? Was he so "in love" with EVE that he could not bear the thought of having her become a sinner while he remained innocent? Was he jealous that her eyes would he opened to good and evil and his closed? Was he AFRAID to trust God with his future life alone and without his HELP MEET? Was the food so appealing to his bodily senses and so pleasant to his eyes that he could not resist?

When Adam sinned his first sin he experienced a CONVERSION DOWNWARDS. He became degenerate and depraved. He developed within himself a FALLEN NATURE which is contrary to God and is EVER PRONE TO EVIL. His constitution was altered fundamentally, and he thus became a wholly different being from the one God had created...NO OTHER human being than ADAM has EVER become a sinner by sinning All others ARE BORN SINNERS. . . . (L. S. Chafer, *Theology op. cit.*, II, p. 217).

DEPRAVITY as a doctrine does not stand or fall on the ground of man's estimation of himself; it rather reflects God's estimation of man. (Chafer, *op. cit.*, II, pp. 218-19, *Theology*).

The DEPRAVITY OR CORRUPTION OF NATURE IS TOTAL . . . . (Shedd, *Dogmatic Theology, II*, p. 257, as quoted in Chafer, *Theology, op. cit.*, II, p. 219).

The BIBLE further teaches with complete unanimity that THE RACE IS DEPRAVED--apart from the saving grace of God--and it is equally evident that no time can be indicated when this came to pass other than the fall of man in the Garden of Eden. (Chafer, *Theology, op. cit.*, II, p. 218).

As C. H. Mackintosh stated:

> *Obedience is due from us to God's Word, SIMPLY BECAUSE IT IS HIS WORD. To raise a question, when He has spoken, is blasphemy, . . . The infidel may call this "blind obedience," but the CHRISTIAN CALLS THIS INTELLIGENT OBEDIENCE, inasmuch as it is based upon the knowledge that it is God's Word to which he is obedient . . . All that we want to know is that God has spoken, and then obedience becomes the very highest order of intelligent acting. When the soul gets up to God, it has reached the VERY HIGHEST SOURCE OF AUTHORITY . . . When God speaks, man is BOUND to obey . . . There is blessing in EVERY ACT OF OBEDIENCE; but the moment the soul hesitates, the enemy has the advantage, and he will assuredly use it to thrust the soul further and further from God . . . A refined rationalism is very near akin to bold INFIDELITY, ATHEISM THAT DENIES HIS EXISTENCE.* ©. H. Mackintosh, Chapter III, *NOTES ON THE BOOK OF GENESIS*).

THINGS TO THINK ABOUT AND DO THIS WEEK

1. **Let's not forget the power of prayer to change us** as HUSBAND-LOVERS from the fretting, frumpy person we were once to the fragrant, friendly wife GOD wants us to become.
2. **Let us "*REJOICE IN THE LORD ALWAY*"** (Philippians 1:4a) in the difficult days and during terrible times as well as in the easy and care-free periods of our lives.
3. HATE STIRRETH UP STRIFES but love covereth all sins (Read 1 Corinthians 13).
4. **Have you considered taking VITAMIN B complex and VITAMIN C?** These are the stress vitamins which we may very well need. You may want

to try the B COMPLEX for a couple of weeks and see how your nervous system is acting.

5. Are you planning a weekend or a twenty-four hour vacation with your husband soon? (Do not take the children.)

6. "*In wedlock, separate ownership of the person ceases.*" (Plummer, from A. T. Robertson).

7. Read and ponder and practice THE KEY TO FEMININE RESPONSE, Chapter 9 of *the ACT OF MARRIAGE* by the LaHayes.

8. Remember that "THE ACT OF MARRIAGE" IS VITALLY SIGNIFICANT TO THE HUSBAND FOR AT LEAST FIVE DIFFERENT REASONS:

   a. It satisfies his sex drive.

   b. It fulfills his manhood.

   c. It enhances his love for his wife.

   d. It reduces friction in the home.

   e. It provides life's most exciting experience.

9. *"Some women will probably take exception to this use of LOVEMAKING as another example of the exploitation of sex. We prefer to think of it as the expression of unselfish love. Because of her love for her husband, this wife created an atmosphere on the* basis *of her husband's need, not his feelings,–not hers, for that matter. It is a beautiful fulfillment of the Bible's description of love: 'Look not every man on his own things* [needs], *but every man also on the things* [needs] *of others."* (Philippians 2:4). [#8 and 9 above are quoted from CHAPTER II of the *ACT OF MARRIAGE* book.]

10. **Read how SARAH obeyed ABRAHAM and called him LORD (1 Peter 3:5-6).** Remember all the while that ABRAHAM was the FATHER of the FAITHFUL, the friend of GOD. Also remember that maybe SARAH didn't start off the minute she said, "I do" being the submissive wife with the meek and quiet spirit. If she didn't, there is much hope for you

and me.

Read Genesis 23:1-20. (Notice that twenty verses are given to the death of SARAH.) What an important woman she was in the history of wifehood. What kind of HUSBAND-LOVER do you think she was?

11. **Remember our consciences MUST BE INFORMED by the WORDS OF GOD.**
12. **Beware how you advise your husband!** Our husbands are influenced by our beliefs, our actions, and our words. There is much DAMAGE that is caused by a wife's UNSCRIPTURAL advice.

a. See Genesis 3:6–When the woman saw, she took, did eat, and GAVE unto her husband . . .

b. Genesis 3:12–"The woman . . . she gave . . . I did eat."

c. Genesis 3:17b—"because thou hast harkened unto the VOICE OF THY WIFE, . . ."

HUSBAND LOVING LESSON #15

WHO HAS TOP BILLING?

A question for you. Who is THE BOSS in your household? Who is the one who receives TOP BILLING? If the children are suddenly sick, who stays home from church or from a pressing engagement?

These are important questions. Your answers formulate your opinion of your husband's position and rating.

An example: Both husband and wife had Christian service jobs in a local church. He was a teacher and she was a teacher. He headed a youth group and she worked in another area of the church's ministry in a leadership position. One morning the children unexpectedly became sick. If this would have happened in your family, who would have stayed home with the sick one, ministering to the needs of the family instead of to the needs of the local church?

In my family? There is no question in my mind that I, as the mother, would have been the partner who stayed home with the sick child. But in the example above, it was the wife who kept her appointment with the local church ministry, and it was the husband who stayed home with the child. This was the wrong decision. The most IMPORTANT person in any family should be the HUSBAND. The HUSBAND should have priority. His local church ministry should be more important to his wife than her position in the same church, because he is the HEAD.

It could be that to other members, a father and husband really does have a lesser position in the church. BUT, in the heart of his wife, HE SHOULD be thought of as being "MR. BIG," "MR. IMPORTANT," "MR. VITAL" FOR THE LORD JESUS CHRIST! **With a backing and supportive love of a faithful woman, what man would not rise to meet his wife's praise with performance of excellence?**

"A" COMES BEFORE "E" IN ANY ALPHABET

Take the case of EVE from EDEN. Should she not have consulted her husband before eating of the fruit of the TREE of KNOWLEDGE OF GOOD AND EVIL? Should she have not spoken forcefully to the SERPENT, "I KNOW WHAT GOD'S WORDS SAY, and I believe it."

I am reminded of a bride's immediate answer of, "Yes, we'll be there when invited to a social affair. I was taken aback by her quick response. Without consulting her husband, she answered. How much better it would have been if she would have kindly responded: "I think it will be fine, but I will check with Stanley first." Sad to say, as I observe this new UNION, she is still making independent decisions which conflict with her new husband's responsibilities.

It is the WIFE who is the HELP-MEET. It is the wife who is the responder to the husband's needs and demands. It is the wife who was made for the man (1 Corinthians 11: 8-9). It is the wife who is to SUBMIT to her HEAD. She is not the CAPTAIN on the ship of matrimony–only the CREW. The CREW is needed for the Captain could not sail the ship alone, but there would be shipwreck if the CREW had no CAPTAIN.

A GOOD WIFE looks into the WORDS of GOD and OBEYS what GOD has written therein. Have you consulted the BOOK lately?

Yes, indeed, "A" for ADAM comes before "E" for EVE!

HAND-SEWN APRONS, A POOR COVERING FOR NAKEDNESS

Let us return to the Book of GENESIS and get back to the lessons the SCRIPTURES have for us as HUSBAND-LOVERS from the failure of EVE to be such in Genesis Chapter Three.

THE QUICKENING OF A CONSCIENCE

And the eyes of them both were opened, and they knew that they were naked; (Genesis 3:7a)

For ADAM was FIRST FORMED, then Eve. And ADAM was not deceived, BUT THE WOMAN, being deceived, was in the transgression: (1 Timothy 2: 13-14)

Let no man say when he is tempted, I am tempted of God; for God cannot be tempted with evil, neither tempteth he any man. But every man is tempted, when he is drawn away of his own lust, and enticed. Then when lust hath conceived, it bringeth forth sin; and sin, when it is finished, bringeth forth death (James 1:13-15).

With the first swallow of the forbidden fruit—the first act of disobedience on our rotating planet—INNOCENCE vanished and CONSCIENCE was quickened. God's WORDS had been doubted by the actions of HIS CREATIONS. Condemnation fell like an avalanche of mud upon the head of ADAM and his posterity. That same condemnation is yours. When you came wet and crying from the womb of your mother, you bore in your inner being a nature like that sinful nature of FATHER ADAM (Romans 3:23)

Those EYES—those first human eyes to ever look upon the trees and stars and bubbling brooks—suddenly "looked" in a different way. In their INSTANT SIN, all of life lost its "glow." With their "rose-colored glasses" of trust and obedience to GOD'S command, shattered at their feet, ADAM and EVE noticed that they were stripped of all garments from the tips of their toes to the top of their heads.

Had not they been naked before? (Genesis 2:25) Had not they romped and played in the GARDEN unclothed since their creation? WHAT was the DIFFERENCE? The difference could not have been in the "look" of their bodies. It must have been in an awareness in their bodies and minds. They must have received a sense of SHAME—never known before—at their outer stripped condition and their inner nakedness and a condemning conscience. Lust had conceived and brought forth sin. *"And sin, when it is finished, brings forth DEATH"* (James 1:15b).

Right here it is IMPORTANT to re-emphasize that the action which produced SIN in man was DIS-OBEDIENCE and UNBELIEF. This is the same rebellion against GOD'S authority that is continued today in the hearts of unregenerated men (Jeremiah 17:9).

"ORIGINAL SIN" WAS NOT THE "ACT OF MARRIAGE"

Many teach and believe that the action which catapulted sin into the world was SEXUAL INTERCOURSE. This is FALSE, Satanic teaching! I cannot say it enough as to the INCORRECTNESS of this thinking! So many couples are plagued with this belief and live in constant defeat, thinking that every time they perform the precious "ACT OF MARRIAGE," they are entering into the SIN SITUATION which led to the fall of ADAM and EVE. UNTRUE! UNTRUE! UNTRUE! UNTRUE!

Let us re-state here for those who are new to these lessons and ignorant of the WORDS of GOD, that GOD has blessed marriage. He made man with a deep, unfinished feeling, with an incompleteness, on purpose. HE created woman from man's side to fulfill and complete man. GOD DID NOT REST UNTIL WOMAN COMPLETED MAN AND THUS COMPLETED CREATION!

The FIRST command in Scripture was for man and woman to be united in sexual union and have babies (Genesis 1:28; Hebrews 13:4).

It is BECAUSE OF THIS PRECIOUS TRUTH that God blesses the marriage union (not the adulterous coming-together). It is sad when married people "abstain" and "defraud" one another, giving way to Satan's temptations! (1 Corinthians 7:5)

TWO SOULS NAKED WITH GUILT AND SHAME

There WAS MORE TO THIS NAKEDNESS of Adam and Eve than meets the eye. It was not only the outer nakedness (I believe), but it was an INNER nakedness. The inner being of the first pair was revealed before their eyes and they knew they were sinners. They knew what evil was—and they possessed it. They KNEW what "good" was and they had lost it. Up until this time, they were blissful and ignorant of "evil." They knew only "good." Truly PARADISE was lost before a flaming sword and Cherubims (as in the KJB, plural of Cherubim) blocked EDEN'S entrance from the evicted couple. The day Adam and Eve disobeyed God, they died spiritually and began to die physically.

> . . . *"that at the time he [ADAM] actually thought more of his nakedness and shame than of his transgression of the divine command, and his consciousness of the effects of his sin was keener than his sense of the sin itself. To awaken the latter, God said, 'WHO TOLD THEE THAT THOU WAST NAKED?'"* (Keil and Delitzsch, *op. cit.*, Vol. I, p. 98)

ADAM TURNED TAILOR & EVE SEWED A SEAM

...And they sewed fig leaves together and made themselves aprons (Genesis 3:7b).

Keil and Delitzsch stated:

> *The discovery of their nakedness excited shame, which they sought to conceal by an outward covering.* (*Keil and Delitzsch, op. cit.*, Vol. I, p. 96).

For by grace [unmerited favor] *are ye saved through faith; and that not of yourselves: it IS the gift of God: NOT OF WORKS, lest any man* [or woman] *should boast*

What did they do? They quickly grabbed the nearest leaves and made themselves aprons. Could the tree of the KNOWLEDGE OF GOOD AND EVIL have been a fig tree? I don't know, but am just asking. The fig tree is the only tree Jesus cursed (Matthew 21:19-20). How much sewing had Adam and Eve done before the day of the fateful feast?

(Ephesians 2:8-9).

They didn't choose big pisang or Indian banana leaves which were twelve feet long and two feet broad. [Cf. *Keil & Delitzsch, op. cit., Vol. I*]. They picked small leaves which required much self-effort to cover their shame. In vain they worked to atone for their sin.

> . . . *"to cover not because any physical change ensued in consequence of the fall; but because with the destruction of the normal connection between soul and body through sin, the body ceased to be the pure abode of a spirit in fellowship with God . . ." (Keil and Delitzsch, op. cit.*, Vol. I, p. 96)

MAN & WIFE PLAYED HIDE & SEEK WITH GOD

And they heard the voice of the LORD GOD walking in the garden in the cool of the day: and ADAM and HIS WIFE HID themselves from the presence of the LORD GOD amongst the trees of the garden.

And THE LORD GOD called unto Adam, and said unto him, WHERE ART THOU? (Genesis 3:8-9)

Daily in the breeze [cool] of the day, God walked in the garden. On that day of INFAMY [the day Adam sinned], the LORD JEHOVAH walked again in the garden to fellowship with MAN. But, where were they? *"WHERE ART THOU, ADAM?" "WHERE ART THOU, EVE?"* He asked.

Did the CREATOR not know where His CREATURES were? Was HE ignorant of their devices? Was He unaware of their disobedience? Oh, no! We cannot surprise God. But Jehovah of the OLD TESTAMENT, as Jesus of the NEW TESTAMENT, was the master Teacher. He was teaching the FALLEN ONES by questions. He was rebuking and convicting by His WORDS.

ADAM and EVE heard God's footsteps [*Keil & Delitzsch*] *"He's coming."* Eve may have cried to ADAM. Perhaps they thought they were ready, dressed in their freshly sewn but quickly fading fig leaves; but soon they discovered their inadequate self-righteousness was as filthy rags (Isaiah 64:6).

But WE ARE ALL AS AN UNCLEAN THING, and ALL OUR RIGHTEOUSNESSES are as filthy rags; and we all do fade as a leaf, and our iniquities, like the wind, have taken us away (Isaiah 64:6).

"So that man and woman stood ashamed in each other's presence, and endeavored to hide the disgrace of their SPIRITUAL NAKEDNESS, by covering those parts of the body through which the impurities of nature are removed. That the natural feeling of shame, the origin of which is recorded here, had its root, not in sensuality or any physical corruption, but IN THE CONSCIOUSNESS OF GUILT OR SHAME BEFORE GOD, and consequently that it was the conscience which was really at work, is evident from the fact that man and his wife hid themselves from JEHOVAH GOD among the trees of the garden, as soon as they heard the sound of His footsteps." [*Keil and Delitzsch*, *op. cit.*, Vol. I, pp. 96-97]

Instead of running out to meet God with tears of repentance streaming down their faces, they hid behind the trees instead of beating their breasts, tearing at their hair, and crawling to their MAKER in anguish of soul, they were like toddlers "hiding" from a parent.

Their conscience—that new governor within them, that "clock" which was started by the ticktocking of sin in their heart—had begun to work and they had a sense of guilt and shame before God.

Could they REALLY hide from the ALL-KNOWING, EVERYWHERE PRESENT GOD? No. They were stripped here before HIM. And, they were afraid. They were too ashamed to meet Him face to face.

Adam was the spokesman for the family as it should have been. But shame upon shame to the WIFE who yielded to such a temptation and urged ADAM'S fall. Eve had to stand by and hear ADAM make up excuses for his sin.

And he said, I heard thy voice in the garden, and I was afraid, because I was naked; and I hid myself (Genesis 3:10).

God's question to Adam still sounds in the ear of every sinner:

> *"Where art thou? It is the call of DIVINE JUSTICE, which cannot overlook sin. It is the call of DIVINE SORROW, which grieves over the sinner. It is the call of DIVINE LOVE which offers redemption from sin. To each and to every one of us the call is reiterated, 'Where art thou?'"* (W. Griffeth Thomas from Pink's *Gleanings in Genesis*, Chapter 5, p. 41).

DIVINE QUESTIONS PIERCING MAN'S SOUL

And He said, WHO told thee that thou wast naked? [Genesis 3:11a]

Did the cow come up to ADAM and moo, *"Thou art naked, oh man"?* Did a bird from the sky sing forlornly to the bees, *"He is stripped and full of sin"?* No!

> "*They had lost 'that blessed blindness, the ignorance of innocence, which knows nothing of. nakedness*.'" [Ziegler as quoted in *Keil and Delitzsch, Vol. I, op. cit.*, p. 26]

Here again we can see the LORD GOD asking questions. The answers were already known to Himself. Here again ADAM was given the opportunity to "come clean" and confess his sin.

Hast thou eaten of THE TREE whereof I commanded thee that thou shouldest not eat? [Genesis 3:11b]

God is asking, *"Why did you disobey me?"* I wonder about their game of hide and seek with God?

Dr. Lewis Sperry Chafer's comments on this matter are timely:

> *"The immediate change in Adam and Eve which their sin wrought is revealed in the record that they were ashamed, having discovered that they were unclothed. . . . In its Scripture use, clothing is the symbol of righteousness. THE SHAME WHICH THESE TWO EXPERIENCED WAS NOT BETWEEN THEMSELVES, BUT RATHER BETWEEN THEMSELVES AND GOD. They had experienced a change in their very constitution which separated them from God. If they were at once to be expelled from the garden it was because of the truth that THEY HAD FIRST VOLUNTARILY BROKEN THEIR RELATION WITH GOD BY HIDING FROM HIS PRESENCE. Whatever may have been their own consciousness at*

> *the time, the faithful record of God's Word offers the UNDISPUTABLE EVIDENCE THAT THEY DEEMED THEMSELVES NO LONGER WORTHY TO MEET GOD FACE TO FACE. Much truth, likewise, lies hidden in the facts that they ATTEMPTED to clothe themselves, which clothing was of no value; and that God clothed them with skins, WHICH MEANT THE SHEDDING OF BLOOD. Thus another great doctrine of the Bible is enacted in type at least: 'WITHOUT SHEDDING OF BLOOD IS NO REMISSION'* (Hebrews 9:22b), *and "BEING JUSTIFIED (declared righteous) FREELY (without a cause) BY GRACE THROUGH THE REDEMPTION THAT IS IN CHRIST JESUS"* (Romans 3:24). (Chafer, *Systematic Theology, op. cit., Vol. II,* p. 218) [Capital letters added by YSW]

> ***"AND THEY . . . WITH ONE CONSENT BEGAN TO MAKE EXCUSE"* (LUKE 14:18a).**

THINGS TO THINK ABOUT AND DO THIS WEEK

1. **Make a list of all the good and wonderful things about your husband.** DO NOT put one bad thing on the list. If you cannot think of any good things to write, shame on you. This reflects what poor taste you had in marrying a man with no good qualities. Don't let that page be blank. Prove to yourself that you married a man worthy of his wife's admiration and marriage.

2. Remember your husband isn't going to want to read books on how to be a better husband. He thinks he is the best. **He only wants to read YOU and how YOU are as a wife.**

3. **"A *Christian woman's adornment should come from within her inner spiritual nature*** *and be truly representative of that nature." (*Kenneth S. Wuest, in 1 *Peter in the Greek New Testament, p.* 79).

4. *"These husbands* [in 1 Peter 3:1] *were of that obstinate, non-persuadable type that will not listen to reason. Their wives*

had often given them the gospel, but they had met it with stiff-necked obstinacy. Peter exhorts them, in view of their husbands' obstinate rejection of the gospel, to STOP TALKING ABOUT IT, and just LIVE a Christ-like life before them. The husband was to be won to the Lord Jesus NOT BY NAGGING BUT BY HOLY LIVING." (Kenneth S. Wuest; in *1 Peter in the Greek New Testament*, p. 72).

5. SOME REASONS FOR SUBJECTION: 1 Corinthians 11:8-9; 1 Timothy 2:11-14.

6. **DO NOT ADMONISH YOUR HUSBAND.** Do not correct him or nag him.
   DEFINITIONS:
   "NAG"—To annoy by faultfinding; to irritate by persistent scolding or *urging.*
   "ADMONISH"—To warn of a fault; to reprove gently or *kindly, but seriously. To exhort; also, to put (one) in mind of something forgotten, by way of a warning* or *exhortation;* as, *he* was *ADMONISHED not to go. To enjoin by a warning;* as *to ADMONISH silence. Syn. & Ant. See reprove.*

7. **What about your personal Scripture reading and prayer time** with the Lord, Christian HUSBAND-LOVER?

8. Think of this verse in the light of today's HUSBAND-LOVING LESSON: Romans 5:12.

9. **Attend a BIBLE-BELIEVING CHURCH regularly** in your area. Besides personally feeding yourself on the WORDS, you must be FED by a CHURCH where you receive the BIBLE PREACHING and teaching, fellowship, and joy of prayer together, so that you might GROW.

10. Read Chapter 10, "THE IMPOTENT MAN," from *THE ACT OF MARRIAGE* by the LaHayes.

11. REMEMBER there is a CULTURAL SHOCK when a woman gets married. **You married a man.** He is not like your college roommate or sister-member of the 4-H-CLUB.

12. A definition of "SELF-CONTROL" is doing the right thing at the right time.

13. What does "lovemaking" mean to a woman?

   a. It fulfills her womanhood.
   b. It reassures her of her husband's love.
      1. Companionship love
      2. Compassionate love
      3. Romantic love
      4. Affectionate love
      5. Passionate love
   c. It satisfies her sex drive
   d. It relaxes her nervous system.
   e. The "ultimate experience." (see below)

14. "The meaning of *oneness resulting from mutual lovemaking is far more important than the time spent in the experience. If a typical couple spends about thirty minutes in a single lovemaking experience an average of three times a week, the act of love would account for only* 1½ *hours per week,* or *nine-tenths of 1 percent of their time. Yet no other repeatable experience is more important to that couple! Probably no powerful human encounter cements their relationship more firmly than the* "act of marriage."" (#13 and #14 above are quoted from Chapter three of *THE ACT OF MARRIAGE* by the LaHayes.

15. One of the girls in my class told us that her husband says "SEX IS THE OIL OF MARRIAGE." Think about it. How long has it been since you've had an oil change?

HUSBAND-LOVING LESSON #16

WRONG ANSWERS TO RIGHT QUESTIONS

THE QUESTION: WHAT HAS THIS CLASS DONE FOR YOUR MARRIAGE?

THE ANSWERS

Answer *#1:* "SEX IS BEAUTIFUL AND CHRISTIAN."

> *"JUST wanted you to know how excited I am about the book and class. My husband and I came to know the Lord only within the last two years. Before, we had been to many x-rated movies. NEVER in our wildest imagination could you know the filth. Anyway, after I was saved, I still had this idea of sex being dirty and bad. After reading this book, I have a different idea. Sex is beautiful and CHRISTIAN!--and even Christian women discussing sex. Praise the Lord!"* (Name withheld).

Answer *#2:* "I DON'T HAVE TO WAIT UNTIL THE KIDS GROW UP TO BE A GOOD WIFE."

"These lessons have made me STOP AND THINK. I have been giving too much of my time to my children; I thought that the time for my husband would be after the children grew up but NOW I've discovered that I DON'T HAVE TO WAIT for the kids to grow up in order to be a good wife."

Answer #3: I HAVE CHANGED MY ATTITUDES IN MY MARRIAGE."

"I have changed my attitudes in marriage and with my husband. I do my HUSBAND-LOVING as unto the LORD. I am submissive unto the Lord. I am sexually aggressive as unto the LORD towards my husband. I've discovered that when I give myself in ALL, my husband gives back."

Answer #4: "I HAVE TAKEN THE 'ACT OF MARRIAGE' FOR GRANTED."

"I'm afraid that: I took the 'ACT OF MARRIAGE' in our lives for granted. After reading the book, I realized some errors in our bedroom. I always wondered what was wrong. I didn't realize that a woman should have a warm-up period."

Answer #5: "I WANT MY MARRIAGE TO BE GREAT."

"I say to myself; "This is the man I married. This is the man I love. I want my marriage to be MORE THAN GOOD. I want it to be GREAT!!"

Answer #6: "I AM LEARNING AND DOING."

"I am learning and doing. I put the sayings and Scripture verses all over the house. This class and the Scripture have helped my husband. He is encouraged."

Answer #7: "I AM LOSING MY 'VICTORIAN' WAYS!"

> *"A woman is what helps a man to blossom." Now my husband WANTS to come home and looks for me at the door. I have become more aggressive with him and he has become more thoughtful. In times past, I would have had a heated argument over some things, but now that I am becoming more submissive and coming out of my 'Victorian ways,' our marriage is changing. Just think. All of this was here before, and I didn't know it. It was all going to waste."*

ANSWER #8: *"I HAVE DISCOVERED BODY LANGUAGE IS IMPORTANT."*

> *"Speaking of holding hands, we like to. I think that bodily contact is very important. Body language is special and necessary in marriage. I want to revive that excited feeling, the heart pounding, etc., that I had when we were engaged and I listened to every word he said."*

What better introduction to the next few verses of Genesis 3? If only Eve had been the eager, learning wife to ADAM which God wanted her to be. If only she had been the obedient child to the commands of God. Lest you become extremely discouraged and enraged over Eve's sin through her influence upon her husband, blasting the human race with sinful cells, lest you wish she had never sinned—don't we all?—thus giving us an escape from the damnation which we have upon our heads because of ADAM'S sin--consider, if Adam and Eve had never sinned, someone else probably would have, and the sin chain would have begun anyway.

ADAM'S ALIBIS

And the man said, The WOMAN whom THOU gavest to be with me SHE GAVE me of the

Just as God was not ignorant of Adam and Eve's "hiding place," HE was not ignorant of Adam's "passing the buck" of blame upon Eve. Look deeply into *tree and I did eat* (Genesis 3:12).

Adam's thoughts, probing Adam's "finger-pointing." Was he not blaming God for creating woman? Was he not saying, *"If you hadn't made woman from my side, I would not have listened to her and have eaten of the forbidden fruit"?*

Yet, Adam had delighted in Eve. He had found satisfaction in her companionship and love. In order to justify his personal guilt, Adam self-righteously said: *"The WOMAN whom thou gavest to me" she did it."*

Finally, Adam confessed, *"I did eat."* But the force of his confession was muffled by blaming others, even God, for his present predicament.

It is true, friends may fail us, husbands may not live up to their "WIFE-LOVING RULES" found in God's Words (and there are plenty of them), but we should not sin because our mates are weak spiritually or in the flesh. We should not blame GOD for the current of trouble washing over our lives.

This question (WHERE art thou?) proved two things—it proved that man was lost, and that God had come to seek,--it proved man's sin and God's grace . . . Man was lost; but God had come down to look for him—to bring him out of his hiding place behind the trees of the garden, in order that, in the happy confidence of faith, he might find a hiding-place in Himself, . . . To create man out of the dust of the ground was

POWER; but to seek man in his lost estate was GRACE... (p. 48. *Notes on the Book of Genesis,* *by C. H. Mackintosh).*

How much more honest if Adam had looked into the face of God, and confessed, *"I HAVE SINNED".*

EVE'S EVASIONS

And the LORD God said unto the WOMAN, What is this that thou hast done? And the WOMAN said, The SERPENT beguiled me, and I did eat (Genesis 3:13).

God knew that Adam was blaming his wife for his failure and his fruit-eating. BEWARE HOW YOU AS A WIFE ADVISE YOUR HUSBAND.

But GOD turned to the WOMAN and accused her with the question, *"WHAT IS THIS THAT THOU HAST DONE?"*

He was saying: *"You naughty, naughty girl. Didn't you realize that your influence was strong in your husband's life? Didn't you know that ADAM loved you passionately? Didn't you know what a strong power you have over your mate? WHY, WHY did you do it, EVE?"*

Enter ye in at the strait gate: for wide is the gate, and broad is the way, that leadeth to destruction, and many there be which go in thereat: Because strait is the gate, and narrow is the way, which leadeth unto life, and few there be that find it

Though Adam USED Eve and even God Himself as a scapegoat for his sin, thus plunging the human race into the pool of uncleanness, God KNEW that EVE had done wrong, too. EVE had listened to the TEMPTER with her itching ears. Eve had had her flesh stirred beyond her ability to refuse temptation. Eve had bowed to KING PRIDE and he had raised the scepter of desire for her to be the GREATEST.

(Matthew 7:13-14).

How often is a wife the step of flesh upon which a husband falls and crashes to the ground? How careful a HUSBAND-LOVER must be to not lead her man about by a ring in his nose, causing him to take the wrong, broad path which leads to damnation.

THE WIFE'S WAYS DISCOURAGE OR ENCOURAGE

What are some of the wrong paths we can merrily skip along? The path of ill-temper and bad testimony for the Lord Jesus Christ; the road of the screaming fish-wife like the clamoring, cawing hawk; the repetitious refusal towards our mate in sexual matters, building a wall between the two of you and lowering the wall of discretion between your husband and the other women he associates with in the business world. These are just a few which come to mind as I write these notes. (See 1 Corinthians 7:5.)

Not forsaking the assembling of ourselves together, as the manner of some is; but exhorting one another: and so much the more, as ye see the day approaching (Hebrews 10:25).

Other paths could be our encouragement in spiritual matters. Perhaps a little probe to attend a Bible-believing church for ourselves or our mates needs to come from us. Perhaps the memorizing of a Scripture passage as a family project would, in a non-directive way, bring much spiritual blessing and unity. Perhaps a prayer of peace and dedication during trials would encourage our mates that GOD still cares and knows the present grief.

But the path of the just

is as the shining light, that shineth more and more unto the perfect day (Proverbs 4:18).

During business conflicts and personal tension, a wife's cool hand, meeting his, or a tender embrace would smooth the rough edges and make decision time for the man easier.

Let us, by our body language, convey our high esteem for the decisions our husbands make and then ask God to give us a thankful heart and a truthful spirit.

"Submission," after all, is really submission to God. Our husbands really benefit from the spiritual exercise we are giving as we yield our innermost self to the sovereign God and keeper of our souls. (Ephesians 5:22; Colossians 3:18).

THE BEGUILED WOMAN CONFESSES

And the WOMAN said, the SERPENT beguiled me, and I did eat (Genesis 3:13b).

Who was there left to blame? Why, the SERPENT, of course! That smiling snake in the grass. By now his grin was from ear to ear. *"I have won."* he must have gloated, and the fallen hosts may have chanted their deadly delight!

Would not it have been the honest thing for this HUSBAND-LOVER (and I say it with some reservation at this point concerning EVE) to have wept in despair, crawling to God in personal grief over her eating of the fruit AND her encouraging ADAM to thus eat?

But I fear, lest by any means, as the serpent beguiled Eve through his subtilty, so your minds should be

But EVE hid behind the SERPENT. Fig leaves could not hide her. The trees of the garden were not able to keep her *corrupted from the simplicity that is in Christ* (2 Corinthians 11:3).

from God's omniscience and omnipresence. So, she tried escaping behind Satan's facade, the SERPENT.

"He beguiled me! He really did," she grimaced. *"I was UTTERLY deceived, I was GREATLY deluded."* Eve had been "out charmed" by the SNAKE.

For Adam was first formed, then Eve. And Adam was NOT DECEIVED, but the woman being deceived was in the transgression. (1 Timothy 2:13-14)

Being deceived by the SERPENT, she seemingly tried to "deceive" God as to her personal guilt in the matter. She did not want to admit to being part of the transgression. BUT SHE WAS.

As Lenski stated:

> *. . . She had sinned and Adam had her before him when she came to him with the forbidden fruit. Thus he was not deceived. Yet when she came with the forbidden fruit, "e did eat"* (Genesis 3:6, 8). *You ask how he could do this. The only answer is: "Both Eve's act and Adam's are irrational." To ask how either could be done is to ask for a rational explanation of an irrational act. No man can give that . . . . We can also certainly say that now, since sin is here, whenever a man is ignorant or when he goes wrong, a woman should lead him aright, but should do this in her divinely appointed position.* Acts 18:24-26 *is one example; Pilate's wife is another although she was unsuccessful* (Matthew 27:19).
>
> *Paul's point is the divinely appointed relation between man and woman. In that relation each must keep his and her place. To point to*

> *ability in leadership deflects the thought. Paul does not here speak of the terrible disobedience to God's command not to eat. Moses does this. Paul first* (v. 13) *makes plain the two positions of the sexes, secondly* (v. 14) *the fact that Eve deserted her position. There is no need to say more, namely that Adam then also deserted his. Verses 9-15 deal with women and their position in the church in relation to men. Let the women remain in their subordinate position . . .* (1 Corinthians 11:9-15)

(*The Interpretation of St. Paul's Epistle to Timothy*: by R. C. H. Lenski, pp. 560-570).

"I did eat." How often you and I willfully sin. We must confess this sin and get right with the LORD (1 John 1:9). *But if you have never received Jesus Christ as your Saviour, you are walking the path of ADAM and EVE in these verses, duped by the biggest CON MAN ever--SATAN.*

The WILL of God was resisted,
the WORD of God was rejected,
the WAY of God was deserted.
(Pink, *Genesis*, p. 5).

WHERE? In that first honeymoon cottage in the GARDEN of EDEN.

SOME QUESTIONS FOR YOU

Question #1: **Are you, as a HUSBAND-LOVER, resisting the will of God?** God wants you to be clothed with a "meek and quiet spirit" and to **place yourself willingly under your husband in subjection, thus bowing to God's authority in your life.**

Question #2: **Are you, as a HUSBAND-LOVER, rejecting the WORDS of God?** Have you looked into the glass of His WORDS and seen the DIRT in your life and walked away, not washing yourselves in those WORDS and keeping a pure heart and clean hands before HIM?

Question #3: **Are you, as a HUSBAND-LOVER, deserting the WAY of God?** In the past, have you walked a plain path with the Lamp of God guiding your feet? Do you know the Scriptures and its commands, yet WILLFULLY have deserted its teachings?

How can you ever expect to be the WIFE GOD intends you to be if you fail to obey and walk by faith and not by sight?

A POEM FOR YOU:

"TRUSTING"

You ask how you learn to trust Him?
Dear child, you must just let go.
Let go of your frantic worry,
And the fears which plague you so;

Let go of each black tomorrow,
Which you try to live today,
Let go of your fevered planning,
He knoweth all your way.

Fear not lest your slipping fingers
Let go of your Saviour, too,

Trusting is only knowing
HE'LL not let go of YOU.

By Martha Snell Nicholson

He hath said, I will never leave thee, nor forsake thee (Hebrews 13:5).

Neither shall any man pluck them out of My hand (John 10:28).

THINGS TO THINK ABOUT AND DO THIS WEEK

1. "***God may take what is just a grain of sand in your life and make it a pearl.***" [Heard over radio WKDN by Jay Kesler.]

2. **When you marry, the only place you should look is UP and FORWARD—never BEHIND.**

3. **THE INITIAL AVENUE OF SPIRITUAL EXERCISE IS IN THE MIND.**

4. *"We may be fundamental in our doctrine, and yet defeat the power of the WORD we give out by the MODERNISM of our appearance."* (p. 76, Kenneth S. Wuest, *1 Peter in the Greek N. T.)*

5. REMEMBER, **WELCOME YOUR HUSBAND HOME** no matter what condition he may be in.

6. REMEMBER that **YOUR HUSBAND is like himself**, and NOT like your father.

7. You either have to live for the LORD or live for the world.

8. **LOVE BEGINS WITH GIVING, not feeling. INVEST yourself in your husband.**
   GIVE.
   LIST the things and actions you can do to GIVE and DO for your husband.
   DO one small thing to please your husband EVERY DAY.
   YOU WILL LOVE BY GIVING--learn to LOVE your husband, if you think you do not.
   [Taken from Jay Adams over the FAMILY RADIO.]

9. Read SANE FAMILY PLANNING, p. 182, from *THE ACT OF MARRIAGE* by Tim and Beverly LaHaye.
10. Learn Psalms 18:30 and put it on a card to catch your eye as you "minister" in your home.

    As for God,
    HIS way is perfect;
    The word of the LORD is tried [proved]:
    He is a buckler [shield] *to all* [Husband-Lovers]
    those that TRUST in HIM (Psalm 18:30).

11. **Continue to make your marriage and your part in that marriage a matter of prayer**. Tell the Lord your innermost concerns and then go out and live in the light of God caring for you. (See 1 Peter 5:7.)

HUSBAND-LOVING LESSON #17

THE SERPENT—CURSED & CRUSHED

Shall we turn to the Book of Genesis and continue our study in HUSBAND-LOVING and the personal & public problems which had entered the lives of the first wife and husband, when she did not heed God's Words.

THE CASE OF THE CURSED SNAKE

And the LORD God said unto the serpent, Because thou hast done this, thou art cursed above all cattle, and above every beast of the field; upon thy belly shalt thou go, and dust shalt thou eat all the days of thy life: (Genesis 3:14)

When God spoke to Adam, HE asked, *"Who told thee that thou wast naked?"* and *"Hast thou eaten of the tree, whereof I commanded thee that thou shouldest not eat?"* When HE spoke to Eve, He questioned: *"What is this that thou hast done?"* BUT when He turned to the SERPENT who was SATAN PERSONIFIED, He IMMEDIATELY PUNISHED!

God imprecated or invoked an oath of EVIL upon SATAN. The CREATOR Who had said when He created the angels, including this angel before he fell, "IT IS GOOD." now bitterly curses that instrument of CRIME [Cf. *Keil & Delitzsch, Vol. I*].

The wolf also shall dwell with the lamb, and the leopard shall lie down with the

Cursed above all cattle. That was the Serpent's doom. *"Crawl on your belly. Eat dust as you slither along life's path."*

kid; and the calf and the young lion and the fatling together; and a little child shall lead them.

And the cow and the bear shall feed; their young ones shall lie down together: and the lion shall eat straw like the ox.

And the sucking child shall play on the hole of the asp, and the weaned child shall put his hand on the cockatrice' den.

They shall not hurt nor destroy in all my holy mountain: for the earth shall be full of the knowledge of the LORD, as the waters cover the sea (Isaiah 11:6-9).

NEVER will the SERPENT be the beautiful creation, the "cattle," it was before that day in EDEN when the "beast" yielded to the EVIL ONE'S embodiment.

SOME DAY the animals and all creation will have "the curse" lifted from their heads. That condemnation which fell upon all creation because of ADAM and EVE'S unbelief and disobedience. BUT never will the snake be released from the sentence executed upon it. *"Because thou hast done this, thou art cursed . . . ALL THE DAYS OF THY LIFE."*

> *The "bondage of corruption" is the consequence of death passing from man into the rest of the creation, and thoroughly pervading the whole. The creation was drawn into the fall of man, and compelled to share its consequences, because the whole irrational creation was made for man, and made subject to him as its head; consequently, the ground was cursed for man's sake, but not the animal world for the serpent's sake, or even along with the serpent.* (*Keil & Delitzsch, op. cit., Vol. I*, p. 98).

AN EMISSARY OF ENMITY

And I will put enmity between thee and the woman, and between thy seed and her seed; it shall bruise thy head, and thou shalt bruise

It is not natural for a woman to like snakes, is it? There seems to be an inborn HATRED within most females to abhor them.

his heel (Genesis 3:15).

If snakes could talk, they probably would tell us of their dislike for woman. There is a mutual distaste, a mutual hostility, between the snake and the woman.

This rancor, this hatred, this mutual antagonism, is in fulfillment of the CURSE which the CREATOR dropped on that crafty character who yielded his body to the EVIL ONE.

BUT MORE than the natural hatred between a female and a reptile is the enmity between SATAN and the WOMAN. Perhaps this is why a fallen woman is so sad to the beholder. Haven't you heard it said, *"There is nothing so bad and sad as a drunken, immoral woman"?* Sin can be camouflaged for a season, but some day that sin will show on the face of the sinner. A film of hardness covers the debauched face, a smirk of toughness and indifference shapes those cursing lips. And the mind has been captured by the ROARING LION and the soul has been DEVOURED. (1 Peter 5:8).

Be sober, be vigilant; because your adversary the devil, as a roaring lion, walketh about, seeking whom he may devour: (1 Peter 5:8)

BEWARE, beware. Oh, CHRISTIAN WOMAN, SATAN wants to catch you in his snare.

And no marvel; for Satan himself is transformed into an angel of light (2 Corinthians 11:14).

BEWARE, beware oh unsaved woman. SATAN wants to blind your eyes to your need of a Saviour.

The hatred will not only be between SATAN and the WOMAN, [The woman here is EVE and, by extension, all

and between thy seed and her seed; it shall bruise thy head, and thou shalt bruise his heel (Genesis 3:15).

womankind], but the hatred will extend to the seed of the woman.

The word "seed" means the POSTERITY of the WOMAN, the child of the WOMAN.

This CHILD (seed) is none other than the LORD JESUS CHRIST who in the future (our past) was to be born of a woman [Mary, His virgin mother].

THE CASE OF THE CRUSHED SEED

Blotting out the handwriting of ordinances that was against us, which was contrary to us, and took it out of the way, nailing it to his cross;

And having spoiled principalities and powers, he made a shew of them openly, triumphing over them in it (Colossians 2:14-15).

Of judgment, because the prince of this world is judged (John 16:11).

What was the SEED [the Lord Jesus CHRIST] to do to the SERPENT [SATAN]? THE SEED of the WOMAN was to crush the head of the SEED of SATAN. This "crushing" was accomplished at Calvary, when the Lord Jesus Christ bore in His body the sins of the world and when He was buried and rose from the dead after being DEAD--dead for three days and three nights. The VICTORY of the bodily resurrection of the Lord Jesus Christ overwhelmed SATAN, it broke SATAN'S power over mankind. Christ's atoning work and His physical resurrection made SATAN a wounded, defeated foe. Though the DEVIL still roams about like a "roaring lion" and though he still is the "PRINCE of the POWER of the air," the BELIEVER in THE LORD JESUS CHRIST is made free from the wicked force which covers the unsaved person like a blanket of poison gas, controlling the mind and body of its victims.

QUOTES ON GENESIS 3:15 FROM CHAFER'S SYSTEMATIC THEOLOGY

And I will put enmity between thee and the woman, and between thy seed and her seed; it shall bruise thy head, and thou shalt bruise his heel (Genesis 3:15).

QUOTE #1

As recorded in Genesis 3:15, God declared that there would be a seed of the woman. While that prediction could have been fulfilled in the first generation to be born, its consummation was, in the plan of God, to be realized only after at least four thousand years of human history. Thus the line of the seed was forecast and is traced faithfully through the genealogies recorded in the Bible.

Special importance is attached to five men in this line:
(1) Abraham, to whom the promise of a glorious seed was given;
(2) Isaac, a type of Christ and a direct removal from the line of Ishmael;
(3) Jacob, the progenitor of the twelve tribes, in whom the line of seed was removed from Esau;
(4) *Judah, the chosen of the twelve sons of Jacob through whom the Messiah was to come--in his prediction, Jacob said of Judah, "The sceptre shall not depart from Judah, nor a lawgiver from between his feet, until Shiloh come; and unto him shall the gathering of the people be."* (Genesis 49: 10)*;* and
(5) *David, to whom was covenanted by Jehovah's oath an everlasting kingdom, and everlasting throne, and an everlasting kingly line (*2 Samuel 7:16, Psalm 89:20-37; Jeremiah 33:17). *Every anticipation of Jehovah regarding the*

seed has been fulfilled both literally and to completeness. "The zeal of the LORD of hosts will perform this" (Isaiah 9:7c), and "Known unto God are all his works from the beginning of the world" (Acts 15:18). (Lewis Sperry Chafer, *SYSTEMATIC THEOLOGY, Vol. IV,* p. 302).

QUOTE #2

That line of prediction began with the declaration of Genesis 3: 15. In that prediction it was asserted that when Christ bruises Satan's head Satan would also bruise Christ's heel. This prediction relative to the bruising of Satan's head is an anticipation of that judgment which Christ secured against Satan by means of the death of the cross (Cf. John 16:11, Colossians 2:14-15), *and the final execution of that judgment which is determined from the beginning.*

There is an order revealed:
(1) Satan would thus be judged at the cross.
(2) He will be cast out of heaven when defeated in the angelic war which is yet to be (Revelation 12: 7-12).
(3) He will be cast into the bottomless pit and sealed for a thousand years (Revelation 20:1-3b).
(4) He will be loosed for a little season for the consummation of his wickedness (Revelation 20:3e, 7-9).
(5) He will be cast into the lake of fire (Revelation 20:10).

This order of events is not subject to possible changes. When God declares that

Satan's head would be bruised, that prediction was fulfilled perfectly. Likewise, when God predicts, as He has done, that Satan will be cast into the lake of fire, it is not with a proviso that some other influence does not arise to defeat that purpose. Nothing could be more certain than that Satan will go to the eternal doom prescribed for him. (Lewis Sperry Chafer, *SYSTEMATIC THEOLOGY, Vol. IV,* pp. 345-46).

QUOTE #3

The death of Christ according to Genesis 3:15, is a preview of the death of Christ. In that Scripture, the fact of Christ's death, its relation to angelic authorities, and its relation to sin and judgment are intimated. It is fitting that a recognition of the cross and its final triumph should appear in those chapters where all beginnings are recorded. (Lewis Sperry Chafer; *SYSTEMATIC THEOLOGY, Vol. III,* pp. 125-26).

QUOTE #4

Only some of the brief predictions of the OLD TESTAMENT which anticipate the death of Christ are to be noted . . .

This proclamation is notable not only for *the direct message which it conveys, but for the early time of its utterance. It is a divine pronouncement, quite apart from human agencies, and concerns but one feature of Christ's death, namely, its relation to Satan and through Satan indirectly to all fallen angels. The great*

And you hath he quickened, [MADE

crisis of the cross as it bears upon Satan is in view and while Christ was to bruise Satan's head, Satan, in turn, was to bruise Christ's heel. By so much it is manifest that Christ's death was to an unrevealed extent and in the permissive will of God, an attack by Satan upon the Son of God. The triumph of the latter is sure, as a wound in Satan's head speaks of destruction while a bruising of the heel is at most but an injury. (Lewis Sperry Chafer, *SYSTEMATIC THEOLOGY, Vol. V,* pp. 185-86).

ALIVE] *who were dead in trespasses and sins; Wherein in time past ye walked according to the course of this world, according to the prince of the power of the air, the spirit that now worketh in the children of disobedience:* (Ephesians 2:1-2)

And I will put enmity between thee and the woman, and between thy seed and her seed; it shall bruise thy head, and thou shalt bruise his heel. (Genesis 3:15)

As you can see, I have quoted extensively from Dr. Chafer's Theology in order to instruct you as completely, yet as simply as I can that you may understand Genesis 3:15 and see the extent and the force of God's curses upon the SERPENT and upon the EVIL ONE—SATAN—who possessed that SERPENT.

GROUND CURSED ALSO

I thought it very interesting that God's judgments towards the three involved in the EDEN sin were called a CURSE only towards the SERPENT [SATAN].

The CREATOR said to the snake, *"thou art cursed above all cattle, and above every beast of the field; upon thy belly shalt thou go, and dust shalt thou eat all the days of thy life:"* (Genesis 3: 14).

Later He says to ADAM that the ground would be CURSED because of ADAM (Genesis 3:17), but God doesn't say. *"I CURSE **you**, ADAM"* though He does punish strongly.

THE BLOOD OF HIS CROSS AVAILS FOR ALL

Oh the love of God. Even in the midst of His judgment towards the first husband and wife team, God promises a Saviour. To encourage their hearts and to make life worth living again for them, He clothed the first sinners in coats of skins. They were looking forward to the SEED which would crush the Serpent's [Satan's] head.

Adam and EVE tried by their own invention to clothe themselves with fig leaves. This work of their hands could not satisfy God's holiness. He caused animals to be killed and the skins from the slain beasts clothed the pair. All of this bloodshed looked forward to the time when the SEED of the WOMAN would come to bruise the HEAD of the SERPENT [SATAN].

"And, having made peace through the BLOOD OF HIS CROSS, by Him to reconcile all things unto Himself—BY HIM, I say, whether they be things in earth, or things in heaven." (Colossians 1:20).

My mother has written a poem which tells of this precious blood.

"THE BLOOD OF HIS CROSS"

The Blood of His cross
Oh, how precious and holy.
It covers the sin
Of the lost, guilty one.

It avails for the souls
Of our *innocent children,*
And those who are sick
And weak and undone.

The Blood of His cross—
That blest cleansing flow—
We are, by its crimson
Made whiter than snow

It availeth forever.
Its power will abide.
That life stream from Calvary
That flowed from His side.

Gertrude Grace Sanborn

THINGS TO THINK ABOUT AND DO THIS WEEK

1. Assume that every person you meet has a sign around his neck which reads "PLEASE MAKE ME FEEL IMPORTANT." The person with that sign in your home IS YOUR HUSBAND!

2. **Make your husband feel like a king** and you will automatically feel like a queen.

3. **Are you sure you are really trying to be a HUSBAND-LOVER approved of GOD?** If you are not, you are only kidding yourself. Everyone else knows you are not trusting the LORD and being dead to self.

4. PRIDE is your biggest enemy in HUSBAND-LOVING!!

5. "*A silent woman is a gift of the LORD . . . a loud crying woman and a scold shall be sought out to drive away enemies.*" (Ben Sira, as quoted in *The Expositor's Greek New Testament*).

6. *Time is too slow for those who wait,*
   Too swift for those who fear,
   Too long for those who grieve,
   Too short for those who rejoice.
   But for THOSE WHO LOVE, time is not.

   By Henry Van Dyke

7. "***REJOICE IN THE LORD ALWAY***" (even when your husband's yelling at you). (Philippians 4:4a)

8. "***GREATER IS HE THAT IS IN YOU,***" than he that is in the world (Even when your husband can't stand you.) (See 1 John 4:4.)
9. **LOOK for the escape** when Temptation walks into your life. *"There hath no temptation taken you but such as is common to* [wo]*man; BUT GOD IS FAITHFUL, Who will not suffer* [permit] *you to be tempted above that ye are able, BUT WILL with the temptation, ALSO make a* [the] *WAY to escape, that ye may be able to bear it"* (1 Corinthians 10:13)

10. Read Genesis, Chapter Three again this week, and meditate on the CREATOR'S conversation with EVE (verse 16).

11. **Pray that GOD will garrison your heart with peace** (Philippians 4:7) and against poor counsel to your husband (Genesis 3:6).

12. READ "SEX SURVEY REPORT," page 195 from the LaHaye book, *THE ACT OF MARRIAGE.*

13. What causes male impotence besides illness, medication, or an enlarged prostate?
    a. Loss of vital energy
    b. Anger, bitterness, and resentment
    c. Fear
        i. The fear of rejection.
        ii. The fear that he will not be able to satisfy his wife.
        iii. The fear of being compared with other men.

iv. The fear that he will lose his erection.
v. The fear of not being able to ejaculate.

d. Ridicule
e. Guilt
f. Unreasonable expectations
g. Obesity
h. Poor physical fitness
i. Heavy smoking
j. Mental pressure
k. Drugs and alcohol
l. Depression
m. Masturbation
n. A sagging vagina
o. Nagging
p. Feminine dominance
q. Premature ejaculation
r. Retarded ejaculation

[From *THE ACT OF MARRIAGE*, Chapter Ten "The Impotent Man" pp. 155-181. Please read this Chapter.]

HUSBAND-LOVING LESSON #18

MULTIPLE SORROWS AND ONE RULE

ANOTHER LETTER FROM A "HUSBAND-LOVER"

Before we turn to the lesson, let's read a letter from an eight-year-married wife of twenty-seven who has been helped by *HUSBAND-LOVING LESSONS*:

> *This class has begun to open up my understanding of the creation in Genesis. There is greater significance than I realized in the unique way in which God created Eve.*
>
> *Also somewhere along the line the "pause" between Genesis 1:1 and 1:2 was introduced into my thinking and your explanation of six twenty-four-hour days for CREATION helped straighten that out in my thinking.*
>
> *I have also realized that I have a hard time accepting these truths on submission.*
>
> *Even though I believe this is the answer to marital difficulties and I've heard these truths many times over (professional counseling included), it is very difficult to consistently and co-operatively live by them.*
>
> *I also appreciate the time and personal effort given by yourself as one person responding with an alternative and answer to what is being offered by "WOMEN'S LIB" to women with genuine needs in regard to her identity and personhood.* (A HUSBAND-LOVER—name withheld).

EVE'S CONDEMNATION IS OURS ALSO

As we approach the WORDS OF GOD, let us do so with unshod feet, for we are on HOLY GROUND. GROUND which is firm and unshakable. Let us face facts as they are recorded and be brave to accept, along with EVE, the punishment given by the CREATOR for her flaunting her wisdom and her way instead of yieldedness and trusting belief in GOD.

None of us is without sin today (Romans 3:23). None of us dares say we are not under the same condemnation that EVE found herself (John 3:18). But, like EVE, we can look for the Saviour. Like EVE, we can confess our guilt and be dressed in the righteousness of the Lord Jesus Christ and once more stand "blameless" before our GOD.

To be "born-again" Christian women [as well as men and children], Paul wrote:

> *According as he hath chosen us in him before the foundation of the world, that we should be holy and without blame before him in love:* (Ephesians 1:4)

EVE WAS SENTENCED SECOND

Unto the woman he said, I will greatly multiply thy sorrow and thy conception; in sorrow thou shalt bring forth children; (Genesis 3:16a)

Now GOD turns to the WOMAN. It is interesting to note God's order in passing out the punishment. First the SERPENT/SATAN curse; second the woman who was "built" from the rib of ADAM; and lastly the MAN IN CHARGE of all of creation – ADAM.

EVE had known that she should not eat of the fruit from the TREE of the KNOWLEDGE OF GOOD AND EVIL. She knew it very well. Yet, she allowed herself to be deceived by the "bewitching" words of the SERPENT. She allowed herself to bend to the beguilement of his beautiful banter.

EVE SENTENCED "IN THE TRANSGRESSION"

And ADAM was not deceived, BUT THE WOMAN, BEING DECEIVED, WAS IN THE TRANSGRESSION (1 Timothy 2:14).

Because she was deceived and ate and gave to ADAM, she found herself part of the TRANSGRESSION.

She wrapped herself in the sin—disobedience to God—and became part of the sin OR became sinful. In "stepping across" the line, in eating of the fruit, she violated GOD'S law; thus entertaining and becoming a sinner.

I can illustrate this point about being IN THE TRANSGRESSION with a homely illustration.

When I was in eighth grade, my family moved to BEREA, OHIO, where the school system was much larger than the little town with 300 people where I'd lived previously.

There were two girls in that school, named Pat and Virginia, who took me under their wing. We were having a great time during the lunch hour in one of the classrooms. I was completely innocent of the fact that it was illegal to be in the classroom during lunch period. They were not innocent of this fact. To make a long story short, we were caught by higher powers, brought to the Dean of Women, and punished by "pink slips."

Can you imagine how I felt?—a little

innocent country girl, getting a "pink slip"? Though the Dean of Women knew I had not known I broke a rule, she had to punish me with Pat and Virginia because they willfully disobeyed the school law.

Though I had been deceived, I was still part of the transgression. So was EVE—but more so, for she was aware of the rule and the penalty.

EVE'S SENTENCE WAS MANY SORROWS

. . . I will greatly multiply thy sorrow. . . (Genesis 3:16b)

Here comes the SENTENCE of GOD'S PUNISHMENT of the willful sinner, EVE.

I WILL! It is GOD who Convicts,
It is GOD who Evicts,
It is GOD who Provides.

To "multiply" means to become greater in number. The worrisomeness, the pain: the toil, the labor, the sorrow of everyday life will be in abundance. It will be enlarged exceedingly. The SORROW will grow up, be heaped, be long, increased, many times and more and more. It will be thoroughly more. EVE will be weighed down with sadness, suffering, and disappointments.

GRIEF will stalk into her life and seldom leave. MOURNING will be her dress and HEARTACHE will pound her temples. Oh, the fruit of the root of sin which she planted in her breast by her willful disobedient action.

Could she erase that taint of sin? Never.

Could she re-do the day of defaming GOD'S WORDS? No. Certain SORROWS are peculiar to a woman's life. (Keil & Delitzsch, op. cit.) And EVE was the "mother of them all."

EVE'S SENTENCE WAS MULTIPLIED CONCEPTION

. . . and thy CONCEPTION. . . (Genesis 3: 16c)

The LORD God (Jehovah—the Lord Jesus Christ of the New Testament] told Eve that HE would greatly multiply her conception.

I think this means that Eve—and thus all women after her—would become pregnant more often than they would have otherwise if Eve had not "fallen."

We looked at the word "multiply" concerning SORROW. Look again. There will be an ABUNDANCE, and exceedingly ENLARGING, and INCREASE MANY TIMES MORE AND MORE: HEAPED, a GREATER NUMBER of times of becoming PREGNANT or of CONCEIVING.

I take it from this wording that Eve could not have conceived as often if she had OBEYED and BELIEVED and NOT EATEN of the fruit of the tree of the knowledge of good and evil.

And ADAM LIVED an hundred and thirty years, and begat a son in his own likeness, after his image; and called his name Seth:

ADAM lived nine hundred and thirty years (Genesis 5:5).

We can assume that EVE lived as many years, if not longer than ADAM. Her age of death is not given. We do know that she

And the days of ADAM after he had begotten Seth were eight hundred years: and he begat sons and daughters:

And all the days that Adam lived were nine hundred and thirty years: and he died (Genesis 5:3-5).

...Be fruitful and multiply, and replenish the earth... (Genesis 1:28a)

was built from Adam's RIB on the sixth day of CREATION—the same day that ADAM was created from the dust of the ground by the LORD God (Genesis 1:24-31).

We are not told in God's WORDS that ADAM had another wife—if he did, it would have been one of his daughters or granddaughters. We presume that EVE was the mother of all his OTHER sons and daughters. How many children do you think they had? How many conceptions? How many miscarriages. How many mentally challenged children did they have? How many lame and maimed? How many blind or deaf? How many had mental breakdowns?

Consider the grief as well as the joy that each offspring brought to the heart and soul of EVE, their mother.

I believe that EVE would not have had SO many children, so quickly, and definitely with less pain, if she had not failed the TREE TEST. Oh, she would have had children, of course. This was part of the command of God (Genesis 1:28).

But, she would have had thousands upon thousands of years of time. Time would not have had its limitations as it does now. There was no sin before the Fall, there was NO END of human life. There was no death. She could have mothered each baby until it was able to stand alone and then conceived and mothered another and another—probably at her convenience (though these thoughts are part of the "silences" of Scripture).

BUT, because of SIN, she would conceive like a rapid-fire machine gun.

EVE'S SENTENCE WAS MUCH TRAVAIL IN CHILD-BIRTH

. . . in sorrow thou shalt bring forth children; . . . (Genesis 3:16b)

Here is the word SORROW again, but its meaning is different from the "sorrow" in the early part of this same verse. Previously, "sorrow" meant "worrisomeness, as in labor or pain;—sorrow, toil." [*STRONG'S EXHAUSTIVE CONCORDANCE, in loco*]

What do I understand from these meanings? It was as if Eve were told by her CREATOR--the one she disobeyed: *"Eve, you are going to have much toil in childbirth. You are going to be like a clay pot being carved out and hollowed out. Your body will suffer BIRTH PANGS. You will have to work, to LABOR in much pain and travail in the delivery of your children. Also your mind will grieve. You will have much disturbance in reproduction because of the vexation of your person."*

What would child-birth have been like if EVE had never sinned? We do not know. But I feel, from these Scriptures, it would have been a BREEZE! And, getting PREGNANT would not have had its difficulties or its HEARTACHES. There would have been a natural birth control—and I don't mean the rhythm method—and there would never have been a need for fertility drugs or birth control pills.

Keil and Delitzsch commented:
The woman, who had broken the divine command for the sake of earthly enjoyment, was punished in consequence with the sorrows and pain at pregnancy and childbirth. (Keil & Delitzsch, op. cit., Vol. I, p. *102).*

. . . but the woman being deceived, was in the transgression. NOTWITHSTANDING she shall be saved in childbearing, if they continue in faith and charity and holiness with sobriety (1 Timothy 2:14b-15).

Again, they commented:
That the woman should bear children was the original will of God, but it was the punishment that henceforth she was to bear them in sorrow, i.e., with pains which threatened her own life as well as that of the child. (*Keil & Delitszch, Vol. I, op. cit.,* p. 103).

EVE'S SENTENCE WAS A LONGING DESIRE FOR HER MAN

And thy desire shall be to thy husband . . . (Genesis 3:16d)

What does this mean? "DESIRE"? "RULE"? (of the latter part of this verse). What? What? What?

When I first began this course, my husband looked these words up for me in his HEBREW books, and I hope that I will be able to convey the flavor of the meaning and force of the WORDS from GOD to EVE that evening as the breeze was cooling the GARDEN for their nightly fellowship. A fellowship with God and with each other which would never be quite the same or on the same plane again.

"DESIRE" is a Hebrew Word, *SHUQ* (pronounced shook), which means:
(1) *A leg, the thigh in the sense of running after.*
(2) The idea to attract, to impel, push towards something.
Noun form means LONGING (for a woman, for a man or *vice versa, or for a beast, to devour.)*

Let's look at the verse again: *"AND THY DESIRE SHALL BE TO THY HUSBAND."* Okay, work with me with the meanings of the words.

I think God is inferring that soon there will be other men on this earth. These men will be EVE'S sons and grandsons and great grandsons. She will live hundreds of years before she physically dies, and she will have many opportunities to commit the sin of adultery, that is, to think another man besides her OWN husband is for her.

So God calls EVE in no uncertain terms, *"Your legs should run after your own husband. You must be attracted to him and to no other man. You must chase after him. You must be impelled toward him to make yourself push towards him and NOT towards any other man."*

"Eve, you must LONG for ADAM, as if you could almost DEVOUR HIM. FACE your mate, look at him. Be drawn to him like a magnet. Run after him, no matter what he is doing or *where he is going. SERVE HIM. WAIT ON HIM. Let your legs be used for HIM only."*

Our imagination can help us as we think of EVE'S legs. All the errands she would "run" for him. The meals she would prepare, running here and there getting the animals ready, the grinding of the meal. Bringing Adam water from the well. Walking here, walking there, always with ADAM on her mind, ALWAYS serving her husband. Always, always!!

Sexually, her legs and thighs were to be DEDICATED to her husband—her ONE FLESH. When she tired of his SAMENESS, his lack of understanding toward her, his cool, matter-of-factness, and his taking her for granted attitude, she was NOT to rove in other directions towards other men or another man. ALWAYS, like a yo-yo, EVE was to bounce back close to ADAM'S SIDE, THE SIDE FROM WHICH SHE WAS TAKEN.

EVE'S SENTENCE WAS TO BE RULED BY ADAM

. . . and he shall RULE OVER THEE (Genesis 3:16e).

Up until this time in Eve's life, she had had a subordinate position—totally—with ADAM. She was not equal with him, neither was she unequal. She was "weaker" than he—made thus by her CREATOR, but she "ruled" the GARDEN with her mate as his HELP MEET.

Part of the curse was the lowering of her position in her eyes, her man's eyes, and in God's eyes. First a lowering because of SIN, and then the loss of the co-rule position she had held before the dreadful day of fruit-eating.

It is only Jesus Christ Who can redeem woman (and man) and bring her up from the mire and muck of sin and stand her on the SOLID ROCK, CHRIST JESUS (Psalm 62:6-7; 1 Corinthians 10:4).

He brought me up also out of an horrible pit, out of the miry clay, and set my feet upon a ROCK, and established my goings.

It is only JESUS CHRIST who can give a woman the ABUNDANT LIFE (John 10:10) of the believer and once again raise her to a worthwhile human being to be loved and cherished. It is only JESUS CHRIST who can give back to a woman her self-worth.

And he hath put a new song in my mouth, even praise unto our God: many shall see it, [even husbands] *and fear, and shall trust in the LORD* (Psalm 40:2-3).

It is CHRIST'S LOVE for His BRIDE—the saved people—which has shown husbands how they should love their wives and how they should treat them by giving their lives for them if necessary (Ephesians 5:25, 28-29).

. . . I am come that they might have life, and that they might have it more abundantly (John 10:10c).

The Lord Jesus CHRIST can turn a woman around. He can reach into her life and CHANGE her heart. He can give her strength to be a SUBMISSIVE wife, obedient, and silent. He can give her joy and strength in the midst of hurt and pain and misunderstanding (Nehemiah 8:10).

. . . teach the young women to be sober, to love their husbands, to love their children, To be discreet, chaste, keepers at home, good, obedient to their own husbands, that the word of God be not blasphemed (Titus 2:4-5).

As *Keil and Delitzsch* stated:

The woman had also broken through her divinely appointed subordination to the man. She had not only emancipated herself from the man to listen to the serpent, but had led the man into sin.

***Wives, submit yourselves unto your own husbands, <u>as unto the Lord</u>* (Ephesians 5:22).

***Wives, submit yourselves unto your own husbands, <u>as it is fit in the Lord</u>* (Colossians 3:18).

**[In the same manner] *ye wives, BE IN SUBJECTION to your own husbands; that, if any obey not the word, they also may without the word be won by the conversation of the wives;* (1 Peter 3:1)

For that, she was punished with a DESIRE bordering upon DISEASE . . . to run to, to have a violent craving for a thing, and with SUBJECTION to the man . . . CREATED FOR THE MAN, the woman was made SUBORDINATE to him from the very first; but the supremacy of the man was not intended to become a despotic rule, crushing the woman into a slave, which has been the rule in ancient and modern heathenism, and even in Mohammedanism also,--a rule which was first softened by the sin-destroying grace of the GOSPEL and changed into a form more in harmony with the original relation, viz. [namely] that of a rule on the one hand, and subordination on the other, which have their roots in mutual esteem and love, (Keil and Delitzsch, op. cit., Vol. I, pp. 102-103).

THINGS TO THINK ABOUT AND DO THIS WEEK

1. *Trust in the LORD with all thine heart; and* ***lean not unto thine own understanding****. In all thy ways acknowledge him, and he shall direct thy paths* (Proverbs 3:5-6).

2. <u>**Pray for your husband's salvation daily.**</u> (Don't tell him necessarily that you are praying for him, BUT JUST PRAY.)

3.

4. <u>**If your husband is born-again, PRAY FOR HIM**</u> that he might hide GOD'S WORDS in his heart that he might not sin against the LORD (Psalm 119:11).

5. **Pray for yourself** that you will love HIS LAW (THE SCRIPTURES) and read and apply it to your life. Pray that you will not be offended by the circumstances and people in your life (like your husband's misunderstanding of you and your Saviour).

   Great peace have they which love thy law: and nothing shall offend them. (Psalm 119:165).

6. READ "THE MISSING DIMENSION" (page 218) from *THE ACT OF MARRIAGE* by Tim and Beverly LaHaye.

7. From Chapter 7 ("FOR WOMEN ONLY") from *THE ACT OF MARRIAGE,* we read on the bottom of page 91: *Although we cannot endorse the sexual revolution, it may be somewhat responsible for exposing the false concept that married love is "dirty," "evil,"* or *"for masculine enjoyment only." Such expressions certainly did not emanate from the Old* or *New Testament* or *from the early church. They sprang from the "Dark Ages" when Roman theologians tried to merge ascetic philosophy with Christian thought. The pagan philosophy that assumed that anything enjoyable must be evil took precedence over the biblical concept that "marriage is honorable in all and the bed undefiled" (*Hebrews 13:4) *It is difficult to describe some of the unbelievable and ridiculous distortion to which the sacred relationship of married love has been subjected.* (*The Act of Marriage, op. cit,* p. 91).

8. We have added **another "s" word** to our collection. It should be at the top of the list. I do not know why it has taken me so long to come up with it. For WIVES, we should be: Subordinate
   Submissive
   Subjective
   Surrendered

   Sexually aggressive
   Sanctified (separated)
   Supportive

***SCRIPTURAL**

9. REMEMBER YOU as the HUSBAND-LOVER must be the one who CHANGES. Do not expect your husband to change. Do not be disappointed if he does not change. **But YOU CHANGE**. As God melts your husband's heart when he observes your BEHAVIOR, he will change. It may take years and years or it may come quickly. YOU be consistent.

10. **A SOUND, SECURE, GOOD MARRIAGE is built upon three mountains: THE MOUNTAIN OF SCRIPTURE**
    THE MOUNTAIN OF SUBMISSION
    THE MOUNTAIN OF SEX
    Without these three points, no marriage can truly stand, for there is a WEAK foundation. It takes three points to determine and to make a plane..

11. **REMEMBER, YOU MARRIED A MAN.**

12. REMEMBER, do not nag, do not admonish. **BE DEAD to sin**. (Ephesians 4:29; Romans 5:11).

13. "*A lot of our praying is giving orders to God*" [J. Vernon McGee]. ***"THE PRIMARY PURPOSE of prayer is to CHANGE us"*** [McGee].

HUSBAND-LOVING LESSON #19

RENDERING, DEFRAUDING & WALL-BUILDING—PART I

. . . We slept that night in the cave wrapped in each other's arms. The temperature dropped way below freezing, but I was warm just feeling her breath sweet and warm against my cheek. There is a mystery of love, a mystery that not only can endure all but can prevail over all; I was warm then, warm and needing nothing more. Two springs later, a drunk lost control of his car in a super *market parking lot in Sacramento, California. I had been cold ever since . . . [Stephen A. Crane, "The Trait" in* READER'S DIGEST, *January, 1977]*

These beautiful, yet tragic words were written by Stephen A. Crane from a piece called "The Trail," which I read in the January, 1977, READER'S DIGEST magazine. It speaks of a special night—a freezing night made warm because of the love that a man and wife shared. His wife was killed in an accident and he has been cold ever since—even though the temperatures outside have not been.

What is the "temperature of your love—that precious, intangible "something" which you and your husband share? You, too, could have an unexpected "accident" snatch your husband from your arms. You, too, could be left cold in the brightest sunshine and frozen in the tropics of your life. Are YOU taking advantage of the GOD-GIVEN opportunity of GIVING YOURSELF in order to WARM your life?

WALLS OF MISUNDERSTANDING PRODUCE STRANGERS, NOT LOVERS. So many women are talking to me about their marriage--their longings, their frustrations, their emptinesses. They hurt because of the unkind tongues of their mates. They smart because of rejections--physical, or mental.

"What should they do? Do they not deserve as much consideration from their husbands as the family dog or the stranger dropping paper on the front lawn?

Is marriage for a woman an endless circle of non-communication and verbal blows?

Anyone who knows the BIBLE a wee little bit, is acquainted with the RULES of the ROAD for the man. These verses of Scripture are precious and upon reading them—a woman thinks marriage will surely be a joy. **But, the SAD THING about men—even CHRISTIAN MEN—is that often they do not follow their rules. THEY do not love, they do not give, they do not care. This leaves the woman with great emptiness and grief of soul.**

Where can she go? What can she do? What will solve her problem--this deep longing to be SPECIAL with the man of her choice? Why does he cut her up? Why does he put her down? Why is he kind to his parents and ugly to her and the children? Why is he never home but off with the boys, or even off doing church work?

The natural reaction (which comes from the "natural" (wo)man.) is to fight back with the SAME weapons and the SAME tactics which her husband has used against her—GREED, EVIL SPEAKING, CLAMOURING, REVULSION, HATE, PHYSICAL ABUSE, MENTAL TORTURE, LOUD TALKING, UNKIND terms, and STREET LANGUAGE. Tears flow in spite of herself or because of herself. She stalks out of the room like a wounded deer. Often she sleeps on the couch or goes to the store and buys a new dress, or begins a chore in the house, accomplishing it in record time with super-human strength brought on by her frustration.

POOR ME. Don't I count? WHY doesn't HE have time for me? Don't I deserve consideration? I'm with these six kids all day—DOESN'T HE CARE?

What is happening? **WALLS are being built between the husband and the wife—HIGHER and HIGHER go the walls and the division between the man and his wife grows stronger and stronger. They grow to be STRANGERS.**

Some women whom I've talked to feel that the whole secret of a happy marriage belongs with the MAN. HE is to be the aggressor sexually. He is to be the "romantic" of the family. In SOME MARRIAGES (but I think very few) THE HUSBAND MAY BE THE PERFECT PERSON—the love-coverer; the one who never gets provoked; the one who always rejoices; the patient, long-suffering one; the one who never envies; the one who never is puffed up in pride; the one who bears the burdens of the house and the job with no tension; the one who never says an unkind word towards his spouse; the one who always is close to her side and never fails her (1 Corinthians 13). SHOW ME this kind of a man and I'll show you the UNUSUAL—the mold was thrown away after his birth..

I believe that the KEY to a SUCCESSFUL MARRIAGE is found in the wife's hands. After all, who was made for whom?

> *And the LORD God said, It is not good that the man should be alone; I will make him an help meet* [FITTING] *for him* (Genesis 2:18).

> *For Adam was FIRST FORMED, then Eve* (1 Timothy 2:13).

> *For the man is NOT of the woman; but the WOMAN of the MAN. Neither was the man created for the woman; BUT THE WOMAN FOR THE MAN* (1 Corinthians 11:8-10).

> *And the LORD God caused a deep sleep to fall upon Adam, and he slept: and HE TOOK ONE OF HIS RIBS, and closed up the flesh instead thereof;*

> *And the RIB, which the LORD God had taken from man, made* [builded] *he a woman, and BROUGHT HER UNTO THE MAN* (Genesis 2:21-22).

Now, wife, you may argue this until you are blue in the face, but I CANNOT SEE ANY OTHER TEACHING THAN THIS IN THE BIBLE. Granted it is much easier to unlock a marriage when one has a willing lock [husband] and a lock which is obedient to the rules of the husband. **THE IDEAL marriage is**

a marriage where both are born-again and where both obey the WORDS of GOD and place themselves under the authority of the BOOK. BUT there are few ideal marriages.

One of the ways to unlock a marriage and walk into a room filled with married beauty is to tear the WALL down between husband and wife and build one against the DEVIL'S devices instead. In this lesson, I wish to review and add to the HUSBAND-LOVING LESSON #9. "PARDON ME, BUT DO I DETECT A POWER FAILURE?" found on pages 119-138 above. **I feel that if there are no "walls" in the bedroom, there will be verbal communication beyond belief.**

WALLS COME DOWN GOD'S WAY

Let us turn to 1 Corinthians Chapter 7, again, with special emphasis this time on the following words:

"RENDER"
"DUE"
"DEFRAUD"
"CONSENT"
"FOR A TIME"
"GIVE YOURSELF"
"COME TOGETHER AGAIN"
"INCONTINENCY"

"RENDER"—A CONTINUOUS ACTION

Let the husband RENDER unto the wife due benevolence: and likewise also the wife unto the husband (1 Corinthians 7:3).

"RENDER" comes from the Greek Word, APODIDOMI.

This is in the present Greek, which indicates a continual, over and over again, repeated action which we are never to stop doing. (My husband, Pastor D. A. WAITE, has helped with the original language and meanings--He is fully qualified in matters of Greek exegesis and I trust his translation and grammatical suggestions completely.]

Most of us are aware of the verse in Matthew 7:7-8, where Jesus tells His disciples to ASK, SEEK, and KNOCK. This SAME Greek present tense (though different verbs are used) indicates a continual, over and over action of never stopping:
CONTINUE to ask
CONTINUE to seek
CONTINUE to knock

What is the wife told to do with her husband in the matter of sexual obligations [which is the subject matter in this context]?

She is to:
"CONTINUE TO RECOMPENSE,"
"CONTINUE TO DISCHARGE AN OBLIGATION,"
"CONTINUE TO RENDER BACK,"
"CONTINUE TO GIVE BACK."

MARRIAGE IS HONOURABLE IN ALL, and the bed [literally, the sexual *act] UNDEFILED: but WHOREMONGERS* [fornicators] *AND ADULTERERS GOD WILL JUDGE* (Hebrews 13:4).

Two more things I want you to especially notice. One is that the tense in the GREEK is NOT in the "AORIST" tense, which would be a once-for-all-action. If the "once for all" action were intimated in this verse, we would say that the first time you and your husband had sexual intercourse should be the ONLY time throughout your marriage. BUT, this verse says: ***"Perform the* ACT OF MARRIAGE *over* and *over and over and over and over and over and over and over. If you are married fifty years, you should***

never stop. If you are married five years and death ends that marriage, you should be able to look back and say, "We obeyed the WORDS of GOD and 'RENDERED' as GOD intended in a marriage" **(Hebrews 13:4).**

The second thing I want to point out is that this command of RENDERING from 1 Corinthians 7:3, is a command for BOTH marriage partners. The HUSBAND is to RENDER UNTO THE WIFE her due and the wife unto the husband.

Perhaps you are willing and want your husband sexually more than he wants you. As we have studied before, HIS BODY is YOUR BODY. He has a CHRISTIAN obligation to RENDER unto you his physical love. [See above, pp. 125-126 on this.] In a kind way point this out to your husband. BE VERY CAREFUL NOT TO OFFEND HIM. If he is a more subdued man sexually, YOU MAY HAVE TO ALWAYS BE THE AGGRESSOR SEXUALLY. He may be overworked, over-tired, over-burdened, or you could be over-admonishing and nagging him, OR HE MAY BE ILL.

Your husband, because he is sexually satisfied, may not realize your great need. You must tell him. BUT most of all, you MUST show him.

[READ the chapter on "THE IMPOTENT MAN" from *THE ACT OF MARRIAGE*, by the LaHayes. I have also listed 22 CAUSES of "male impotence" above, in

LESSON #17, p. 240]

But MAYBE the shoe is on the other foot. Maybe your husband is the one with the great need sexually. [Read Chapter 2 of *THE ACT OF MARRIAGE* and see "THINGS TO DO" on page 201 for five different reasons the "ACT OF MARRIAGE" is vitally significant to your husband.]

Maybe YOU are the one REFUSING, "DEFRAUDING," and "NOT RENDERING" HIS DUE" to him. Maybe you are the one who says, *"I didn't get married just for sex."* Maybe you are the one who would be satisfied with a "ONCE A WEEK" appointment or "ONCE A MONTH" contact sexually with your husband. If so, SHAME ON YOU. Do you realize that you are letting SATAN have an entrance into your husband's life?

Suppose some woman with a "hankering" would saddle up to your man and cause him to sin with her. What guilt would hang upon your head, my dear. What shame would come to you and your children. Everyone's tongue would wag because of your husband's indiscretion, but, in your heart, you would know that you were equally guilty because you did not do your "RENDERING." Because you did not obey the WORDS of GOD in the matter of this phase of wifesmanhip.

Think it over and ask God to give you strength and grace to be the wife He intends to have you be. Bring back the bliss of EDEN into your lives. Bring back the sparkle into your husband's eyes and the spring in his step. You will be rewarded. Yes, you will.

REMEMBER—WIVES MUST "DO" TO DESTROY THE WALL

OFTEN a wife thinks she is changing, but she isn't. She is hanging on to her old, old habits of whining and selfishness. **God wants to grip our hearts and knock down that pride which causes us to want to be "IT"—the RULER of the HOME and not the one ruled over.** CHANGE! CHANGE! CHANGE! is the factor which will bring about results in a marriage. **DON'T look for the change in your husband—that takes longer** [men differ]. **LOOK for the CHANGE in YOURSELF.** MAKE YOURSELF CHANGE. GET OFF YOUR KNEES AND DO!! Stop your pious platitudes and put yourself in place. SMILE! (Philippians 4:4).

"DUE" MEANS THE "ACT OF MARRIAGE"

Let the husband render unto the wife DUE benevolence [her DUE]: *and likewise also the wife unto the husband* (1 Corinthians 7:3).

"DUE" comes from the Greek Word," OPHELLEO.

The question has been asked to me by wives who do not want to "RENDER" unto their husbands their "due" in sexual matters—*"How do we know that this word, 'DUE' means SEXUAL INTERCOURSE? We OWE our husbands many things like cooking for them, doing their wash; making the beds; cleaning their clothes, etc., etc., etc."*

Look at the previous verses. The question was asked of Paul, *"Is it okay if a man doesn't want to 'know' a woman sexually* [the meaning of the word, "touch" in 1 Corinthians 7:1]? And Paul affirms that's fine, BUT to avoid fornication [please consult HUSBAND-LOVING LESSON #9 above, pp. 119-138 on this], you better get married! Of course you should have your own wife, or to the women, your OWN HUSBANDS. Marriage is a PERSONAL POSSESSION!

BUT, CHRISTIAN, when you have your own mate, you must dish out the potatoes. You must "RENDER" over and over the sexual function which is needful for your mate. WHY? So you and so your mate do not commit adultery in thought, word, or actions. It's as plain as ABC and why CHRISTIANS cannot see this fault of going without the "ACT OF MARRIAGE," I'll never know.

So, wife, [and if I were teaching men, and I am NOT—I certainly would tell them, but it is up to you, WIFE, to kindly inform your husband either through your actions or some way what God's Words say—without NAGGING--that's why it would be easier with actions. You know, that ACTIONS speak louder than words]--You OWE, YOU'RE UNDER OBLIGATION. YOU OUGHT, MUST, SHOULD.

If you, as a mate, do not RENDER HIS (your husband's) DUE, you are failing in your obligation. It BEHOOVES you to do this. YOU are BOUND or in DEBT. It IS your duty to have the "ACT

OF MARRIAGE" with your husband (and vice versa). Don't be guilty. THERE IS A NEED!!

REMEMBER--AN UNSAVED HUSBAND WILL NOT ACT LIKE A CHRISTIAN

NOW, remember this: IF you are married to an unsaved man, he is a child of DARKNESS, and he has not the Holy Spirit living in his body, but is only a "NATURAL MAN" and has only the sinful nature within him, NOT LIGHT from the LORD, no insight into His Words, no Holy Spirit to direct his life. DO NOT EXPECT HIM TO ACT LIKE A CHRISTIAN for he has not the LORD'S LOVE AND POWER. JUST LOVE him, and SUBMIT TO HIM, OBEY him, and let the Lord Jesus Christ be your Helper. "*The joy of the Lord is your strength*" (Nehemiah 8:10d). Don't let any man [husband] take this JOY from you (John 16:22d).

A GOOD MARRIAGE—BUILT ON THREE MOUNTAINS

In speaking of a wounded marriage, a friend of mine said, *"They need more than a sexual union three or four times a week. They have serious problems. They need counseling."* Perhaps this is a true statement, but I say that frequent physical closeness is a good beginning and opens the doors to understanding of one another. Marriage is like a ball—sex and kindness, communication and serving roll into one

If SEX is used, not as a reward, but as a DUTY; if SEX is a giving of oneself; I say that it IS a very good beginning in breaking down the non-communication wall.

As I have said over and over again in our classes, a good MARRIAGE is built upon three mountains for the WIFE: the SCRIPTURE, SUBMISSION, and SEX. If you know your Bible and attend a Bible-believing church every time the doors open; if you contribute regularly and cheerfully to the offerings of that church; if you read your BIBLE daily, and spend time in personal prayer; if you memorize Scripture until you are a walking Bible; etc., etc., etc., and ARE NOT A SUBMISSIVE WIFE to your husband, YOU HAVE AN INSECURE MARRIAGE.

If you are submissive as a wife and WALK the Scripture road and do not "RENDER" unto your husband his "DUE," you do not have a secure marriage.

If you are "RENDERING" and READING, and not SUBMISSIVE, you do not have a complete, finished marriage. IF you are SUBMISSIVE and SEXUALLY active towards your mate, and not SCRIPTURALLY sound, you do not have a stable marriage. IT TAKES THREE POINTS FOR A PLANE TO BE STABLE—and a marriage too!!

TOO many women are fighting the WORDS and WILL of God for their lives. Refusal to walk GOD'S way is the same old story--PRIDE, DISOBEDIENCE, and UNBELIEF. The woman of today is no different from that woman who was built from the side of ADAM so many years ago.

"WE DARE NOT FAINT"

Our work is solemn
Therefore, we dare not trifle.

Our task is difficult
Therefore, we dare not relax.

Our opportunities are brief
Therefore, we dare not delay.

Our path is narrow
Therefore, we dare not wander.

Our prize will be glorious
Therefore, we dare not faint.

(Author unknown)

RENDER, STOP DEFRAUDING, & WALL BUILDING--PART II" will be continued in the next lesson, Lesson *#20,* beginning on page 269 below.

THINGS TO DO AND THINK ABOUT THIS WEEK

1. **RE-READ 1 Corinthians 7 this week and re-read the notes from *<u>HUSBAND-LOVING LESSONS</u>* <u>pertaining to this chapter:</u>**
   a. Chapter *#9,* "PARDON ME, BUT DO I DETECT A POWER FAILURE?" (pp. 119-138)
   b. Chapter #10, "TO STAY, OR NOT TO STAY--THAT IS THE QUESTION" (pp. 139-154)
   c. Chapter #11 "BLOOM WHERE YOU ARE PLANTED" (pp. 155-166)

2. **CONTINUE TO PRAY—NOT IN A SELF-RIGHTEOUS WAY**, BUT AS the Lord Jesus Christ in The Garden, *"nevertheless not my will but thine be done."*

3. **Put legs on your prayers.**

   God is ready to answer your prayer.
   What have you DONE about your problem?
   God answers prayer how, when, and where HE pleases.
   Prayer becomes a springboard for Biblical ACTION.
   PRAY AND OBEY. [Jay Adams, from his WKDN Radio program over Family Radio].

4. **BE INWARDLY SATISFIED, in spite of CIRCUMSTANCES.**

5. Ask yourself this question concerning your marriage: *"DO I WANT TO WIN HIM* [my husband] *or DO I WANT MERELY TO WIN ARGUMENTS"?*

6. "<u>You marry not only a sinner, but a man</u>. **You marry a man**, not a woman. Strange how easy it seems to be for some

women to expect their husbands to be women, to act like women, to do what is expected of women. Instead of that, they are men, they act like men, they do what is expected of men and thus they do the unexpected." [from *LET ME BE A WOMAN*, by Elisabeth Elliot, Chapter 24, "You Marry a Man" (page 83)].

7. Continue reading *THE ACT OF MARRIAGE* by the LaHayes, Chapter 14. "PRACTICAL ANSWERS TO COMMON QUESTIONS" page 234.

8. It is important for you to become familiar with the basic terms and parts and their locations of yours and your husband's reproductive system. See pp. 47-58 for this in *THE ACT OF MARRIAGE.*

9. **STOP NAGGING your husband.**

10. Are you attending a Church where the clear gospel of the LORD JESUS CHRIST is presented with no strings attached? **Are you attending a church where the WORDS OF GOD are opened and taught?** If not, why not?

11. CONSCIENCE NEEDS TO BE INFORMED BY THE WORDS OF GOD.

HUSBAND-LOVING LESSON #20

RENDERING, DEFRAUDING, & WALL-BUILDING—PART II

"A WORD ABOUT WORDS"

Learn how to use words with purpose,
Learn to express *your heart's feelings*
Softly , kindly,
With expression from your soul—
Practice the use of WORDS,
Their sound, their force,
Roll them 'round your tongue like candy.

Discover the sum of their intent,
Hearken to your inner voice
And translate it to sound—
Sound expressed in WORDS,
English words, French WORDS, Spanish WORDS.
TAKE CARE lest *they cause a cacophony*
From their effect upon the hearer.

Do you desire the result
Of a fighter, boxing in the ring?
Or *of the* wrestler, *straining*
For his opponent's pin?
Then use WORDS which bring about
The aggressive spirit of a fighting cock.

Do you desire a response of love,
Tender and warm?
Then, take care what WORDS you choose
For such a tender moment.

Use lover's WORDS which speak
Of sunset's golden red
Of sands warm, and sea gulls flying,
Of happy days . . .

Don't speak of mundane, common things
As broken cars, *business debts,*
Or *telephone rings.*
Speak WORDS of heart, of soul, of spirit,
Recall a kiss, a night,
A prayer, a baby's laugh,
A hand held tight in time of stress . . .

Think thoughts which bring response
Within YOUR hungry soul,
THEN SPEAK OUT IN WORDS
Those inner feelings.
Speak them in whispers,
As you walk the street hand in hand,
As you work together at the job,
As you look upon a sick and dying one . . .

SHARE YOUR SOUL–
And you will gain your love.

[Dedicated to my sons]

By Yvonne S. Waite
"FROM THE TENT DOOR"
THE BIBLE FOR TODAY NEWSREPORT
April 11, 1975, page 3

DOES YOUR MARRIAGE NEED NEW SPARK PLUGS?

To be perfectly truthful, I cannot remember any sermons preached on 1 Corinthians 7 with such detail as I have tried to write down for you to read. I am sure there have been some written, but I haven't heard them. In fact, the only preacher I've ever heard expound these verses such as 1 Corinthians 7:1-5 in detail has been my husband.

If the matter of fornication, adultery, and marriage was a problem to the church of Corinth in that wicked generation [see pages 119-120 above, for the summation of Corinth in Paul's time] it is DOUBLY SO TODAY.

The longer I am into this ministry to the married woman and to those contemplating marriage, I am convinced that 1 Corinthians 7 is not only misunderstood, but it is a closed chapter among born-again Christian men and women.

I have been in many WOMEN'S meetings especially called to help women, the Pastor's wife, etc., and as far as I'm concerned, the ISSUE of the DAY (marriage and what to do about it) is skirted with some devotional or humorous ditty about keeping your house clean or making well-balanced meals. These are important, but not FIRST in marriage..

There is a dearth--a sickness--of ignorance. No wonder Christian couples are operating with half of their spark plugs burned out.

Let us turn now to the FIFTH verse of the SEVENTH CHAPTER of 1 CORINTHIANS (1 Corinthians 7:5) and brave the commands of SCRIPTURE wherein you and I, as HUSBAND-LOVERS will find our rules for marriage.

THE RULE: STOP DEFRAUDING YOUR MATE

Defraud ye not one the other, except it be with consent for a time, that ye may give yourselves to fasting and prayer; and come together again, that Satan tempt you not for your incontinency (1 Corinthians 7:5).

"DEFRAUD" is the Greek Word, *APOSTEREO*; *APO* means "away from, or off;" *STEREO* means "to harden, make firm, or make stiff"

It carries the force of saying, **"STOP DEFRAUDING,"** because it is a prohibition in the PRESENT Greek tense. **You've been defrauding your mate, CHRISTIAN, Paul wrote, so stop it right now!**

"DEFRAUD" means: "To deprive; to debar (forbid, set up a barrier) to detach

These Corinthian Christians must have thought it was more Christian to defraud, to be detached from their mates sexually. But Paul says, *"On the contrary, do not stiffen away from each other; don't be firm away from each other; don't build a wall between the two of you in regards to the* ACT OF MARRIAGE.*"*

Each day you are not with each other, a WALL is being built. By the end of the week, the wall is taller. If you go two weeks or a month or longer, the wall is taller and stronger and much harder to knock down. Paul exhorts: *"WIVES, husbands, don't do this. Don't let anything come between you and your partner when it comes to the marriage relation."* NOTHING could be plainer. Why then, is there so much "WALL-BUILDING," so much "DEFRAUDING" one another as husbands and wives--even in Christian circles where the Bible SHOULD be understood and obeyed?

AN EXCEPTION TO THE RULE: A MUTUAL DISCUSSION OF "DEFRAUDING"

Defraud ye not one the other, EXCEPT IT BE WITH CONSENT for a time . . . (1 Corinthians 7:5a)

"WITH CONSENT" is from the Greek word *SUMPHONOS*. Meaning:
"with voice" (together)
"agreeing in sound"
"accordant"

"harmonious"
[THE SAME SOUND]
"agreeing"
"to sound together"

[THE TOGETHER SOUND]
"to be in unison"
"to agree with"
"to harmonize with"

[NO CACOPHONY!]

It is the same word from which we get "SYMPHONY." And you all know what a "SYMPHONY" is supposed to be. So if your husband and you decide to "DEFRAUD" or "REFUSE" each other sexual relations; If you agree in harmonious sound, or have unison accord together that you are going to deprive one another of his or her "DUE" in sexual matters, you may—according to this verse—"BUILD A WALL" between you.

A MUTUAL "DEFRAUDING" FOR A SHORT PERIOD OF TIME

Defraud ye not one the other, except it be with consent FOR A TIME (1 Corinthians 7:5b)

"TIME" or "SEASON" is from the Greek Word, *KAIROS* which means: "a limited period of time;" "a short season of time as opposed to a long time or season."

In other words, STOP DEPRIVING your husband your body sexually, BUT if you both AGREE on the subject of defrauding, okay, but only for a tiny, weeny, period of time!

A MUTUAL "DEFRAUDING" FOR LIMITED DEVOTIONAL REASONS

Defraud ye not one the other [STOP DEFRAUDING], *except it be with consent* [unless you are in accord on the matter], *for a time* [a short period of time], *THAT YE MAY GIVE YOURSELVES TO FASTING AND PRAYER* [the reason] . . . (1 Corinthians 7:5c).

Now we have the reason:

"GIVE YOURSELF" is the Greek Word *SCHOLAZETE* meaning: *"to devote oneself entirely to a thing;" "to be at leisure" [like a 'scholar' has leisure to study).*

Here is the REASON for the harmonious agreement to set up a barrier between husband and wife in the bedroom for a very brief, short period of time. The reason is *"for fasting and prayer."* [There might be OTHER good reasons for this agreement for brief periods of time but the Scripture gives us just this one.]

You decide you want to go on a spiritual retreat with the ladies from the church, or he decides he wants to pray and fast for a certain reason. BOTH of you say, *"Okay, honey, you may do this. I will really miss your body, but for the LORD'S sake, I'll refrain from asking for what is mine (your body) and let you pray."*

HOW long should this fast or this praying go on? How many days would you agree to go without food and to remain on your knees in prayer? Maybe you don't know. Should it be like the Lord Jesus Christ in the wilderness—forty days? Do you think you could go without food for forty days? Do you think you could pray for forty days? Do you think you could pray for twenty-four hours? Just wondering. Perhaps you can; I don't know. These words, "FASTING AND PRAYER" bring into the picture a TIME factor, just as *KAIROS* indicates a BRIEF time only. [See pp. 130-137 for more discussion on "frequency" of married love.)

A MUTUAL RETURNING TO ACTIVE SEXUAL PLEASURE WITH ONE'S MATE

Defraud ye not one the other, except it be with consent for a time, that ye may give yourselves to fasting and prayer; and COME TOGETHER AGAIN . . . (1 Corinthians 7:5d)

"COME TOGETHER AGAIN" is the Greek Word, *SUNERCHOMAI*. It is in the present tense and therefore indicates a continued, over and over again action, which means: *"to continue to come together (in the sense of cohabiting matrimonially)," "don't stop coming together," "keep coming together all your life* as *husbands and wives."*

The same word is used in Matthew 1:18 to indicate that Joseph did NOT "come together" or "cohabit matrimonially" with Mary until AFTER the birth of the Lord Jesus Christ.

So, agree on a SHORT PERIOD OF TIME for a good Scriptural reason, BUT COME TOGETHER AGAIN. Continue NOT DEFRAUDING one another. Don't stop your previous correct sexual pattern; keep on going as you were before the "devotional wall" was built between you. COHABIT again. WHY the rush? Why the immediacy?

TOO MUCH "DEFRAUDING" WITH ONE'S MATE LOWERS OUR RESISTANCE TO ADULTERY

. . . that SATAN TEMPT YOU NOT for your incontinency (1 Corinthians 7:5e).

BECAUSE SATAN IS A ROARING LION. walking about, seeking whom he may devour (1 Peter 5:8).

Here you are little Miss Devotions herself (or your husband, Mr. High and Mighty Holiness himself). You are praying and fasting. You are devoting all your life for a short season for a spiritual goal.

> **BE CAREFUL. TAKE CARE. TEMPTATION will walk in quietly, while you THINK you are spiritual. You may be praying with the opposite sex and wham. You'll discover that the WALL between you and this man whom you are NOT MARRIED TO has come down.**

Your husband may be devoting his time to teaching the BIBLE to some Miss Lovely. You and he have agreed to build a wall between you both so he can do this. What happens? He might discover that the WALL which should be there between him and Miss Lovely has dissolved. And WHAM! TEMPTATION! And a fall!

While you are in the weakened condition of fasting and the "humble" position of praying, you could suddenly discover that between you and the opposite sex

there are temptations because of your "*incontinency.*" [these are the few of the meanings of the Greek Word for "*incontinency*"]
"no restraints,
"no hindering,
"no keeping under reserve,
"no getting under one's power,
"no retaining wall,
"no harnessing of the loins."

WHICH WALL ARE YOU BUILDING?

BUILD THE RIGHT WALL BETWEEN YOU AND THE "OTHER" MAN, NOT BETWEEN YOU AND YOUR MATE. We all can count on our fingers and toes couples who have been tempted of the DEVIL because of their "INCONTINENCY" (without self control, no restraints, no retaining WALL). For one reason or another, a WALL has been built between husband and wife:

He was overseas in the service.
She was home with the children.
He was traveling "for the Lord."
She was involved in CHRISTIAN WORK—the organist.
He yelled at her all day.
SHE said all he wanted was sex and she refused him at night.

Slowly, the WALL was built. The time between their love-making was farther and farther apart. They were like strangers to each other.

There could have been illness, death, whatever--but a WALL had been built because one of the partners didn't realize the physical need of the other. Then there was exposure to another person who had a need. Another person who enticed, who sought, and the WALL OF SELF RESTRAINT crashed, and adultery was committed—in thought, word, or in deed itself!!

Oh, the heartache which could have been prevented, if the married people would have STOPPED DEFRAUDING OR REFUSING ONE ANOTHER married love.

My personal opinion is that there should be VERY LITTLE REFRAINING from sexual activity within a marriage for devotional purposes. WHY? Because SATAN and his hosts are active, waiting to pounce on the separated wife or husband.

True, there are times, such as during menstruation, surgery, or childbirth, where normal married love relationships cannot be continued, but a loving wife is able to compensate for certain restrictions in other "ways." A wife's aim and goal should be to keep her husband faithful to her and to be faithful to her husband. The reason being *"that the ministry be not blamed"* (2 Corinthians 6: 3b).

But I speak this by permission, and not of commandment (1 Corinthians 7:6).

These teachings in 1 Corinthians 7 are nowhere else in the SCRIPTURE. No other commandments tell us such things. The Holy Spirit is teaching you and me these truths from the pen of Paul. The Corinthians were the first to hear them.

Praise God we are blessed by these teachings so that we can have HAPPIER MARRIAGES, and be faithful mates and not blaspheme the Words of God (Psalm 74:10; Titus 2:5).

"O God, how long shall the adversary reproach? Shall the enemy blaspheme thy name forever? (Psalm 74:10)

THINGS TO THINK ABOUT AND DO THIS WEEK

1. LET'S SEE SOME ACTION in our marriages this week. **Let's "DO"--not only sexually, but also in DOING! in caring!** with no expectation of returns!!

2. **REMEMBER, YOU MARRIED A MAN.**

"They [husbands] *surprise their wives by being men and some wives wake up to the awful truth that it was not, in fact, a man that they wanted after all. It was marriage, or some vague idea of marriage, which provided the fringe benefits they were looking for—a home, children, security, social status. But somehow marriage has also insinuated into their cozy lives this unpredictable, unmanageable, unruly creature called a man. He is likely to be bigger and louder and tougher and hungrier and dirtier than a woman expects, and she finds that bigger feet make bigger footprints on the newly washed kitchen floor; they make a bigger noise on the stairs. She learns that what makes her cry may make him laugh. He eats far more than seems necessary or even reasonable to a woman who never ceases her vigil against excess weight, etc., etc., etc."* (From *LET ME BE A WOMAN* by Elisabeth Elliot, pp. 83-81 from Chapter 24 "You Marry a Man.").

3. Continue to pray for your husband's salvation and let GOD work HIS Way. **His way includes your being a submissive wife** (Ephesians 5:22; Colossians 3:18; and 1 Peter 3:1).

4. You are either living for the LORD or living for the WORLD.

5. **CHANGE YOUR ATTITUDES and become a HUSBAND-LOVER the BIBLE WAY.**

6. *"the things which come out of him, those are they that defile the man* [or woman]." (Mark 7:15b, 20-23). *"And he said, That which cometh out of the man,* [or woman] *that defileth the man* [or woman]. *For from within, out of the heart of men,* [or women] *proceed evil thoughts, adulteries, fornications, murders, Thefts, covetousness, wickedness, deceit, lasciviousness, an evil eye, blasphemy, pride, foolishness: All these evil things come from within, and defile the man* [or woman]."

(LOOK UP THE MEANINGS OF THESE WORDS)

After you discover the definitions of the above words, **DO NOT POINT your finger at your husband, point it at yourself and then DO SOMETHING—first** starting with confession, if you know the Lord Jesus Christ as your Saviour (1 John 1:9).

7. What are some changes which have come into your life since becoming a SCRIPTURAL HUSBAND-LOVER?

8. "*The art of mutually enjoyable love-making is not difficult to learn, but neither is it automatic. No one is a good lover by nature, and the more selfish the individual, the more difficulty he will have in learning this art.*" [From *THE ACT OF MARRIAGE*, by Beverly and Tim LaHaye, Chapter 5, "The Art of Lovemaking" pp. 78-79.]

9. **Read 1 Peter 3:1-6 again, and also**
   Genesis 1:26-5:5, and also
   1 Corinthians 13.

10. **NEVER SLEEP ON THE COUCH**--alone, that is!

11. **"*RENDER*," "*DEFRAUD NOT*" your own husband**, but build a wall between you and any other man.

IN CLOSING

As these ***HUSBAND LOVING LESSONS*** come to an end, **I want to remind the reader that marriage, in my opinion, is the most difficult assignment that a woman can have**. Why? It involves two people united as one in God's eyes and with their personal assent. They each have desires, loves, goals, and wills. *The two shall become one flesh* in the eyes of God. Often these same two people who loved each other cannot agree on many things and hence live as if they are separate entities.

Sad to say, many times, with the responsibility and

the title of *husband*, a man can become a bossy person, ordering his wife around like a child and, apparently, showing no appreciation for her in any area of her life. This is the person he promised to love and to cherish. He misunderstands what it means to be *the head of the house*. He assumes it means to be separate entities. At least that is how the wife looks at the situation. Often, the truth of being a husband brings the man to the realization that the responsibility of marriage is overwhelming.

The wife is full of plans making her house into a home. She has ideas for the present and the future, excited over being a wife and the intimate life she has with her husband, often becoming pregnant early in the marriage. Perhaps in her exuberance she forgets to yield to her husband's wishes, wants, and commands.

Often, that which was so precious in the courting days, disappears after the honeymoon is over. They each had ideas what their marriage was going to be like, and often it did not turn out like they dreamed. The potential of a good marriage evaporated with the many differences which both of them did not handle in a Scriptural way. What went wrong?

It isn't always easy to blend two personalities. Some women are pliable and flaccid. Others are imaginative and exciting. The years together as man and wife should be a time of yielding to one another and learning the proper Scriptural posture that we learn about in the Bible. They must not forget the Scriptural order of leadership and submission, as well as to love as the Lord Jesus Christ loves the Church. It is when two separate personalities clash within a marriage, that the couple wonders what have they gotten themselves into when they said,"I do" a few years before.

Perhaps it is not the man's fault in the unhappy marriage. It may not be the wife's fault either. They have bumped into companionship problems, not only because of personality differences and family backgrounds, but because of the wrong understanding of God's way and will in their marriage union. That is when we women should look into the Words of God to help us in our heartaches and unhappiness. How we need help to have, Christ-like marriages!

This book tries to help the woman who finds herself

feeling unloved and unappreciated by her mate. It is also a book of lessons that can help good marriages to be better and more Scriptural. Many couples are married for many years who do not know the sin of habitually refusing one's mate in the "act of marriage." So much sorrow comes into a couple's life if the marriage bed is neglected. Also, much sorrow comes into a marriage if a husband orders his wife around the house like a ignorant disobedient child. **A wife is a responder to her husband's treatment of her**. May she find it easy to respond to him and reflect his love for her back to him.

Though this book is for women to help them in their marriages, it is imperative for husbands to read their rules in the Bible and practice them always. One will be very surprised when one sees how God honors His Words in the very personal matters of marriage manners and love when the husband and/or the wife practice marriage-loving the Bible Way!

1 Corinthians 13

"Though I speak with the tongues of men and of angels, and have not charity, I am become as sounding brass, or a tinkling cymbal. And though I have the gift of prophecy, and understand all mysteries, and all knowledge; and though I have all faith, so that I could remove mountains, and have not charity, I am nothing. And though I bestow all my goods to feed the poor, and though I give my body to be burned, and have not charity, it profiteth me nothing. Charity suffereth long, and is kind; charity envieth not; charity vaunteth not itself, is not puffed up, Doth not behave itself unseemly, seeketh not her own, is not easily provoked, thinketh no evil; Rejoiceth not in iniquity, but rejoiceth in the truth; Beareth all things, believeth all things, hopeth all things, endureth all things. Charity never faileth: but whether there be prophecies, they shall fail; whether there be tongues, they shall cease; whether there be knowledge, it shall vanish away. For we know in part, and we prophesy in part. But when that which is perfect is come, then that which is in part shall be done away. When I was a child, I spake as a child, I understood as a child, I thought as a child: but when I became a man, I put away childish things. For now we see through a glass, darkly; but then face to face: now I know in part; but then shall I know even as also I am known. And now abideth faith, hope, charity, these three; but the greatest of these is charity" (1 Corinthians 13:1-13).

ABOUT THE AUTHOR

Her Experiences. Saved since childhood, Yvonne has had years of walking with the Lord Jesus Christ on the "narrow way" in the good and bad times of daily Christian living. She wrote:

> ***"I desired from girlhood to go where God wanted me to go. One thing was certain, much to my surprise, staying with the stuff--being a mother and wife--was my life's work!"***

Yvonne Sanborn Waite looks at life through the eyes of a mature, godly woman, having experienced personal, physical, emotional, and spiritual battles. Many of her private crises and convictions are reflected on the printed page--as well as heard devotionally from a speaker's platform. These personal feelings and experiences contribute to making the portrayals of FANNY CROSBY and FRANCES HAVERGAL "real" to her audience.

Her Education. Mrs. Waite and her husband graduated from Berea High School in 1945. In 1948, she graduated from the Moody Bible Institute, the same year Dr. Waite received his baccalaureate degree from the University of Michigan. In 1996, she was given an honorary Doctor of Humanities degree by the Great Plains Baptist Divinity School in Sioux Falls, South Dakota. Even though she is a graduate of the Moody Bible Institute, along with other studies, Yvonne feels that her greatest educational enrichment has been that of being married to her husband. It has been a marriage union since August 27, 1948. Her husband's knowledge and wisdom has influenced her life through his teaching and godly insights. Also, the early training and example of her parents (Ren and Gertrude Sanborn), in a Bible-believing home, taught invaluable lessons. Now that she is the mother of five adult children, she has found satisfaction in their wisdom and Biblical leadership, too, as well as the invaluable lessons learned from their spouses.

Her Husband. The Waites were married on August 27, 1948, in a small independent Baptist church--then bordering the Cleveland Hopkins International Airport near Berea, Ohio. Dr. D. A. Waite graduated from the University of Michigan with a B.A. in Classical Greek and Latin; from the Dallas Theological Seminary with a Th.M. in New Testament Greek Literature and Exegesis, and with a Th.D. in Bible Exposition; from the Southern Methodist University with an M.A. in Speech; and from Purdue University with a Ph.D. in Speech and Public Address. He is the founder and director of **THE BIBLE FOR TODAY, INC.**, as well as being the president of **THE DEAN BURGON SOCIETY** since its founding in 1978. One of her husband's many books is the well-received ***DEFENDING THE KING JAMES BIBLE*** **(BFT #1594-P @ $12.00 + $8.00 S&H)**. This was the first of many other books defending the King James Bible and its underlying Hebrew, Aramaic, and Greek Words that he has written.

Her Writings. Since January, 1974, Mrs. Waite had penned a column in the ***BIBLE FOR TODAY NEWSREPORT*** called *"FROM THE TENT DOOR"* until it ceased publication. Through this column she was able to speak to women about issues of the day, Scriptural truths, and "women things." Years ago, Yvonne was published in the REGULAR BAPTIST PRESS adult Sunday School take-home papers, and, for a time, in a church-sponsored digest. She said, "*It was fun while it lasted*!" For more years than she can remember, she has authored a monthly newsletter called *The Bible For Today Update* which is sent out around the world into **BFT-LAND**. She chats about places, people, convictions, books, articles, and tracts that Dr. Waite has written, as well as the Bible teaching meetings where Dr. Waite preaches. Also for twelve years, (until 2013) Yvonne had a radio program called **"JUST FOR WOMEN."** It reached into many hearts around the world.

Her Variety. The Waites are the parents of five adult children (four sons and one daughter) and have thirteen grandchildren and thirteen great grandchildren as of 2013. Their second-born son, David William Waite, went Home to be with the Lord on April 15, 2008. He is greatly missed!

Yvonne has followed her husband where he has followed the Lord as a student's wife, a Navy chaplain's wife, a pastor's wife, a teacher's wife, and the wife of a writer, editor, radio speaker, and publisher of ***THE BIBLE FOR TODAY NEWSREPORT***, and its daily & weekly radio broadcasts. She has supported her husband as he founded and led the **Dean Burgon Society** since 1978. That is a society that defends the ***Authorized King James Bible*** and its underlying Hebrew, Aramaic, and Greek original Bible Words.

Her Travels. As a couple, Dr. and Mrs. Waite have traveled to Liberia, Sierra Leone, Ivory Coast (in West Africa), Singapore, Japan, Taiwan, Korea, Switzerland, France, Holland, England, Northern Ireland, Israel, Jordan, Egypt, Hawaii, Mexico, hijacked to Cuba, as well as dozens of other states in the United States, and into several provinces of Canada. As a Navy chaplain, Dr. Waite found himself stationed in Okinawa for a year, at Subic Bay in the Philippines, stopped in Guam, docked in Germany, stationed in Panama, and docked at Guantanamo Bay in Cuba. During much of this time, Yvonne was home in the United States with the children.

Her Ministries. Mrs. Waite has taught the Bible to a whole age-spectrum from nursery through adolescents to adult women's classes. In years past, she taught Bible clubs of forty or fifty children in her home as well as leading two Junior-church choirs. It has been her privilege to speak at women's meetings, mother-and-daughter banquets, Bible classes, and on many other occasions.

As of 2013, Mrs. Waite has presented ***A TRIBUTE TO FANNY CROSBY*** over 400 times as well as scores of Frances Havergal presentations. Her readers may know her through the *Bible For Today Update*, a letter which is composed monthly for contributors and friends of the **Bible For Today Ministries**. Her radio program, *Just For Women*, was heard for twelve and one half years by many, not only by radio, but also around the world by means of the Internet. For many years, she was the

Bible For Today's videographer and has made hundreds of videos of her husband's teaching.

Her Blending. It has been said of Yvonne Waite's portrayal of Fanny Crosby in ***"THE TRIBUTE TO FANNY CROSBY*** that it is as if *the first lady of gospel songs* were in the very room. Her blending together of the two personalities--that of the sightless hymn writer and that of the actress portraying her--results in a dramatic presentation which captures the hearts of her audiences. She presents this portrayal to small groups, or to as many 1,000 in Singapore.

Her Presentations. In 1978, at the invitation of her church's music director, Yvonne studied, wrote, and caught the joyful spirit of blind Frances Jane Crosby. Also, in May, of 1986, she researched the life of the devotional English poet and hymnist, frail Frances Ridley Havergal, one of Fanny Crosby's contemporaries.***THE PORTRAIT OF FRANCES HAVERGAL*** has been well received also. Complimenting Mrs. Waite's unique monologues, in both presentations, is the professional narration of her husband, Pastor D. A. Waite, Th.D., Ph.D.

Her Compositions. Her ***HUSBAND-LOVING LESSONS***, this present book, covers over 300 pages, and gives practical applications from God's marriage manual, the Bible. Her work was a result of teaching on the subject of marriage to women in her local area. Recently, Mrs. Waite has written ***My Daily Bible Blessings From My Daily Bible Reading***. It is a 649-page book that follows her husband's *Yearly Bible Reading Schedule* of 85 verses per-day to read the Bible in one year. It takes one blessing or teaching from each daily Bible reading and puts it on the page. The *Daily Bible Blessing* book teaches, comforts, and reflects on life for the Biblical education and edification for women and their children.

Another study written for women by Mrs. Waite is ***FOR AND ABOUT WOMEN*** which is a manual of four in-depth, original studies about Sarah, Hannah, Lydia, and Mary Magdalene. Her play called ***THE EVE OF CHRISTMAS*** is a drama bringing Adam and Eve back to our present century, searching for the Christ-Child amidst the commercialism of Christmas. It was presented to a Christian High School in Maryland, and to a Bible-believing Church in New Jersey, with convicting impact.

Another Bible study, in written form, is called *THINGS CALLED LOVE*, which covers, in 56 pages--three chapters of original writing--a Biblical definition of what love is and what love is not. ***REFLECTIONS OF A DAUGHTER*** is a gracious tribute to Yvonne's mother, Gertrude Sanborn, which tells of the first days after her mother's death; and continues into the example, consecration, and purity taught by her mother which were spiritually planted in Yvonne's life and also grounded into the life of Yvonne's daughter.

Two other booklets are available. The first is entitled ***WITHIN THE BORDERS OF OUR LIVES*** (Psalm 16:6) It tells about how the times, trials, and temptations of a woman's life are revealed as her "pleasant places." The second booklet is called ***MARRIAGE DEFRAUDING AND OTHER MATTERS ESPECIALLY FOR WOMEN.*** It is a series of articles concerning marriage and the proper deportment for a Christian woman. There is also a ***STUDY ON RUTH*** which was given in West Africa as well as Singapore. (All of the above and other Bible & devotional subjects are available upon request from the **Bible For Today**.) Both of her hymn writers' portrayals are not only in audio-tape form but are on video, as well as other talks by Mrs. Waite which may be ordered from the **BIBLE FOR TODAY.**

Her Impact. Teaching women the verities of their Faith has been Yvonne's pleasure. Her series titled ***HUSBAND-LOVING LESSONS*** has awakened many a married woman "*to walk within her house with a perfect heart*" (Psalm 101:2b). Her talk on *THOSE PESKY 'THEE'S' AND 'THOU'S'* was well received by **The Dean Burgon Women**. She was the first person to reveal in print the homosexuality of one of the NIV language consultants, not only by writing and speaking about Virginia Mollenkott, but also interviewing her personally (**BFT #697 @ $4.00 + $2.00 S&H**). This was before this lesbian speaker was officially "out of the closet"!

Her Assessment. It has been said of Yvonne Waite's writing that it shows the curiosity of a child, the frankness of an adolescent, the humor of a comedienne, the sarcasm of a philosopher, the truth of a prophet, the wisdom of a sage, and the beauty of a poet. The thrust of her ministry is to be herself with no pretense, to be the genuine person and use the personality which God has given her--not a copycat of anyone. When God asked her, as He did Moses many years ago, *What is that in thine hand*? (Exodus 4:2), Yvonne desired to use what she found there for God's glory. Thus, in emptying her hand into His, Yvonne Sanborn Waite has found a pen. Thus it became her duty to use that discovery and penetrate hearts with words to thousands all over the world!

According to the Scripture, Mrs. Waite, born in 1927, feels that she is in the "bonus" years of her life (Psalm 90:10), and her desire is to serve the Lord Jesus Christ in every way He leads before she *flies away* to Heaven.

The lines are fallen unto* [her] *in pleasant places, yea*, [she has] *a goodly heritage (Psalm 16:6).

INDEX OF WORDS AND PHRASES

CPSIA information can be obtained at www.ICGtesting.com
Printed in the USA
BVOW06s1431310716

457373BV00004B/31/P